FARMING
An Industry Accounting and Auditing Guide

Second Edition

Gary J Markham
Grant Thornton

Accountancy Books
40 Bernard Street
London
WC1N 1LD
Tel: 020 7920 8991
Fax: 020 7920 8991
E-mail: abgbooks@icaew.co.uk
Website: www.icaew.co.uk/books.htm

© 1999 The Institute of Chartered Accountants in England and Wales.

ISBN 1 85355 984 9

British Library Cataloguing-in-Publication Data.

A catalogue record for this book is available from the British Library.

First Edition 1996

Typeset by J&L Composition Ltd, Filey, North Yorkshire
Printed in Great Britain by Bell and Bain Ltd, Glasgow

THE COLLEGE of West Anglia
LANDBEACH ROAD · MILTON · CAMBRIDGE
TEL: (01223) 860701

WITHDRAWN

LEARNING *Centre*
The ticket - holder is responsible for
the return of this book

I would like to dedicate this book to my wife Anne and my children Tamsyn, Jamie and Kieran who have been very patient in allowing me to update this edition of the book.

Contents

Contents

Foreword

There are a number of books available on farm business management and farm management accounting, but none is at all recent and none covers the same wide spectrum as Gary Markham does in this book, now updated in this new edition.

The agricultural scene in all its many aspects is moving so fast that it is almost impossible to keep up. Event follows event thick and fast and even the specialist agricultural press has problems in keeping pace, let alone the national news media. This book, however, is as up-to-date as anyone could possibly expect.

Agriculture is no hick industry. Farm economists and accountants have long been in the forefront in developing and applying relevant management principles and techniques to the practical situation. Furthermore, a high proportion of the modern generation of farmers and farm managers have a strong knowledge of their businesses as well as the technical side of farming, with computerisation much in evidence. They have had to have this knowledge in order to stay in business during some bad times, economically speaking, since the mid-1970s. Contrary to what many of the general public seem to think, farming profits have been severely squeezed at times in those years, never more so than in 1998/99.

In addition, the average size of farms has inexorably increased and personal farm businesses and farming companies covering more than 10,000 acres, with turnovers of well over £20 million, are now far from uncommon. Having said that, there are far more considerably smaller successful family farm concerns and it is good that this should be so.

The future is extremely problematic for the agricultural industry. The imminent World Trade Organisation negotiations seem certain to lead to freer trade, i.e., lower tariffs and government support, making it increasingly essential for farmers to raise their competitiveness. At least for some years ahead, world food supply looks likely to exceed effective demand. Within Europe, the probable entry of the Central and Eastern European countries into the European Union will create many tensions. In addition, substantial further changes are sure to be made to the Common Agricultural Policy.

At the same time as these developments are taking place, farmers will be under sustained pressure to conserve and improve the environmental aspects of the countryside and animal welfare. More and more legislation to curb the individual farmer's freedom of action is certain and most of the general public would agree that this is desirable.

For all the above reasons an authoritative, up-to-date book that assists all those involved in the agricultural industry, facing all these pressures, is extremely welcome. The coverage of the book is remarkably wide. The content is not only comprehensive but also very well presented, with lots of headings and sub-headings to guide the user. No words are wasted: waffle is absent.

Gary Markham is an ideal author for such a book. His background and breadth of experience could hardly be bettered. He is someone who has been both an academic and a practitioner – both in the world of accountancy and in practical farming. It is a combination that few could match. It shows in this book.

John Nix
Emeritus Professor of Farm Business Management
Wye College
April 1996

Preface and acknowledgements

Since the first edition of this book, published in the autumn of 1996, the agricultural industry has been through dramatic changes and experienced a sharp decline in profitability in most enterprises which is resulting in financial and personal pressure on many farming businesses.

Over the past two to three years the industry has faced the full impact of BSE, relative high value of sterling, Working Time Directive, the launch of the Euro, National Minimum Wage and CAP Agenda 2000 changes. In the future we shall be facing World Trade Organisation talks, the introduction of Eastern Europe within the EU, and further changes to the CAP.

As a result of these increasing pressures on the industry farmers, more than ever, need a wide range of skills in order to cope with the physical, technical and financial issues of running a business.

It is because of these increasing pressures on the industry that I decided to update this book.

It is unlikely that the profitability of agriculture, apart from some specialist enterprises, will recover over the forthcoming few years. This inevitably means major restructurings within the industry, some of which we are beginning to see. At times like these financial and business management skills are vital in order to adapt and survive, for example, to recognise when to cut costs and streamline existing businesses, when to combine skills and resources with others or when to expand.

Farmers need to have the technical and husbandry skills that are required to achieve the desired level of production at an optimum cost and also an increasing amount of business management skills. A large number of farmers now possess these skills and also have an awareness and working knowledge of the accounting and taxation aspects of their businesses; for example, whether to lease or hire purchase a new machine, or the taxation aspects of the timing of grain or livestock sales.

I have been involved with the agricultural industry all of my life and spent the last fifteen years advising farmers. During this time, I have been fortunate to encounter numerous interesting and challenging situations, businesses and individuals. Because of my farming background the approach in the book is from a practical rather than a technical angle; I apply the accounting concepts and taxation legislation to practical farming business situations.

Broadly speaking there are three dimensions to the financial management of farming businesses, namely:

- accounting;
- business management; and
- taxation.

All three are interrelated and need to be considered in all business decisions; the farm accounts need to be interpreted, identifying strengths and weaknesses enabling business management decisions to be made with regard to the taxation consequences.

In this book I have attempted to bring all three aspects together explaining their relationships.

The book has been written for a range of individuals, but primarily for accountants in general practice, who would not normally deal with a large number of farming clients on a regular basis. In addition, the book is also aimed at all individuals who are involved in farm business management ranging from the rural land agent, bank managers, farm secretaries, consultants and students through to the farmer or manager of the business.

The first section has been completely updated and deals with the structure and description of the industry including the CAP changes announced at the end of March 1999. It is aimed at a reader who is not familiar with the farming industry thereby enabling accountants to understand their farming clients and to approach new farming clients with confidence. This book sets out to provide the information and techniques required by both the accountant to prepare meaningful accounts and the farmer to understand them.

Throughout the remainder of the book I have assumed that the reader has a working knowledge of the principles of the subjects covered. I have concentrated on the particular aspects that tend to be peculiar to the agricultural industry and their application to specific circumstances.

The chapters on accounting and auditing include sections on the role of the accountant and the information required to prepare annual accounts, thereby providing a wider understanding. The objective is for the accountant and the farmer to fully understand their respective aims, hopefully resulting in an efficient and effective service. The examples have been updated throughout this chapter and a new section included on accounting for euros.

The financial management practices chapter has been aimed at all individuals to enable them to understand the farming business in greater depth and the relationship between annual accounts and traditional gross margins. For example, a section has been included on the interpretation of annual accounts for management purposes. A new section has been added on the working capital requirements of expansion.

The taxation chapter deals on a practical level with the areas of taxation that are specific to agriculture. VAT in particular has become a complex tax and sections include common problem areas encountered in farming businesses.

The final chapter is based upon the most common questions, problems and situations I have encountered in farming businesses over the past years. Most are based on the application of accounting, taxation and management advice to individual practical circumstances faced by farmers. New sections include borrowing in euros, capital gains tax planning, working time regulations, business reorganisation and quota. All these are based on my experience of the key issues that farming businesses are currently facing.

In some sections of the book I have used either metric or imperial measurements depending upon the circumstances. I make no apology for this as each one has been carefully considered and, in my opinion, the most appropriate measurement has been used.

I would like to thank Aubrey Davies of Ashton Hughes & Co, Chairman of the Agricultural Group of the Institute of Chartered Accountants in England and Wales, who kindly reviewed this edition, also many of my colleagues at Grant Thornton who have assisted in the production of this book by reviewing and commenting upon the content as it was being updated.

Gary J Markham
April 1999

Chapter 1 – Industry description and background

1.1 Introduction

Agriculture is a unique industry because it uses what most of the population term the 'countryside' to produce most of its goods. In addition, the output of the industry is governed to some extent by the weather and it produces one of our basic needs – food. The production systems of this food industry, as opposed to most other industries, are usually in full view of the general public. Therefore countryside maintenance, welfare issues, visible pollution and other similar issues are important. Also, there are demands for tourism and leisure which are not always compatible with food production. This has placed the industry under increasing pressure from most interested parties.

The source of most of the following data is from *Agriculture in the United Kingdom, 1997* produced annually by the Ministry of Agriculture, Fisheries and Food (MAFF) as a requirement of the Agriculture Act 1993.

1.2 Industry structure

Agriculture is one of the country's largest industries. It currently contributes £7,563 million or 1.1 per cent of the UK's gross domestic product. This has reduced from over £9,000 million or 1.5 per cent in recent years.

1.2.1 Number and size of holdings

Each farming business has a MAFF 'Holding Number' enabling a record to be maintained of all agricultural holdings. The size of holdings is measured in 'European Size Units' (ESUs). This is a measure of the financial potential of an agricultural business based on standard gross margins. Holdings of under 8 ESUs are considered to be part time holdings. The number of holdings above and below this threshold and therefore considered to be full time or part time is (excluding minor holdings):

Table 1.1 *Number of holdings*

	Number of holdings '000	Percentage
Under 8 ESU	107.1	45
8 ESU and above	130.6	55
Total number of holdings	237.7	100

Therefore nearly half the holdings in the UK are officially recognised as not being able to financially support a family and therefore being part-time. The National Farmers' Union predict that by the year 2005 there will be a 13 per cent decrease in full-time farmers with a corresponding 18 per cent increase in part-time farmers. (NFU Publication: *Is UK Agriculture Competitive?*)

Table 1.2 *The number and size of holdings in terms of area*

	Number of holdings '000	Percentage
Above 0.1 Ha under 20 Ha	102.8	43.2
Above 20 Ha under 50 Ha	54.9	23.1
Above 50 Ha under 100 Ha	38.9	16.8
Above 100 Ha	40.1	16.9
Totals	237.7	100

The largest 3 per cent of holdings account for around 26 per cent of the agricultural activity.

1.2.2 Land use

Agriculture uses around 18.294 million hectares (45.2 million acres) of land in the UK. This is in the region of 76 per cent of the total land area of over 24.1 million hectares (59.5 million acres).

The 18.294 million hectares in agriculture are used as shown in Table 1.3.

Table 1.3 *Use of land*

	'000 Ha	*Percentage*
Crops	4,989	27.3
Set-aside	307	1.7
Bare fallow	27	0.1
Grass under 5 years old	1,393	7.6
Permanent grass	5,241	28.6
Owned rough grazing	4,374	23.9
Common rough grazing	1,221	6.7
Other land; roads, buildings, woodlands	742	4.1
Totals	18,294	100

The areas of individual crops grown on the 4,989 hectares used for cropping are shown in Table 1.4.

Table 1.4 *Areas of individual crops*

	'000 Ha	*Percentage*
Cereals		
Wheat	2,036	40.8
Barley	1,358	27.2
Oats	100	2.0
Rye and mixed corn	12	0.2
Triticale	8	0.2
Other crops		
Oilseed rape	446	8.9
Sugar beet	196	3.9
Hops	3	0.1
Peas and beans	197	3.9
Linseed	73	1.5
Potatoes	166	3.3
Other crops	210	4.2
Horticulture		
Vegetables	127	2.6
Orchard fruit	30	0.6
Soft fruit	11	0.2
Nursery stock, bulbs and flowers	14	0.3
Glasshouse crops	2	0.1
Totals	4,989	100

3

1.2.3 Livestock numbers

The number of cattle and sheep is generally dictated by quota: milk quota in the dairy herds and headage quota in beef and sheep. The number of pigs and poultry generally follow their profitability. Pig numbers in particular tend to be cyclical as a result of producers responding to their profitability.

Table 1.5 *Livestock numbers*

	Numbers '000	Average size of herd/flock
Dairy cows	2,473	66.1
Beef cows	1,856	25.8
Heifers in calf	847	
Ewes and shearlings	20,543	245.4
Lambs under one year old	20,926	
Breeding sows	677	80.9
Gilts in pig	116	
Table poultry including broilers	76,621	26,754
Laying poultry	31,962	

1.2.4 Self-sufficiency

The UK is 53 per cent self-sufficient in total food and feed of all types, and 69 per cent self-sufficient in indigenous food and feed. The self sufficiency of individual products is shown in Table 1.6.

Table 1.6 *Self-sufficiency of individual products*

Commodity	% self-sufficient
Wheat	119
Barley	123
Oats	112
Rye, mixed corn and triticale	100
Oilseed rape	92
Linseed	96
Potatoes	92
Sugar	66
Hops	84
Apples	26
Pears	26
Cauliflower	67
Tomatoes	26
Beef and veal	76
Mutton and lamb	94
Pork	106
Bacon and ham	51
Poultry meat	96
Butter	73
Cheese	67
Cream	145
Condensed milk	128
Skimmed milk powder	148
Eggs	96
Wool	46

1.2.5 Workforce

There has been a gradual decline in the workforce in agricultural over the past number of years to around 531,000 persons, representing 2.0 per cent of the total employed workforce. Table 1.7 shows the decline in numbers over a five-year period.

Table 1.7 *Decline in workforce*

	Numbers in '000's				
	1993	1994	1995	1996	1997
Regular full-time					
male	96	93	90	89	88
female	14	13	13	13	13
Regular part-time					
male	30	30	30	31	31
female	25	24	24	23	23
Seasonal or casual					
male	55	54	56	55	55
female	30	28	27	26	26
Salaried managers	8	8	8	8	8
Farmers, partners and directors					
whole-time	180	176	173	170	168
part-time	110	113	114	117	120
Totals	548	539	536	532	532
Spouses of farmers, partners and directors engaged in farm work	79	78	76	75	74
Totals	643	631	624	623	615

The largest decline has been in regular whole-time workers and whole-time partners and directors. Part-time workers, partners and directors have increased.

Survey work conducted by Grant Thornton on 95,000 acres of combinable crops in East Anglia and the East Midlands shows over recent years a reduction in the overall employment costs on farms excluding directors' remuneration, with a corresponding increase in machinery costs. This trend has reversed in the 1997/98 year.

Table 1.8 *Labour and machinery costs*

	1993	1994	1995	1996	1997
Labour costs (£ per acre)	40	37	38	34	39
Total machinery costs (£ per acre)	87	90	99	94	85
Total	127	127	137	128	124
Top 10% of farming businesses in terms of management profit					
Labour costs (£ per acre)	36	20	21	29	12
Total machinery costs (£ per acre)	75	69	75	68	70
Total	111	89	96	97	82

1.2.6 Farming income and productivity

The agricultural industry has a very good record of increasing output as a result of increases in productivity. In particular, yields of crops and milk have increased over the years. This, coupled with the decrease in the labour force, also results in an increase in efficiency as shown below. The gross product is a result of total output less inputs including stock valuation movements but excluding depreciation. The figures are in 1995 prices indices.

Table 1.9 *Gross output and efficiency*

	1993	1994	1995	1996	1997
Gross output including subsidies	99.0	100.3	100.0	99.9	100.5
Gross output per unit of all inputs	103.0	101.9	100.0	101.3	103.2
Gross product per whole-time person equivalent	98.3	99.9	100.0	103.3	106.6

Farming income peaked in 1995 and has dropped dramatically over the past two years. The figures in Table 1.10 are based on total income from farming which is gross output including subsidies, less gross inputs, depreciation, interest, rent and hired labour.

Table 1.10 *Total income from farming £ million*

	1993	1994	1995	1996	1997
Total income from farming	4,358	4,406	5,297	5,139	3,363

As a comparison, the income for previous years peaked in the late eighties and generally declined to 1991. Mainly as a result of EC support packages introduced in 1992 and the weakness of sterling, there was an increase to 1995 with a sharp decline of around 35 per cent in 1997 with the industry currently in a relative recession.

1.2.7 Capital

The capital employed in individual farming businesses is discussed in Chapter **4**. The balance sheet for agriculture in the UK from a lender's point of view is very strong. This is because of the value of the land and property. The value of tenanted land is also included in the following table.

Table 1.11 *The aggregate balance sheet for agriculture in the UK – December 1996*

	£ million
Assets	
fixed	
land and buildings	50,950
plant, machinery and vehicles	8,350
breeding livestock	5,050
Total fixed capital	64,350
current	
trading livestock	3,150
crops and stores	2,650
debtors and cash	4,200
Total current	10,000
Total assets	74,350
Liabilities	
long- and medium-term	
bank loans	1,900
other	2,100
Total long- and medium-term	4,000
short-term	
bank overdraft	2,550
other	2,450
Total short-term	5,000
Total liabilities	9,000
Net worth	65,350

The percentage equity of the industry is 87.9 per cent, mainly as a result of the relatively high value of land.

The increase in profitability in most agricultural enterprises up to 1995 resulted in an increase in investments during the early nineties. There are indications that this has fallen in 1997 with a further drop expected in 1998.

Table 1.12 *Investment in assets*

	1994 £ million	1995 £ million	1996 £ million
Buildings and works	576	523	559
Plant and machinery	1,076	1,182	1,246
Vehicles	241	275	243
Total	1,893	1,981	2,048

1.3 The Common Agricultural Policy (CAP)

The EC Common Agricultural Policy was introduced to provide a mechanism of support for a number of farm products. It also aims to improve farm structure and the means of agricultural production, to ensure that food continues to be supplied to the consumer at a fair price and that farmers have a fair standard of living through the operation of stable markets.

The financing of the CAP is through EU member governments and The European Agricultural Guarantee and Guidance Fund (EAGGF). The Guidance section of the EAGGF, also known by its French acronym FEOGA, provides grants of up to 50 per cent for projects involving the modernisation of holdings, the processing and marketing of products and agricultural development measures. The Guarantee section is responsible for common pricing arrangements for about 90 per cent of the EU's supported farm output. The CAP was reformed in 1992 to its present structure as detailed in this chapter. It is now under renewed pressure for further amendments as a result of the General Agreement on Tariffs and Trade (GATT) agreed on 15 December 1993. In particular, cuts in the volume and value of subsidised exports will be required as well as a move to more market oriented support policies. Total public expenditure under the CAP was £4,081 million in 1996/97 and is forecast to decrease to £3,403 million. The total to include national grants and subsidies was £4,329 million in 1996/97 and is forecast to be £3,692

9

million in 1997/98. The reduction is mainly as a result of a reduction in BSE related expenditure.

1.3.1 Agenda 2000

The European Commission introduced proposals in July 1997 for reform of the CAP. In broad terms these included a move from production support to agri-environmental cross compliance. Agricultural ministers reached an agreement on the CAP reform on 11 March 1999 but this was amended by the Heads of State on 25 March 1999 to retain the total cost within budget. The details below are a summary of the interpretation of the latest information available converted to sterling at 0.675 pence per euro. It should be noted that the sterling equivalent will change with exchange rates.

(a) *Beef*

A reduction in the intervention price by 20 per cent in three stages commencing July 2000, 2001 and 2002. A safety net intervention and private storage aid system introduced from 1 July 2002. To compensate for these reductions there are increases in headage payments in three steps to 2002. Suckler cows to include 20 per cent for heifers (SCPS) to £135, steers (BSPS) to £101 and bulls (BSPS) to £142. There is an increase in extensification payments and provision for national aid. A slaughter premium has been introduced paying £54 for over seven months animals and £34 under seven months.

(b) *Dairy*

A reduction in support prices by 15 per cent over three years in stages starting July 2005. The introduction of a Dairy Cow Premium in 2005. Milk quota to be retained until March 2006 with a 1.5 per cent increase in the total European quota as from 2003.

(c) *Extensification*

The stocking density calculation has been amended to include all cattle over six months of age rather than cattle subject to a subsidy claim, which excluded heifers. Payments will be subject to decreasing stocking rates with increasing payments to £54 per head for stocking rates less than 1.4 livestock units per hectare in 2002. The payments will no longer be automatic and will have to be applied for (**1.9**).

(d) *Arable*

A reduction of 15 per cent in intervention price in two steps in 2000 and 2001. An increase in the area payments for cereals in two stages to £256 per Ha in 2001. Oilseeds and linseed area payments reduced in three steps to £256 per Ha in 2002. Protein crops to receive a premium to a total of £282 per Ha. Compulsory set-aside set at 10 per cent for 2000 to 2006 at cereals rate. The payment period for area aid is 16 November to 31 January.

(e)   *Cross compliance*
Member states will be obliged to introduce environmental conditions and requirements on all direct aid payments. The actual condition and penalties for not complying at the discretion of each member state.

(f)   *Capping and modulation*
It was proposed that total subsidy payments per business are restricted in stages with the first 100,000 euros per business being paid at 100 per cent (equivalent to around £70,000 and 257 Ha or 640 acres of arable land), the second 100,000 Euros at 80 per cent and the remainder at 75 per cent. The level of employment within a farming business may be taken into account. These measures have not been implemented in the latest agreements but are available to Member States to adopt.

(g)   *Separate businesses*
To obtain separate IACS status at present businesses must comply with certain financial and managerial criteria. The capping and modulation proposals have led farmers to consider reorganising their businesses to avoid the proposed ceiling. In order to be considered as a separate business it is likely that complete separate financial responsibility and managerial control by different individuals may be required with individuals not having a financial interest or being involved in the management in more than one business It is understood that the Commission proposes to introduce anti-avoidance measures to avoid the ceiling being circumvented. It is suggested that the IACS Separate Business Questionnaire issued by MAFF (reference IACS 26 (11/97)) is obtained and studied in the first instance.

1.3.2 Agrimonetory system – Green Pound

The common prices within the community are expressed in European Currency Units (ECU), now in Euros. For agricultural commodities, the conversion of EC prices in Euros into pounds sterling, was by a rate of exchange called the 'Green Pound'. As the value of the pound fluctuates the conversion to sterling changes, therefore as the pound has strengthened the support prices have reduced. However there has been a mechanism to compensate for the reduction in support prices which at the end of 1998 allowed the subsidy payments to be 11.5 per cent above the market exchange rate.

The United Kingdom, together with Denmark, Sweden and Greece has remained outside the Economic and Monetary Union (EMU) and therefore will continue to require a mechanism to convert support payments from Euros into national currencies. The green rate has now disappeared, the conversion of ongoing support such as intervention prices will operate on a daily spot basis and the arable and livestock support payments will continue to be converted on the dates as before.

- Arable area payments: exchange rate on 1 July each year.
- Livestock payments: exchange rate on 1 January each year.
- Flax and hemp: exchange rate on 1 August each year.

There is a provision for compensation over a three year period if payments are reduced as a result of the withdrawal of the Green Rate. Therefore the current 11.5 per cent gap between the market exchange rate and the previous green rate will be fully compensated by the EC in the first year but will require a contribution from the UK government in the second and third years.

1.3.3 European Enlargement

There are ten Central and East European Countries (CEEC) who are candidates to join the existing 15 countries in the European Union. Current Agenda 2000 proposals include provision for agricultural and rural development aid for the ten candidate countries to bring their production methods up to date and in line with the existing members. The addition of the ten countries will:

- double the current agricultural workforce with workers who earn around 40 per cent of current EU workers;
- increase the arable area by around 50 per cent;
- increase the total population within the EU by around 30 per cent;
- increase total agricultural production considerably.

1.4 Economic and Monetary Union (EMU)

There has been much debate in the farming industry as to whether the industry will be better or worse off should the UK enter into the EMU. The industry has been lobbying government to provide a euro payment option for support payments. The new EU regulation allows member states the option for farmers to receive support payments in euros. MAFF has indicated that intervention buying and export refunds can be paid in euros by the autumn of 2000 but there is no indication as to whether direct support payments will be available in euros.

The main advantages for agriculture are (**6.14**):

- a fixed exchange rate would stabilise support payments and commodity prices;
- no longer a need for the agrimonetary system;

12

- the possibility of receiving support payments in euros, however a greater degree of financial management will be required to ensure that exchange rate risks are minimised;
- the ability to take out loans in euros at lower interest rates although interest rates are likely to converge in the next 3 to 4 years;
- the ability to purchase machinery and inputs from European countries although they may not be significantly cheaper.

1.5 The Integrated Administration and Control System (IACS)

This system of administering the subsidies available commenced in April 1993 where in order to claim subsidies, details of all land farmed and crops grown have to be submitted to a local MAFF regional office in England, and the Welsh Agricultural Department in Wales, by the 15 May every year. The only exception is headage subsidies for sheep where the completion of the forms is optional. This has enabled the MAFF to compile a computerised database of all fields in the UK.

This scheme is very complex with many detailed rules. The following paragraphs provide an overview and do not attempt to cover all aspects. Booklets are produced annually by MAFF and are freely available from their regional centres. The regional centres can also be contacted by telephone to answer any queries on the scheme. Inevitably there are many grey areas within the complex rules and clients will constantly be raising queries regarding their personal circumstances. It is not advisable for any accountant to attempt to interpret the rules without a detailed knowledge of the schemes. It is recommended that all queries regarding the interpretation of the rules for individual circumstances should be made in writing to the local MAFF regional centre, advising them of all the facts and requesting a written reply. A response is normally obtained within a reasonable time.

MAFF amalgamate farming businesses where they are not financially independent and the principals have interests in other farming businesses (**1.3.1**). This is to ensure that the various schemes are being correctly claimed. In particular, the Beef Special Premium Scheme which is subject to 90 animals per holding or business (**1.6**) and where there are dairy and suckler cow enterprises where restrictions apply (**1.7**). In the future total subsidies may be subject to a maximum per business (**1.3.1**).

These points should be borne in mind when there is a reorganisation of family businesses or when a new farm is purchased.

The support systems governed by the IAC System are:

- Beef Special Premium Scheme (BSPS)
- Suckler Cow Premium Scheme (SCPS)
- Sheep Annual Premium Scheme (SAPS)
- Extensification Premium
- Hill Livestock Compensatory Allowances (HLCA)
- Arable Area Payments Scheme (AAPS)
- Grain Legumes Scheme

1.6 Beef Special Premium Scheme (BSPS)

This is based on a payment per animal and was introduced to compensate farmers for a reduction in the price of beef cattle as a result of a reduction of 15 per cent in the intervention price. It is payable on up to 90 male, or castrated male, cattle per age category, per holding, per annum. The BSPS is not subject to a quota system and any number of farmers can claim. However there is a regional maximum number of claims based on the number of claims made in 1991. The regions are:

- England and Wales
- Scotland
- Northern Ireland

When total claims exceed the regional threshold the payment is scaled down.

A claim can be made twice per castrated animal, once for male animals:

(a) Animals that reach the age of 10 months old. A claim can be made when they are eight months old and they have to be retained on the holding for the two months after the claim is made, called the 'retention period'.
(b) Animals that reach the age of 23 months old. A claim can be made at 21 months, again with a two month retention period on the farm.

Therefore a claim can be made on a total of 180 castrated male cattle, including the two age groups, per holding, per annum.

Prior to 28 September 1998 all animals had to have Cattle Identification Documents (CID's) in order to claim the subsidy and for them to be sold. These documents were colour coded based on whether a claim had been made. Animals registered after 28 September 1998 require the new cheque book style cattle passports issued by the British Cattle Movement Service which replace the CIDs.

1.6.1 Stocking rates

The payment is made subject to a maximum stocking rate of two Live-stock Units (LU) per hectare (0.81 per acre). A further premium per animal called 'Extensification Premium' (**1.9**) is available when stocking rates are below 1.4 LU per hectare (0.57 per acre) with the subsidy increasing if the stocking rate is below 1.0 LU per hectare (0.4 per acre).

Stocking rates are calculated on the total claimed forage area of the holding based on the following animals upon which premium is claimed:

- Ewes   0.15 LU
- Cows, bulls and male cattle over two years old   1.00 LU
- Male cattle 6 months to 2 years   0.60 LU

Therefore the ewes and beef suckler cows included in the calculation will be calculated on the appropriate quota.

Dairy cows are calculated on the total milk quota divided by a notional yield per cow of 5,195.7 litres rather than the number of cows.

Heifers and male cattle not subject to a claim are not included in the stocking rate calculation.

The forage area used in the calculation is all land farmed on a holding that is not included in a claim for arable area payments (**1.11**). The forage area does not have to grow grass, for example, a crop of wheat or barley can be grown as long as a claim is not made for arable area payments.

1.6.2 Payment of premium

The payment is usually made in two instalments; the first, being 60 per cent, after 1 November with the balance the following spring in April, May or June. The Extensification Premium payment is also made, where applicable, with the second instalment.

In 1988 as a result of the low market prices for beef following the BSE crisis, 80 per cent of the payment was made in October.

The payment in 1998 is 108.70 ECU per head and was based on the Green Rate on 1 January 1998 of 1 ECU per £0.775745 (taking account of the 11.5 per cent threshold (**1.3.2**)) giving a payment per head of £84.32 for castrated males and £104.73 for bulls. Both these are before a possible scale down (**1.6**).

The payment of Extensification Premium (**1.9**) in 1998 was 36 ECUs, giving a payment of £27.93 for stocking rates up to 1.4 LU per hectare, and 52 ECUs, giving a payment of £40.34 for stocking rates below 1 LU per hectare.

The accounting treatment of these payments is discussed in **2.8**.

1.7 Suckler cow premium scheme (SCPS)

The premium is restricted to the suckler cow quota which is allocated to a producer rather than a holding. Therefore unlike milk quota it is not attached to land.

Cows and replacement in-calf heifers must be a beef breed or a cross, must be retained on the holding for six months after a claim is made and must be used for breeding beef calves. Dairy producers with a quota above 116,500 litres are not eligible to claim under this scheme.

Extensification Premium (**1.9**) per head is also payable when stocking rates are below 1.4 LU per hectare (0.57 per acre) with additional payments when stocking rates are below 1 LU per hectare (0.4 per acre).

1.7.1 Stocking rates

The same stocking rates as for the BSPS apply with in calf heifer replacements included in the calculation.

1.7.2 Suckler cow quota

These were allocated to producers in 1993 and can be sold or leased within geographic areas. The market price has varied depending on the geographic area allocated:

Table 1.13 *Market price of suckler cow quota 1997/1998*

	Less favoured area *£ per unit*	*Lowland* *£ per unit*
Sale	110	115
Lease	30	30

Quota sold without the sale of the whole holding is subject to a 15 per cent transfer to a national reserve without compensation. There are restrictions on minimum amounts that can be sold or leased.

At least 90 per cent of the quota must be used by a producer or leased out in the 1997 Scheme year, otherwise it may be confiscated to the national reserve.

1.7.3 Payment of premium

Payments limited to the quota are paid in two instalments as in the BSPS. The payment rate in 1998 was 144.90 ECUs per head at a green rate of 1 ECU per £0.775745 (taking account of the 11.5 per cent threshold (**1.3.2**)), giving a payment per head of £112.41. The payment of Extensification Premium in 1998 was 36 ECUs, giving a payment of £27.93 for stocking rates below 1.4 LSU per hectare (0.57 per acre) and 52 ECUs, giving a payment of £40.34 for stocking rates below 1 LSU per hectare (0.4 per acre).

The accounting treatment of these payments is discussed in **2.8**.

1.8 Sheep annual premium scheme (SAPS)

This premium is subject to quota allocated in 1993 to individual producers. Headage payments are made on female sheep that:

- have lambed, or
- attained the age of 12 months,

by the end of a 100 day retention period from 4 February until 15 May. Prior to 1996 there were two retention periods. Because there is not a requirement for the sheep to lamb, a number of farmers have developed a system of purchasing ewe lambs that will fulfil the age criteria by the end of the retention period, therefore claiming the premium, and selling the young ewes for breeding the following summer. This reduces the workload as the sheep do not lamb.

There are strict rules regarding losses during a retention period and detailed records of all sales and purchases must be maintained throughout the year.

1.8.1 Sheep quota

Sheep quota has been amended since its introduction in 1993. In particular, initially there was a maximum of 500 ewes in lowland holdings and 1,000 ewes in upland holdings at full rate, with the balance, if any, at a rate of 50 per cent. The number of quota at 50 per cent have now been halved and converted to full rights.

Sheep quota can be sold or leased with or without land. However, a sale without land will attract a 15 per cent siphon, without compensation, to the national reserve. Sheep quota cannot be sold out of a Less Favoured Area (LFA). There is a minimum amount of quota that can be sold or leased depending upon the total amount of quota held by the producer.

The prices of leasing and sale have varied considerably and have been in the region of:

Table 1.14 Approximate prices of leasing and sale of sheep quota 1997/1998		
	Less favoured area £ per head	Lowland £ per head
Lease	10	6
Sale	30	15

At least 70 per cent of the quota must be used by a producer otherwise it will be confiscated to the national reserve. Similarly, at least 70 per cent of the quota in any two consecutive years out of five must be used when the quota is leased out.

1.8.2 Payment of premium

Payments limited to the quota are usually paid in two or three instalments; up to 60 per cent in the autumn as two payments with the balance before the following 31 March. The payment is not fixed at the outset as in the BSPS and the SCPS. It is based on the difference between the price set by the EU and the average market price for sheep. Therefore the initial payment is an estimate with the final balance not announced until the following spring.

The total payment in 1998 has been finalised at £17.44. Two advance payments were made in the autumn of 1998. Therefore the final payment in March 1999 will be £7.01 per head.

An additional supplement is normally payable to eligible ewes in Less Favoured Areas.

• In 1998 this supplement was £5.15.

The accounting treatment of these payments is discussed in **2.8**.

1.9 Extensification Premium

This is paid automatically as an additional payment to the BSP and the SCP when stocking rates are below 1.4 LU per Ha (0.57 LU per acre). A higher rate is payable when stocking rates are below 1 LSU per hectare (0.4 per acre). It is paid with the second instalment. This payment is subject to a scale back as in the BSPS and SCPS.

The payments in 1998 converted to sterling at the green rate of 0.775745 on January 1 1998 after adjustment for the 11.5 per cent threshold (**1.3.2**) are:

- Stocking rates below 1.4 LSU per hectare   36 ECU   £27.93
- Stocking rates below 1 LSU per hectare   52 ECU   £40.34

The calculation of stocking rates has been amended in the latest amendments in Agenda 2000 (**1.3.1**).

1.10 Hill Livestock Compensatory Allowances

These are additional headage payments to the BSPS, SCPS and SAPS and apply to holdings in Less Favoured Areas subject to certain criteria. There are two rates of payment based on whether the land is in:

- a disadvantaged area; or
- a severely disadvantaged area.

The payments in £ per head in 1998 are:

Table 1.15 *Payments in 1998 (£ per head)*

	Severely Disadvantaged Area	Disadvantaged Area
Hardy breeding ewes	5.75	N/A
Breeding ewes	3.00	2.65
Breeding cows	47.50	23.75

There are an increasing amount of environmentally based criteria being imposed on these payments to minimise the effect of overgrazing. These criteria include:

Disadvantaged areas
- minimum area of 3 hectares (7.4 acres);
- maximum amount of payments of £97.65 per Ha (£39.52 per acre);
- maximum of 1.4 LU (0.57 per acre) and 9 ewes per Ha (3.64 ewes per acre).

Severely disadvantaged areas
- maximum amount of payments of £121.49 per Ha (£49.17 per acre);
- maximum of 1.4 LU (0.57 per acre) and 6 ewes per Ha (2.43 ewes per acre).

A sheep annual premium scheme supplement of £5.15 is paid on all eligible sheep in less favoured areas. In addition £0.50 per head in lowlands and £0.73 per head in less favoured areas was paid in 1997 to compensate for the adverse exchange rates.

1.11 Arable Area Payments Scheme (AAPS)

1.11.1 Introduction

The accounting treatment of arable area payments is included in **2.14**.

This scheme offers payments based on the areas of the following crops and set-aside, on eligible land:

- cereals including wheat, durum wheat, barley, oats, rye, maize, triticale, sweetcorn, sorghum, buckwheat, millet and canary seed;
- oilseeds including oilseed rape, sunflower seed and soya beans;
- proteins including peas and field beans for harvesting dry, sweet lupins;
- linseed;
- set-aside land, lying fallow or growing an industrial crop.

These payments were introduced in the 1993 harvest, increasing to their current level over the first three years, to compensate farmers for a phased reduction in the price of these crops by a reduction in intervention and target prices.

The scheme is not compulsory. There are two main options:

(a) *Main scheme*
   A proportion of the eligible land on a holding must be set aside in order to receive the area payments.

(b) *Simplified scheme*
   There is no requirement to set aside any land under this scheme but the land area claimed must be less than a standardised area that at average yields would produce 92 tonnes of grain. This equates to an area of 15.62 Ha (38.6 acres) in England and 18.22 Ha (45.02 acres) in Wales. The area payments are at the cereals rate irrespective of the crops grown. Therefore, the benefit is that there is no set aside requirement but the higher area payments for oilseeds, proteins and linseed will not be available.

1.11.2 Eligible land

This is based on the use of the land as at 31 December 1991. The land must have been growing cereals, oilseeds, proteins or linseed or a grass ley less than five years old. In addition, land is now treated as eligible if the following crops were grown as at 31 December 1991: raspberries, gooseberries, cranberries, loganberries, black currants, or other such crops, or asparagus, artichokes or rhubarb.

1.11.3 Transfer of eligibility

The rules on transferring eligible and ineligible land were relaxed in February 1999 with the Commission rewriting the regulation. MAFF have issued an explanatory booklet AR28 which is available from Regional Service Centres (Appendix **4**).

1.11.4 The payments

The payments are set every year on the exchange rate from ECU to sterling on 1 July. The support payments are set in ECU per tonne converted to ECU per Ha using a regional yield.

Each region in the UK has a base area and if all claims exceed the base area the payments paid to farmers in that region will be reduced. In addition there will be an uncompensated increase in the set-aside rate.

Forage maize has a separate base area which has been exceeded in previous years.

The green rate on 1 July 1998 was 1 ECU equivalent to £0.775249 after an adjustment for an exchange rate buffer of 11.5 per cent (**1.3.2**). The arable area payments for the regions are converted from ECUs per tonne by a standard yield in each region to ECUs per Ha. The yields for cereals vary from 5.03 tonnes per hectare in Northern Ireland to 5.89 tonnes per hectare in England; oilseeds vary from 2.84 tonnes per hectare in Scotland LFA to 3.45 tonnes per hectare in Scotland non LFA. These yields are set out in Table 1.16.

Table 1.16 *Yields for cereals and oilseeds*

		ECU/Ha	£/Ha	£/Acre
Cereals	England	320.06	238.34	96.46
	Wales LFA	274.42	207.26	82.70
	Wales non LFA	280.94	212.18	84.66
	Scotland LFA	283.11	213.82	86.53
	Scotland non LFA	308.11	214.55	86.83
	N. Ireland LFA	273.33	206.43	83.54
	N. Ireland non LFA	283.65	214.23	86.70
Oilseeds*	England	565.75	298.83	120.93
	Wales LFA	576.78	308.98	125.04
	Wales non LFA	576.78	308.98	125.04
	Scotland LFA	521.67	279.46	113.09
	Scotland non LFA	633.72	315.38	127.63
	N. Ireland LFA	536.36	287.33	116.28
	N. Ireland non LFA	536.36	287.33	116.28
Proteins	England	462.31	344.27	139.32
	Wales LFA	396.37	299.36	121.15
	Wales non LFA	405.79	306.47	124.03
	Scotland LFA	408.93	308.85	124.99
	Scotland non LFA	445.04	312.35	126.41
	N. Ireland LFA	394.80	298.18	120.67
	N. Ireland non LFA	409.72	309.44	125.23
Set aside	England	405.41	301.90	122.18
	Wales LFA	347.59	262.52	106.26
	Wales non LFA	355.85	268.76	108.76
	Scotland LFA	358.80	270.84	109.61
	Scotland non LFA	390.27	273.91	110.85
	N. Ireland LFA	346.21	261.48	105.82
	N. Ireland non LFA	359.29	271.36	109.82
Linseed	England	619.04	460.98	186.56
	Wales LFA	530.76	400.86	162.22
	Wales non LFA	543.37	410.38	166.08
	Scotland LFA	547.57	413.55	167.36
	Scotland non LFA	595.92	418.24	169.26
	N. Ireland LFA	528.65	399.27	161.58
	N. Ireland non LFA	548.62	414.35	167.68

* The oilseeds payments in sterling are after the 29.07 per cent reduction in 1998.

1.11.5 Payment dates

Payments for all crops and set-aside apart from oilseeds are made during the period 16 October and 31 December, although in practice some farmers have received payments later than this. Agenda 2000 (**1.3.1**) proposes to amend the payment of these to the period 16 November to 31 January.

Oilseed payments are paid in two instalments; up to 50 per cent is made in September with the balance subject to a scale back (**1.11.6**) in the following April.

1.11.6 Oilseed payments

The oilseed payments are subject to an EU 'Maximum Guaranteed Area' and if this threshold is exceeded payments are reduced in all Member States who exceed their base area. In addition, payments may be further adjusted as a result of the level of world prices. Payments have been reduced in most years with a considerable reduction in 1998.

1.11.7 Set-aside

Land must be eligible for set-aside. Initially it must be eligible for the AAPS as set out in paragraph **1.11.2** or be accepted as eligible for transfer of eligibility (**1.11.3**).

The minimum area that can be set-aside per applicant is equal to or greater than 0.3 Ha (0.74 acres). The period of set-aside is from 15 January to 31 August; guaranteed set-aside is subject to specific management all year.

The following two criteria have been waived in 1998:

(a) Previously the land must have been cultivated with the intention of producing a harvestable crop or have been in set-aside in the previous year.
(b) Previously the land must have been farmed by the claimant in the previous two years subject to certain exemptions such as land inherited, taken back in hand or rented. In these circumstances only the obligatory minimum set-aside was allowed.

There are a number of set-aside options:

(a) *Obligatory set-aside*
The area can be rotated, remain in the same place or a mixture of both. Therefore a great deal of freedom is allowed as long as the

correct percentage of land is set-aside. The set-aside rules have relaxed over the past two years with this category replacing 'rotational' and 'flexible' set-aside. The area that must be set-aside in 1998/99 is 10 per cent of the total cropped and set-aside area.

(b) *Guaranteed set-aside*

This option is no longer available unless linked to the Countryside Access Scheme or for biomass production. The land must remain in set-aside for five years and in return the payments are guaranteed to remain at their ECU level for the five years.

(c) *Voluntary set-aside*

Land can be set-aside in addition to the obligatory amount and receive area payments, up to a maximum of the area of land which is being cropped and upon which area payments are being claimed. Therefore in most cases 50 per cent of the farm can be set-aside. New rules now allow more than 50 per cent if all the land is used for biomass.

(d) *Additional voluntary set-aside*

This is only available to participants in the previous '5 Year Set-Aside Scheme' where it is possible to enter land from the previous five year scheme into additional voluntary set-aside. Therefore up to 100 per cent of the eligible land.

(e) *Penalty set-aside*

This is imposed when a regional base area is exceeded. No payment is received.

(f) *Transfer of eligibility for environmental, plant health or agronomic grounds.*

The rules were relaxed in January 1999 (**1.11.3**).

(g) *Transferable set-aside*

The obligation can be transferred to other land and businesses within a 20 Km radius. It is sometimes called importing or exporting set-aside.

1.11.8 Set-aside rates

The set-aside rates are as follows:

Table 1.17 *Set-aside rates*

	Rotational %	Non-rotational %
1993 harvest	15	18
1994 harvest	15	18
1995 harvest	12	15
1996 harvest	10	10
1997 harvest	5	5
1998 harvest	5	5
1999 harvest	10	10

1.11.9 Set-aside links with other schemes

Set-aside is linked to several other schemes with payments in addition to the set-aside payments apart from the Woodland Scheme:

(a) *Countryside Access Scheme*
Started in 1995 on land in guaranteed set-aside allowing permissive (not permanent) access as 10m wide routes (£90 per hectare (£36 per acre)) and open field spaces (£45 per hectare (£18 per acre)).

(b) *Woodland Schemes*
Land entered into Woodland Schemes can count as set-aside. The woodland grants are available but set-aside payments are not (**6.10**).

(c) *Nitrogen Sensitive Areas (NSA)*
Land in this scheme can count as set-aside.

(d) *Habitat Scheme*
Land in this scheme can count as set-aside.

(e) *Environmentally Sensitive Areas (ESA)*
Land in this scheme can count as set-aside provided it has not reverted from arable to grassland.

(f) *Countryside Stewardship Scheme*
Land in this scheme can count as set-aside provided it has not reverted from arable to grassland.

(g) *Organic Aid Scheme*
Land in this scheme can count as set-aside and arable area payments.

1.11.10 Non food or non feed crops on set aside land

Annual or perennial crops for a non food or non feed use can be grown on set-aside land provided the value of the non food or non feed product exceeds the value of any by product used for food or feed. The most common crop grown is industrial oilseed rape and linseed. The crops must be grown under contract.

Crops with no feed use include short rotation coppice and elephant grass (Miscanthus).

1.11.11 Commercial implications of set-aside

There are gains and losses as a result of the introduction of set-aside which will be different in every farming business. Many farming businesses have now accepted set-aside as part of their management of the land and take the opportunity to achieve timeliness and carry out land maintenance work.

Gains
• Many farms have had a timeliness benefit from establishing crops

such as winter oilseed rape early on land that was previously in rotational fallow set-aside.

- Larger farms in the early years of set-aside were able to reduce their labour and machinery costs. As the set-aside area has reduced over the years these farms are now more efficient in this cost area.
- There can be a reduction in working capital when crops are not grown on the set-aside land.
- Some farms have reduced the amount of the lower gross margin crops.
- Set-aside can allow the least productive areas on the farm to be set-aside.
- Set-aside allows some operations of land maintenance to be carried out without any damage to growing crops, such as ditching and hedging.

Losses
- The gross margin is lost when the land is fallow and non food crops grown on set-aside land tend to have lower margins.
- Set-aside can interrupt the cropping rotation on the farm although it has now been integrated into the rotation in most businesses.

The area payments for oilseeds have been subject to a scale back (**1.11.6**) in 1998 which has reduced the commercial margin below the non food crop margin. Consideration should be given to including areas of oilseed rape in voluntary set-aside to benefit from the set-aside area payment.

1.11.12 Husbandry rules and arable area payments

To be eligible for arable area payments farmers must conform to detailed rules which have been amended over the years. It is possible for individual farmers to apply to MAFF for exemptions from some of the rules depending upon individual circumstances. It is essential that permission is obtained in writing for any deviation from the standard rules, otherwise part or all the arable area payments on the holding may be withdrawn.

The rules and regulations for the 1999 cropping year together with some key dates are summarised below and provide an indication of the management requirements that farmers have to adhere to. The detailed rules are published by MAFF every year and are available from their regional centres.

(a) *After 1998 harvest*
A green cover must be sown or natural regeneration must be allowed to establish on land destined for fallow set-aside for the 1999 harvest.

(b) *1 October 1998*

A green cover need not be established if crops are still in the ground on land destined for set-aside.

(c) *15 January 1999*

Set-aside period starts for 1999 harvest. Any remaining crops on the land must not be harvested nor grazed. This has been extended to 28 February in 1999 because of the exceptionally wet conditions. The land cannot be put to any use for any return or cash apart from grazing private, non-agricultural livestock such as family ponies.

(d) *15 May 1999*

IACS area aid application forms must be with MAFF by this date.

(e) *15 May 1999*

All crops subject to a claim for the 1999 harvest must be sown by this date apart from forage maize grown below 250 metres above sea level, sweetcorn and sunflower seed.

(f) *31 May 1999*

Forage maize and sunflower crops must be sown.

(g) *15 June 1999*

Sweetcorn crop must be sown.

(h) *1 July 1999*

Set-aside land can be cultivated to control weeds.

(i) *15 July 1999*

Cereal, oilseed and protein crops for harvest in 2000 and some horticultural crops can be sown on 1999 set-aside land. A grass ley can be sown but it can not be grazed or cut before 15 January 2000.

(j) *15 July to 15 August 1999*

Deadline for cutting any green cover on set-aside land apart from guaranteed set-aside land.

(k) *31 August 1999*

Set-aside period ends for 1999 harvest for flexible and rotational set-aside but restrictions remain for the use of any green cover.

(l) *1 September 1999*

Set-aside land can be grazed by animals belonging to the farm. Hay or silage can be harvested for own use only.

(m) *15 January 2000*

Green cover from 1999 set-aside land can be harvested for sale after this date if the land is not set-aside for the 2000 harvest.

1.12 Land classification

1.12.1 Introduction

The type of farming and the enterprises found in farming businesses are largely dictated by the land type and quality. Therefore different enterprises are found in different regions of the country. The Ministry of Agriculture Fisheries and Food (MAFF) classifies land in England and Wales into five grades according to its suitability to farming based on soil type, climate and relief.

1.12.2 Grades of land

(a) *Grade 1*
Soils capable of growing a wide range of crops with high yields. They are mostly loams, sandy loams and peats with good drainage and water availability. They have a high level of natural fertility or are highly responsive to fertilisers.

(b) *Grade 2*
Soils capable of growing a wide range of crops but with limitations which exclude them from Grade 1. These limitations restrict the range of crops capable of being grown and their yield potential.

(c) *Grade 3 (split into A and B)*
Land which is still capable of growing good crops but only a more restricted range than Grade 2. At the top of the grade, the less demanding horticultural crops, i.e, cereals, roots and grass can be grown. At the bottom of the grade, oats, barley, grass and feed crops for animals can be grown.

(d) *Grade 4*
This land has restricted potential, the choice of crops being limited, yields moderate and the timing of cultivations restricted to times when the weather is favourable. This land is mostly down to grass, with smaller areas of oats, barley and feed crops for animals.

(e) *Grade 5*
Land with very severe restrictions, being mostly rough grazing.

1.13 Farming systems – geographic location

There are large variations in the range and type of enterprises carried on by farmers. The choice is largely dictated by the quality and type of land (**1.12.2**), topography, rainfall, proximity to markets and processing facilities and the quota or eligibility for subsidies.

The western parts of England and Wales are more suited to grass growth than cropping because of the topography and rainfall, therefore livestock enterprises predominate. The better quality land in these areas usually supports dairy enterprises, with the remainder, including the hill areas, supporting beef and sheep. The drier eastern parts support cropping systems with the land type dictating the type of crop grown, which is discussed in more detail in paragraph **1.14** below. Sugar beet is only grown in the proximity of sugar beet processing factories located as follows:

- Allscott, Shropshire
- Bardeney, Lincolnshire
- Bury St Edmunds, Suffolk
- Cantley, Norfolk
- Ipswich, Suffolk
- Kidderminster
- Newark, Nottinghamshire
- Wissington, Kings Lynn
- York

The best quality land will be used for growing vegetables, particularly where irrigation is available. In general these areas are located in East Anglia, Worcestershire, Lincolnshire, Herefordshire and Kent.

1.14 Arable and cropping

1.14.1 Introduction

Plants are grown to produce various primary and secondary products, for example:

Table 1.18 *Various primary and secondary plant products*		
Crop	*Primary product*	*Secondary product*
Cereals	Seed	Straw
Potatoes	Root tubers	
Sugar beet	Root	Tops for grazing
Peas	Seed	Haulm silage from vining peas
Oilseed rape	Oil from seed	Rapemeal for animal feeds
Herbage seed	Seed	Forage for hay or grazing

1.14.2 Soil and nutrients

Soil used for crop production must have a suitable tilth and structure in the surface layer of the seedbed to provide air and water for seed germination. The lower layer of the soil must be free draining and surplus water is usually removed by drains, clay tiles, plastic pipes and mole drains.

The higher value crops such as potatoes and vegetables are usually irrigated. It is very difficult to obtain licences to irrigate crops and specialist growers are considering investing in the construction of reservoirs to store winter water for irrigating in the summer.

For optimum crop growth soils should contain the correct balance of the required nutrients. The main nutrients are:

- nitrogen
- phosphate
- potash

Phosphate and potash are applied depending upon the existing reserves in the soil and this is usually measured every two to three years by soil chemical analysis. Different crops have varying requirements and the required amount of fertiliser is generally applied in the seedbed. There are very little reserves of nitrogen in the soil, therefore the crop is provided with the required amount, usually at its active growth stage and in two or three applications. Some crops such as peas and beans, being leguminous, manufacture their own nitrogen and therefore will not require any application.

In addition, the soil must have the appropriate level of acidity or alkalinity for the crop grown, which can be governed by the application of lime. Depending upon the inherent acidity of the soil, lime may be applied every five to eight years.

Many soils suffer from compaction either in general or have compacted layers at specific depths. These are as a result of the heavy equipment used and many soils are now broken up by dragging a 'subsoiler' through, thus opening up the soil allowing surplus water to drain through the top layers to the drainage system installed at a lower depth.

1.14.3 Rotations

Crops are commonly rotated around the farm to maintain soil nutrients and structure and to control weeds, pests and diseases. These objectives can mostly be achieved by the use of disease resistant varieties, artificial fertilisers and chemicals and some farmers grow continuous cereals. However, because of the costs and environmental considerations most farms rotate different crops around the farm. Poorer grades of land are less able to support continuous cereals. Winter wheat currently has the potential to produce the highest margin, therefore this crop predominates. The yield potential drops in the second year, however many farmers are now growing the crop two years in a row, the second year's crop termed 'second wheats'. In most rotations land is given a break from growing cereals for a year to increase subsequent yields. The break crop is normally oilseed rape, peas or beans or a grass ley when there are also livestock on the farm.

1.14.4 Chemical control

Chemical sprays are used to control weeds, diseases and pests. Weeds will compete with crops for soil nutrients, water and light, contaminate the crop and can contribute to pest and disease carry-over. The range of weed sprays is vast but in general they are used to control annual and perennial broad leaved weeds and grass weeds. The control of pests and diseases begins with a variety that may not be so susceptible to certain diseases than others. A number of diseases may be controlled by treating the seed prior to sowing.

Chemicals sprayed to control weeds tend to be applied routinely, but because of the cost of the chemical and its application, spraying for disease and pests is carried out when there is thought to be an economic benefit from spraying.

1.14.5 Inputs or variable costs

The inputs normally used to grow crops are:

- seeds of a correct variety dressed in chemicals
- fertilisers
- chemicals.

The cost of these inputs is deducted from the output of the crop to produce the standard gross margin per acre or hectare. Their costs vary depending upon the crop: being £20 per acre for seed, £35 per acre for fertiliser and £45 per acre for chemicals on a crop of winter wheat, down to £30, £6, and £25 respectively for spring sown beans. The total inputs for potatoes including casual labour is in the region of £1,800 to £2,000 per Ha (£730 to £810 per acre).

The application of fertilisers and chemicals is usually made with a set arrangement of wheelmarkings called tramlines. These ensure the tractors travel along the same lines on each application therefore keeping crop damage to a minimum and avoiding an overlap of the application. After the cultivations and drilling in the autumn, the number of times that tractors and machinery travel through the crops, before harvest, can be in the region of eight times, comprising two nitrogen fertiliser applications and up to six chemical applications.

Some farming businesses apply liquid fertiliser with their sprayer, therefore a fertiliser applicator is not required and this reduces the investment in machinery.

1.14.6 Cereals

Wheat and barley are the most common cereals, with wheat more common on the heavier land and potentially providing a higher margin than barley. Oats are grown where other cereals would not thrive in the wetter conditions.

31

Wherever possible, winter varieties of cereals are grown. These are sown from mid to late September to mid to late October. Spring cereals are sown from late February to the end of March. One of the main determinants of yield is time of sowing. Generally, the earlier the sowing the greater the yield. Because of the longer growing season, yields from winter sown crops are up to about 30 per cent higher than spring varieties.

Cereals may be grown for:

- feed wheat
- milling wheat
- seed grown under contract
- malting barley
- feed barley

Milling wheat and malting barley varieties produce less yield than feed varieties. However they command a premium if the required quality is achieved.

1.14.7 Spring sowing

Spring sown crops normally yield less and result in a lower margin but they become necessary where the previous crop cannot be harvested early enough to allow autumn cultivation and sowing to proceed. Potatoes, sugar beet and forage maize are three crops which are harvested from October to December and sometimes in January.

Farms that have heavy soils usually only have a relatively short time period after harvest to sow the following year's crops before the ground becomes too wet and unworkable. In wet autumns these farms have to resort to spring crops on land not sown in time.

In some instances land is left fallow over the winter period for weed control coupled with a cultivation programme. Normally, where winter cereals are grown in sequence there may only be a period of a few weeks between harvesting one crop and sowing the next. Any problems with carry over of weeds, pests and diseases will have to be dealt with by chemicals and the costs of the chemical and its application will have to be compared with a lower yield from a spring sown variety. Spring sown crops usually require less variable costs, therefore less working capital for a shorter period is required.

1.14.8 Seed production

The production of seed free from pests, diseases, weed seeds and other cultivated crop seed is a highly specialised business. Crops for seed production are grown on isolated land to avoid contamination. Cereal seed must be preceded by two years of non cereal crops, and the equipment used, particularly the combine harvester and grain trailers, must be meticulously clean. All seed is sold on contract with the crop being regularly inspected by the buyer. Only licensed seed merchants are allowed to sell seed. Many farms now use their own seed by treating and cleaning their own grain which can save a considerable amount in seed costs.

New regulations have been introduced whereby the British Society of Plant Breeders Ltd (BSPB) collect 'farm-saved seed' levy payments on EU protected varieties of most combinable crops. Farmers other than small farmers (**1.11.1**) must make payments for their use of all farm-saved seed. The rates for 1998/99 are as follows and will vary every year subject to discussions between BSPB and the farming unions.

Table 1.19 *Farm-saved seed payments 1998/99*

(a) *Seed processed on the farm*

Crop	£ per ha
Wheat	4.76
Winter barley	3.77
Spring barley	3.75
Oats	3.14
Peas	5.73
Beans	5.48
Oilseed rape	8.57
Linseed	7.60

(b) *Seed processed by a BSPB registered cleaner*

Crop	£ per tonne
Wheat	25.03
Winter barley	20.95
Spring barley	22.06
Oats	17.45
Peas	27.27
Beans	27.42
Oilseed rape	1,225.00
Linseed	146.32

Great care must be taken by farmers who operate as contractors under contract farming agreements (**2.15.4**) to avoid taking farm saved seed from their home farm to the contract managed farm. This will constitute a sale of seed and is illegal.

1.14.9 Wheat

Table 1.20 *Wheat crop data*

Area grown '000 Ha			2,036
Typical yield tonnes per Ha (acre)			
	feed	winter sown	7.27 (2.9)
		spring sown	5.5 (2.2)
	milling	winter sown	6.75 (2.7)
		spring sown	5.5 (2.2)
Straw	tonnes per Ha		3.0
	small rectangular bales per Ha		120
Drilling date	winter wheat		Sept to Nov
	spring wheat		Feb to April

Wheat is harvested in August or September with a combine harvester and dried if necessary down to a moisture content of between 14 per cent and 16 per cent. Since the banning of straw burning, straw is either baled for bedding down stock or chopped by a straw chopper on the back of the combine to be incorporated in the seedbed.

There are numerous varieties but two main categories; feed varieties for animal feed and milling varieties for bread and biscuit making. Milling varieties yield less but command a price premium. It is debatable whether the premiums over the past few seasons have made up for the yield reduction.

1.14.10 Barley

Table 1.21 *Barley crop data*

Area grown '000 Ha			1,358
Typical yield tonnes per Ha (acre)			
	feed	winter sown	6.25 (2.5)
		spring sown	5.25 (2.1)
	malting	winter sown	5.25 (2.1)
		spring sown	4.40 (1.75)
Straw	tonnes per Ha		2.0
	small rectangular bales per Ha		80
Drilling date	winter barley		Sept to Oct
	spring barley		Jan to April

Barley is usually harvested earlier than wheat and is sometimes included in the rotation in order to spread the harvest workload. Barley straw is often baled for livestock feed; it has greater nutritional value than wheat straw and is more palatable. Many livestock farms in the western part of the country purchase barley straw from arable areas.

Barley is either grown for malting or feed. Malting varieties are often spring sown and require special husbandry if a malting quality is to be achieved. A good sample will have a nitrogen content of less than 1.5 per cent, therefore late dressings of nitrogen to encourage growth should be avoided.

1.14.11 Oats

Table 1.22 *Oat crop data*

Area grown '000 Ha			100
Typical yield tonnes per Ha (acre)			
	feed	winter sown	6.00 (2.4)
		spring sown	5.00 (2.0)
Drilling date	winter oats		Oct to early Nov
	spring oats		mid Jan to mid April

Oats are harvested late August to September. They have declined in importance as they have a high husk content which is not popular for animal feed. Contracts are available for growing for oatmeal and porridge.

1.14.12 Oilseed rape

Table 1.23 *Oilseed rape crop data*

Area grown '000 Ha		467
Typical yield tonnes per Ha (acre)		
	winter sown	3.00 (1.2)
	spring sown	2.10 (0.85)
Drilling date	winter oilseed rape	mid Aug
	spring oilseed rape	early March to mid April

Harvest is in August. There are two methods for harvesting:

(a) The crop is desiccated with a chemical and cut direct with a combine harvester fitted with a vertical side cutter bar to cut through the thick crop.

(b)   Cut into windrows and left to ripen before being picked up by a combine harvester.

Rape seed is crushed for its oil, which falls into two categories:

- human consumption – low erucic acid content for margarine and cooking oils;
- industrial use – high erucic acid content for lubricants and detergents.

The resultant rape seed meal is used for animal feed.

Oilseed rape fits well into a cereal rotation as it does not require any additional machinery. It is harvested and drilled earlier than cereals therefore spreading the workload.

1.14.13 Sugar beet

Table 1.24 *Sugar beet crop data*

Area grown '000 Ha	195
Typical yield tonnes per Ha (acre)	44 (17.5)
Drilling date	20 March to 10 April

Grown within a quota system of 'A', 'B', and 'C' categories operated by British Sugar. The 'C' quota is excess production and the price received by the grower can vary from £6 to £25 per tonne.

Harvest is normally complete by early December when they are temporarily stored on concrete pads on the farm awaiting delivery to the processing plants. It is important that the beet do not get frosted during this period.

1.14.14 Potatoes

Table 1.25 Potato crop data		
Area grown '000 Ha		
	early potatoes	15.9
	maincrop potatoes	149.6
Average yield tonnes per Ha (acre)		
	early potatoes	25 (10)
	maincrop potatoes	42 (17)
Sowing dates		
	first earlies	Feb to early March
	sprouted maincrop	April
	unsprouted maincrop	March to April

Production is dependent on the intended market of the potatoes.

(a) *Maincrop or 'ware' potatoes*
These produce the highest yields, they are lifted when they are fully mature, producing medium to large potatoes.

(b) *Early potatoes*
Producing new potatoes for the early summer market. They are lifted immature when prices are at a premium. This crop is grown in mild, frost-free areas including Cornwall, Pembrokeshire and the Channel Islands.

(c) *Processing*
The crop is usually grown under contract for a range of products:
- potato crisps
- chips or French fries
- dehydrated potato
- canned new potatoes
- canned potatoes.

(d) *Seed production*
This is a highly specialised form of production which traditionally has been practiced in Scotland, Northern England and Northern Ireland where there is less incidence of pests and diseases. The crop is increasingly grown in other parts of the country.

Whole tubers or sprouted seed are sown. In the latter case, seed potatoes are allowed to sprout (chit) in a controlled environment. Sprouted seed normally produces a yield increase in early potatoes.

Potato blight is a major disease particularly in warm, humid conditions.

Maincrop harvest takes place from mid September to mid October. The leaves are normally desiccated with a spray to prevent the spread of blight to the tubers and then left in the ground for the skins to harden.

Potatoes can be stored in controlled atmosphere storage buildings on farms for selling early in the following year.

The Potato Marketing Board no longer controls the production by quota (**5.14.5**). Prices are very volatile with the 1997 prices being low and those for 1998 significantly higher.

1.14.15 Peas and Beans

Table 1.26 *Pea and bean crop data*

Area grown '000 Ha	dried peas		78.3
	field beans		99.0
Typical yield tonnes per Ha (acre)			
	peas		3.7 (1.5)
	beans	winter sown	3.6 (1.4)
		spring sown	3.4 (1.3)
Drilling date	dried peas		Late Feb to early March
	winter beans		late October
	spring beans		mid Feb to mid March

Vining peas are controlled by the processor and are harvested by pea viners which separate the peas from the pods. The timing is crucial as the quality quickly deteriorates, therefore they are transported to the processing plant immediately.

Dried peas are harvested usually in August.

Field beans are harvested in September.

Peas and beans are legumes which have the ability to convert atmospheric nitrogen into the soil for use by subsequent crops.

1.14.16 Herbage seed

Table 1.27 Herbage seed crop data	
Area grown '000 Ha	11.3
Typical yield kg per Ha (acre)	
Italian ryegrass	1,000 (400)
Perennial ryegrass	900 (360)
Clovers	375 (150)

Plant breeders rely on commercial farmers to grow the many varieties of grass and clover under contract. The crop can fit in particularly well with cereal and sheep enterprises, providing a break from cereals, grazing and hay and also an entry into wheat.

The crop can be established in two ways:

- As a crop on its own in the summer.
- As an undersown crop to cereals where a cereal and grass crop are sown at the same time. The cereal crop is harvested leaving the grass crop to be grazed and produce seed the following year.

The crop is harvested by a combine harvester with the remaining grass baled to make hay for feeding to livestock.

1.14.17 Fruit, vegetables and hops

Table 1.28 Fruit, vegetable and hops crop data	
Area grown '000 Ha	
Orchard fruit	27.8
Soft fruit	10.5
Vegetables in the open	170.8
Hops	3.5

There are numerous vegetables grown on a field scale commercially. The performance and yield is usually measured in the amount of marketable crop after processing rather than bulk off the field. Sales are through wholesale suppliers and packers with the product being packaged ready for the supermarket shelf. Many of these crops are labour intensive with high volumes and low margins. The prices are often volatile and dictated by supermarkets.

Pick-your-own and fruit shops have become more important but the quality, marketing and presentation are important. Many pick-your-own and farm shop enterprises have failed on farms.

Hops are marketed through cooperatives.

1.14.18 Minority crops

Some farmers are continually looking for alternative enterprises to increase their total incomes, particularly when the margins from conventional cropping are low. Over the last few years the general profitability of conventional crops has increased, lessening the need to look elsewhere for income. Below are some of the crop enterprises that have been of interest to farmers. The details and potential margins from these crops are detailed in J Nix, *Farm Management Pocketbook* and *The Agricultural Budgeting and Costing Book*, the details of which are in Appendix **2**.

- durum wheat
- grain maize
- naked oats
- navy beans
- soya beans
- lupins
- borage
- opium poppies
- evening primrose
- sunflowers
- quinoa
- flax
- hemp
- mushrooms
- turf
- vineyards
- short rotation coppice
- Christmas trees
- commercial woodlands and forestry.

1.14.19 Horticulture

Horticulture has become a very specialised industry with strong economic and marketing links to supermarkets and marketing groups. The total area in horticultural production is in the region of 184,000 hectares (455,000 acres) and has declined over the last few years. The prices and yields for many crops are volatile, although there is support for several crops such as apples. The main crops grown in the UK in terms of value of output are:

- cabbages
- carrots
- cauliflowers
- lettuce
- mushrooms
- peas
- tomatoes
- apples
- pears
- raspberries
- strawberries.

1.15 Livestock farming

1.15.1 Introduction

Apart from some intensive systems having a minimal requirement for land, livestock are dependent upon land mostly cropped to grass. The majority of grass in the UK is in poor growing situations, often with high altitude, shallow soil and steep slopes. Although output from this grassland is low per acre, the extent is so vast, mainly in the upland areas, that it provides breeding and store sheep and cattle for use on more fertile, lowland farms.

The main livestock products are:

- meat
- milk and milk products
- eggs
- wool

1.15.2 Dairy farming

The Friesian and Holstein breeds predominate in the UK, with many herds being a cross between both breeds.

The number of dairy cows and heifers in calf, being their replacements, in the UK are as follows.

Table 1.29 *Number of dairy cows and heifers in-calf in the UK*

	'000 head
Dairy cows	3,031
In calf dairy heifers	640

Milk production from dairy cows and heifers is as follows.

Table 1.30 *Milk production from dairy cows and heifers*	
Average yield per cow	5,810 litres per annum
Milk production from dairy herd	14,400 million litres
Milk production from beef herd	7 million litres
Less milk fed to other stock	244 million litres
Total milk for human consumption	<u>14,163</u> million litres
Of which: liquid consumption	6,719 million litres
manufacture	7,141 million litres
other net of import/exports	303 million litres
Average total return	22.27 pence per litre
Value of output	3,154 £ million

Dairy farms rear most of their own replacement stock. These calve at the age of two years to two and a half years when they start milk production. Milk is obtained from heifers and cows for about 300 days after calving. This lactation period ends when milking is stopped and the cow is dried off in order to gain body condition prior to her next calving. The cow will be ready for serving (mating) six to ten weeks after calving and will return on heat every three weeks if she does not hold to service. A heifer is normally first served at 15 to 20 months of age, the gestation period lasting for 280 days, thus calving between two and two and a half years old.

The timetable for milk production for an individual animal, on average, is as follows:

Table 1.31 *Average timetable for milk production for an individual animal*			
	Days		
Calving	0	{	
Served/mated	64	{ Lactation	
Possible return to service	85	{ 305 days {	
Dried off	305	{	{ Gestation
			{ 280 days
Calving	365		{

It can be seen from the above table that if the cow or heifer returns to service, the following calving and therefore the following lactation will be delayed by three weeks. This is called the calving pattern and the aim is a 365 day calving pattern. In practice the calving patterns of most herds is longer than this, therefore a gross margin per cow, normally based on a period between two calvings, will cover a period longer than 12 months. The annual accounts will therefore show a lower gross margin for the herd as they will be based on a 12-month period (**4.11**).

During the lactation period, milk yield increases to a peak from 40 to 60 days after calving and then decreases, this is called the lactation curve. The maximum daily yield, and therefore the figure which governs the size of the bulk milk tank, is about 0.5 per cent of the lactation total. For a cow yielding about 5,000 litres the maximum daily yield is about 25 litres per day.

The profitability of dairy herds has increasingly involved the careful management of grass production and its utilisation. On average about 55 per cent of the grassland area is grazed and 45 per cent conserved. There are various systems of grazing management:

(a) Strip grazing – electric fencing allows the herd access to strips of the fields at a time.
(b) Paddock grazing – fields are split up by electric fencing into areas that are capable of supplying the required quantity of grass for the herd for one day.
(c) Set stocking – the herd is kept on the same block of land throughout the growing season.
(d) Buffer feeding – excess grass over and above the requirement for winter fodder is conserved, usually in the early summer in the form of big bale silage, and fed to the herd outside when grass growth reduces, such as mid summer during dry periods.
(e) Zero grazing – the herd is kept in the buildings throughout the year and grass is cut and fed fresh to the animals.

The area of land required per cow per annum is in the region of one to one and a half acres (0.4 to 0.6 Ha). Concentrate feeding stuffs for milk production are typically about 15 per cent of milk value, therefore feeding management is critical to profitability.

Silage is made by eliminating air and fermenting fresh grass. Self-feeding of silage is common involving the rationing of the silage by an electric fence at the silage clamp face. A cow will typically require eight to ten tonnes of silage per winter. Complete diet feeding is popular, being the mixing of silage, concentrates and feed supplements mixed in a special trailer called a 'feeder wagon', which can be towed by tractor into the buildings housing the cattle where it discharges the feed along a manger.

Slurry and silage pollution cause many problems on dairy farms. This is a particular problem on the smaller dairy farms in the western part of the country where rainfall is high, where there is an abundance of watercourses and the ground often slopes. The facilities to handle slurry and effluent are very expensive and the investment is not matched by an increase in production.

Some diseases causing problems in dairy herds are:

(a) Mastitis, which is a bacterial infection of the udder causing inflammation and contamination of the milk and loss of yield.
(b) Infertility is usually related to feeding and management and directly related to profitability.
(c) Lameness causes difficulties particularly where there is a predominance of concreted areas. It may be associated with feeding problems.
(d) Bovine Spongiform Encephalopathy (BSE) has become a particular problem although the incidence of the disease has reduced as a result of slaughter and the banning of offal in feed. It has become a political and public perception problem.

Milk can now be sold to any processor whereas previously the Milk Marketing Board was a monopoly buyer. The price of milk is based on a number of factors depending upon the contract offered by the buyer.

(a) Compositional payments constitute the largest proportion of the price, calculated on the percentage of butterfat and protein in the milk.
(b) Seasonality adjustments encourage summer milk production by increasing the basic price during June to September and making deductions during the winter months. Many dairy farmers have adjusted their calving patterns according to the seasonality adjustments.
(c) Adjustments for 'Total Bacterial Count' (TBC) and 'Somatic Cell Counts' are usually in the form of a penalty on a sliding scale as milk quality reduces.
(d) Some purchasers of milk charge collection charges.

When the Milk Marketing Board lost its monopoly powers, a number of milk buyers, including Milk Marque, attempted to encourage producers to sell milk to them by offering a relatively high contract price per litre. This has led to receivership in some of the buyers and the milk price received by producers has declined.

1.15.3 Beef

The size of the UK beef herd is as follows:

Table 1.32 *Size of the UK beef herd*

	'000 head
Beef cows	1,856
In-calf beef heifers	249
Cattle marketed	
steers, heifers and young bulls	2,264
calves	21
cows and adult bulls	8
Average dressed carcass weights (dcw)	*Kgs*
steers, heifers and young bulls	306.4
calves	47.5
cows and adult bulls	308.7

Table 1.33 *Production of meat*

Home-fed production	697 '000 t dcw
Value of meat produced	1,166 £ million
Subsidies and associated payments	697 £ million
Total value of home-fed production	1,863 £ million
% self-sufficiency in beef	76%

Beef systems are largely dependent on grass, although a large amount of the energy requirements of beef are supplied by grain and other concentrate feeds. All beef production systems aim to achieve the highest market value of product consistent with a controlled level of feed intake. The performance is measured by assessing the average daily live weight gain and the cost of the gain in pence per kilogram.

The particular system of beef production adopted on the farm depends upon many factors: the source and type of cattle available; availability of feedstuffs including by-products from other farm enterprises and nearby food processing plants; and availability of grassland and buildings.

Cattle are commonly fattened to maturity at 12, 18 and 24 months old, although there are many variations to these basic systems. The liveweight at maturity varies as follows:

Table 1.34 *Live weight at maturity*

	Kilograms liveweight
• 12 month cereal beef	350 to 420
• 18 month beef	400 to 425
• 24 month beef	450 to 500

Generally the longer the system, the greater the use made of grassland for grazing and forage; grass being the cheapest feed. The shorter, more intensive systems require a substantially higher concentrate input, greater labour input and cost of accommodation.

Twelve-month beef system
This system is based on the animals being housed with ad lib feeding of cereal, usually rolled barley, however, this can be partially supplemented with wheat, oats, sugar beet pulp, turnips and swedes. Calves are kept from about three months of age, or are home reared to sale at 10 to 14 months. Target daily live weight gain (DLWG) is high, given the short period. DLWG ranges from 1.0 to 1.3 kg per day from a calf weight of around 100 kg. Some systems use bulls which are taken to a heavier slaughter weight but do require careful handling.

High feed conversion ratio, being the ratio of the weight of concentrate food eaten to live weight gain is vital to this system. The use of bulls rather than steers, achievement of higher sale weights and prices, and lower feed costs are all targets to aim for a higher gross margin.

Eighteen-month system
The 18-month system takes autumn born calves after weaning at two to three months old. The calves are fed and housed during their first winter, grazed in the spring and summer and then wintered and finished whilst housed for sale the following spring. The weaned calf is fed on hay or silage plus concentrate until turnout to grass in the spring to a target live weight of about 180 kg. During grazing, the target DLWG is about 0.9 kg with a target liveweight of 300 to 350 kg at the end of the grazing period.

During the final period of indoor feeding the cattle are fed concentrates at the rate of up to 4 kg per day plus hay or silage. Target DLWG in this period is up to 1.0 kg with a target live weight of 400 to 425 kg at slaughter. The final weight at sale depends upon the breed of animal and the market requirements for type of carcass and fat cover. English beef breeds and their crosses tend to have more carcass fat at lower weights than Friesian steers. Holstein steers are very difficult to fatten. Continental beef and their crosses tend to develop carcass fat at higher weights, thereby producing higher finishing weights.

Highest gross margins using this system tend to result from a higher DLWG, slaughter weight and stocking rate on grass and a lower level of concentrate feed usage. Higher stocking rates result from better grassland management and higher fertiliser usage.

In order to avoid finishing on grass, and consequently lower beef prices in the autumn, spring born calves may be finished at 15 months on a concentrate diet in the winter. This system depends upon the achievement of high levels of DLWG at grass, which may involve concentrate supplement whilst grazing, and is more suited to breeds which mature later and therefore benefit from the high level of concentrate feeding during the finishing period.

Twenty-four month system
The 24 month system uses spring born calves finished on grass in their second summer. During the winter, prior to finishing on grass, they are fed a store ration of hay or silage and up to two kg concentrate per day, with the aim of slow muscle and skeletal growth but little fat formation.

Table 1.35 *DLWG targets*

	DLWG kg
● Winter prior to finishing	0.5
● Turned out to grass	1.0

Suckler cows

Calves which are reared by beef suckler cows may be autumn or spring born. In upland and hill areas spring born calves are more common and are usually sold as store animals for fattening in lowland areas. These calves are weaned at the end of the summer period and are then either finished:

- on a concentrate diet during the winter months; or
- off grass at the end of their second summer; or
- indoors at the end of their second winter.

Suckler cows are normally kept on a low level of feeding, but nutrition does need to be raised for calving, lactation and serving. The value of beef suckler cows as a means of utilising low quality feeds is recognised in the suckler cow premium, and, in the uplands, the additional hill livestock compensatory allowances. This support is needed to compensate for an otherwise low gross margin resulting from feed and other costs required to produce only one calf per annum per cow.

Some suckler cows are kept on lowland farms, particularly where they are able to utilise by-products. The feed requirement is substantially higher under an autumn calving system because of the lack of grass for the cow and her growing calf.

1.15.4 BSE and livestock industry crisis support

The beef and, to some extent, the dairy and sheep industry in the UK has been described as being in chaos since 1995 (**6.2**). The drop in the prices of beef, sheep and dairy cull animals has resulted in temporary support schemes being implemented and the introduction of recording and traceability systems.

(a) *The Calf Processing Aid Scheme* (CPAS)
     Came into effect on 23 April 1996 and is operated by the Intervention Board. Aid is paid to slaughterhouses for pure bred male dairy calves and from December 1996, to beef breeds which are slaughtered and disposed of by approved means. The rate of aid was 120.8 ECU (£103.47) per calf paid directly to the slaughterhouse who deducted slaughtering and other costs. The rates have reduced over the years as a result of a reduction in the subsidy and the exchange rate. The scheme was extended to beef breeds in December 1996 and the upper age limit extended from 10 to 20 days. The scheme was scheduled to end on 30 November 1998 but was extended to April 4 1999 as part of a £120 million government aid package announced at the end of November 1998 and has since been further extended to 31 July 1999. It has been stated that the scheme will close on this date. Payments were reduced further to 80 ECUs (£56) as from 1 December 1998.

     The total number of calves slaughtered under this scheme at the end of 1998 was in the region of 1.5 million.

(b) *The Over 30-Month Slaughter Scheme*
     Introduced on 1 May 1996 to remove these animals from the food chain. The initial basic rate of aid was 1 ECU (85.66 pence) per kilogram live weight or double this rate for dead weight. There was a top-up payment for the first six months. The rates have reduced over the years. The total number of animals slaughtered under this scheme at the end of 1998 was in the region of 2.5 million.

(c) *Selective cull*

A selective cull of animals commenced on January 24 1997 with specific animals identified, based on birth dates. Compensation is paid per animal based on a professional valuation of 90 per cent of the replacement value (**6.2.4**). The total number of animals slaughtered under this scheme at the end of 1998 was in the region of 74,000.

(d) *Beef marketing aid*

£29 million was paid out to beef producers who sold cattle slaughtered for human consumption during 20 March 1996 to 30 June 1996. The payments amounted to £66.76 per head.

A further £29 million was paid out to beef producers in December 1996. Payments were £55 per head for cattle slaughtered between 1 July and 30 September 1996 and £34 per head for cattle slaughtered between 1 October and 9 November 1996.

(e) *Additional subsidies*

Compensation for the reduction in beef prices was announced in June 1996. An additional £19.70 per head was paid for Beef Special Premium and £19.70 per head for Suckler Cow Premium. Further additional payments were paid for Suckler Cow Premium; £30 per head announced in February 1997 and £44.20 in the spring of 1998.

(f) *Livestock aid package*

A £120 million aid package was announced on 16 November 1998 as a result of the crisis of the livestock industry. This has resulted in a 55 per cent increase in Hill Livestock Compensatory Allowances (HLCA's) payable on beef and sheep and an increase in the Suckler Cow Premium scheme of around £29.50 per cow.

(g) *Compulsory cattle passports*

Cattle passports are now required on all cattle born or imported from 1 July 1996 replacing CIDs (**1.6**).

(h) *Other measures*

A Beef Assurance Scheme was launched to register beef herds that had no connection with any incidence of BSE.

A Certified Herd Scheme and a Date-Based Export Scheme were introduced to enable cattle which met with strict criteria to be exported.

1.15.5 Sheep

Table 1.36 *UK sheep population*

	'000 head
ewes	20,543
lambs under 1 year	20,926
other sheep	1,089
Sheep marketed	**'000 head**
clean sheep and lambs	15,991
ewes and rams	2,042
Average dressed carcass weights	**dcw kg**
clean sheep and lambs	18.2
ewes and rams	28.9
Production of meat	
home fed production	350 '000 tonnes
value of meat produced	774 £ million
value of subsidies and other income	341 £ million
Total value of home fed production	1,114 £ million
Per cent self-sufficient in UK	94

Sheep are kept predominately in the west and north. Sheep systems are based on the production of meat and wool from grass. There is a varying dependence on concentrate feeding, temporary leys, permanent grass, hay, silage and forage crops. The system adopted depends upon the farm type and location, weather conditions, other farm enterprises and the markets supplied.

Husbandry

Most systems of lamb production aim to ensure that the ewes have their lambs at the start of the period of most rapid grass growth. Some systems produce fat lambs in time for the high-priced Easter market, which requires the lambs to be born in the December/January period. For upland and hill flocks, lambing can be as late as May and lambs sold as stores for lowland fattening.

Lambs are born after a gestation period of about five months at a birth weight of between four or five kg and are fattened normally for a period of 12 to 16 weeks to be sold at a live weight of around 40kg. The carcass weight at slaughter averages around 18kg based on a killing-out percentage of 45 per cent. Intensive systems ensure good grass supply by early April by careful selection of grass mixtures and fertiliser application. Lowland lambing increasingly occurs indoors, even when the flock is not housed during the latter part of the winter. Outdoor lambing may be on catch crops or grass with hay or concentrates.

Ewes are put to the ram in October or November. In hill and upland areas tupping is more likely in November; for early lambing flocks, tupping will occur in July or August after hormone-impregnated sponges have been used to induce heat. Rams are fitted with a colour crayon harness which is changed every 16 days in order to identify ewes which have held to service. This enables ewes to be lambed in groups to ease management and marketing. Lambs born per ewe will be higher in lowland flocks, lower with upland flocks and lowest with hill flocks.

The achievement of a high lambing percentage has two contrary effects. When a high proportion of the lambs born are reared and sold, then growth will be slower for larger lamb litters. Larger litter sizes, however, result in higher meat production per acre. Farm costings indicate that lambs reared of between 1.7 and 2.0 per ewe are reasonable targets for lowland production. As the lambing percentage rises it becomes more difficult to fatten all of the lambs and an increasing proportion of them will have to be sold as stores or fattened on root crops during the winter.

The level of stocking of the ewes and lambs depends upon the quality of the grass and other feed available and its management. Grazing management may be minimal through set stocking, allowing ewes and lambs access to all grass at all times, to being more developed through paddock grazing systems. The rotational grazing ensures that the lambs have the greatest quantities of digestible grass. Less intensive lowland systems are more likely to be based upon permanent grass such as parkland, rather than leys with heavy nitrogen input. Stocking rates will be half as much as in more intensive systems.

To supplement grassland, forage crops may be grown either as an annual crop such as kale and swedes, or as a catch crop such as rape and stubble turnips. Forage crops have good dry-matter yields, and are most valuable in the period from October to February when little grass is available and when it is important for the ewes to be on a rising plane of nutrition. Rather than planting forage crops specifically for sheep it may be possible to utilise arable by-products. These include sugar beet tops, pea straw, and so forth. Many hill and upland farms send sheep to lowland farms for winter grazing.

1.15.6 Pigs

Table 1.37 *National pig herd*

	'000 head
sows	677
gilts in pig	116
other	7,199
Pigs marketed	
clean pigs	14,996
sows and boars	377
Average dressed carcass weights	
clean pigs	69.0
sows and boars	132.7
Production of meat	
home fed production	1,123 '000 tonnes
value of meat produced	1,140 £ million
Percentage self sufficient	
pork	106%
bacon and ham	51%

The principal market for pig meat is pork, ham and processed products. The live sale weights are as follows.

Table 1.38 *Live sale weights*

	kg live weight
• Pork	67
• Cutter	85
• Bacon	90
• Heavy pigs	112

Killing out percentages increase from just over 70 per cent for pork to just below 80 per cent for heavy pig.

Husbandry

Gilts are usually first served at about six months old, around 100 kg live weight. Gilts and sows which have not held to service return to heat at 21-day intervals. During pregnancy sows are kept in groups, the diet being increased shortly before farrowing and then during lactation. Gilts and sows usually farrow at around 115 days and may have between 10 and 12 piglets at an average weight of 1.5 kg. Whilst it is vital for sows to suckle their young, creep feed for pigs is introduced very early, in order to wean as early as possible. Weaning of piglets weighing about seven kg takes place at three to four weeks of age although some systems delay this until five or six weeks in order to increase piglet survival. The sow comes back into heat about a week after weaning and is served with the objective of producing 2.25 to 2.5 litters per sow per annum.

Feed for pigs varies from carefully formulated concentrate rations through to by-products such as milk, whey and potatoes. Waste products must be cooked before feeding in order to prevent the spread of diseases. Daily liveweight gain for pigs can be as high as one kg under ad lib feeding conditions. The objective of good management of fattening herds is the achievement of low-cost conversion of feed into meat.

Feed conversion ratios and fattening performance factors for indoor systems are as follows.

Table 1.39 *Feed conversion ratios and fattening performance factors for indoor systems*

Feed conversion ratio (kg of feed per kg of LWG)	Pork	Cutter	Bacon	Heavy pig
Average	2.9	3.25	3.3	3.6
Target	2.6	2.9	2.9	3.4
		Average	*Target*	
Weaners per sow per annum		21	24	
Feed per annum (kg) including boar and creep feed		1,800	1,500	

Food comprises over 90 per cent of variable costs for breeding herds and over 95 per cent for fattening herds.

Outdoor pigs
There has been an increase in recent years in outdoor pig breeding enterprises and it is estimated that around 20 per cent of breeding sows in the UK are kept outdoors. The production is lower with the weaners reared per sow per year around 18 to 19. The capital cost can be as low as one fifth of indoor units. Outdoor pigs can only be kept on light, free-draining soils, they require a mild climate and low rainfall. There are many outdoor pig enterprises in Norfolk and Wiltshire on lighter land. The stocking rates for outdoor pigs is five to six sows per acre.

1.15.7 Poultry

Table 1.40 *National poultry flock*

	'000 head
chickens and other table fowls	76,621
the laying flock	31,692
hens for breeding	7,570
turkeys	12,408
ducks	2,505
geese	142
Poultry marketed	*millions*
fowls	785
turkeys	36
ducks	17
geese	1
Value of output	
fowls	983 £million
turkeys, ducks, geese	446 £million
Percentage self sufficient	96 %

The formulation of poultry diets is complex, and compounds are usually produced by feed manufacturers. Most diets are designed to ensure adequate intake of protein and minerals based on the limiting factor of energy intake. Feeding may be ad lib in order to simplify management. Mechanically controlled feeding provides opportunities for restricted feeding to reduce feed costs. For both broiler and egg production systems, feed constitutes over 90 per cent of all variable costs. Its control is therefore critical to the achievement of adequate returns.

The environment in which the poultry are kept is controlled for temperature, humidity and lighting. The requirement for particular conditions is determined by the growing stage of the flock. Temperatures can generally be lowered with increasing age, whilst increasing amounts of light can be used to stimulate egg production.

Laying birds are normally kept in battery houses or on a deep litter system. There are many variations on these basic systems, all reconciling in some way the need to provide a suitable environment with lower feeding and labour costs. Lower running costs usually have to be purchased by higher initial capital outlay. Free-range egg production, where laying birds are allowed to roam in large outdoor pens, produces eggs commanding a premium price.

Poultry may be kept for one of four principal markets. Apart from egg and broiler meat production, some poultry farmers keep breeding flocks to supply fertile eggs to hatcheries to produce either broiler or laying chicks. Specifically bred birds are kept for the purpose of meat or egg production.

As poultry enterprises involve large numbers of birds the financial planning and control has to be maintained with precision.

Table 1.41 *Main performance criteria*	
	Layers
● Weeks to point of lay	18 to 20
● Egg production per annum	270 to 300
● Feed per annum from point of lay (kg)	40 to 50
	Broilers
● Age at sale for killing (weeks)	6 to 7
● Weight at sale (kg)	1.8 to 2.4
● Feed consumption from day old to sale (kg)	4.0 to 4.7

Generally livestock production has suffered recently, particularly in the red meat sector, by a move towards diets containing less animal fats. Consumer demand has forced the industry to produce leaner and lighter carcasses. The 'white meats' chicken and fish, have been less affected. Periodic 'health scares' such as salmonella in eggs and the current BSE situation have lasting effects on the livestock industry. This together with the volatility and cyclical effect of prices in some of the livestock enterprises has forced many producers to cease trading.

1.15.8 Minority enterprises

In conjunction with farm diversification (**1.17**) there has been an increase in alternative livestock enterprises in the industry over the past few years. Some of the enterprises listed below have become established although they are still a minority in terms of numbers, such as red deer for venison. The details and potential margins from these enterprises are detailed in J Nix, *Farm Management Pocketbook* and *The Agricultural Budgeting and Costing Book*, the details of which are in Appendix **2**.

● wild boar
● camelids
● red deer
● dairy sheep

- dairy goats
- yoghurt and ice-cream
- carp
- crayfish
- salmon
- rainbow trout
- cashmere and mohair
- ostriches
- table ducks
- table geese
- quail
- angora rabbits
- meat rabbits
- snail farming
- worm farming

1.16 Organic farming

The area of organic farming has steadily increased in the past few years and is currently estimated to be in the region of 32,000 Ha (80,000 acres). The concept of organic farming tends to go beyond the commercial production of organic food. It also embraces the wider aspect of sustainable farming systems.

The economics of organic farming are based on a premium being obtained for the product compared with conventional farmed products.

The main differences and the key issues in production of an organic cropping system compared with a conventional system are as follows:

- Lower yields.
- Higher prices.
- Lower variable costs with the absence of spray costs.
- The reliance on rotations including fallow and grass ley breaks.
- The reduction in overall margin as a result of fallow breaks.
- Being able to establish profitable enterprises on the additional grass breaks.
- Labour requirements are generally higher.
- Cultivation costs tend to be higher as they are used for weed control instead of the reliance on chemicals.
- The balance of supply and demand and the price premiums available.
- There is a conversion period before the full organic status and associated premiums are available; the Organic Aid Scheme has been introduced to assist farmers through this period.

Organic Aid Scheme

This scheme was introduced in 1984 with the purpose of increasing the area of land farmed organically. It provides financial aid for the conversion of land to organic standards but no aid thereafter. Land already registered as organic is not eligible. All participants have to be registered with the United Kingdom Register of Organic Food Standards (UKROFS) to be eligible.

Table 1.42 *Subsidy payments under the Organic Aid Scheme introduced in 1984*

	Non-LFA		LFA	
Year	£ per Ha	£ per Acre	£ per Ha	£ per Acre
1	70	28	14	6
2	70	28	14	6
3	50	20	10	4
4	35	14	7	3
5	25	10	5	2

In addition £30 per Ha was paid for the first five Ha.

Annual subsidy payments announced in 1998 and brought into effect on 12 April 1999 under the Organic Aid Scheme are:

Table 1.43 *Subsidy payments under the Organic Aid Scheme 1999*

	AAPs Eligible		Not Eligible for AAPs	
Year	£ per Ha	£ per Acre	£ per Ha	£ per Acre
1	225	91	175	71
2	135	55	105	42
3	50	20	40	16
4	20	8	15	6
5	20	8	15	6

Different rates of subsidy are available on unimproved grassland or rough grazing:

Table 1.44 *Subsidy payments on unimproved grassland or rough grazing – Organic Aid Scheme 1999*

Year	£ per Ha	£ per Acre
1	25	10
2	10	4
3	5	2
4	5	2
5	5	2

In addition, single payments per unit are available to assist during the conversion period. The payments are £300 in year one, £200 in year two and £100 in year three.

1.17 Diversification and alternative enterprises

There has been a dramatic increase in public interest in the countryside (**1.1**) which has provided the opportunity for many farmers to create additional income from non-agricultural sources. The government has encouraged farmers to diversify in the past with the availability of grant aid for capital expenditure on diversification projects.

Many farmers consider diversification or alternative enterprises in order to create additional income for the business. Unfortunately there are many instances where the existing business may not be providing sufficient income because of poor technical performance and lack of managerial ability by the farmer. Most alternative enterprises demand capital and business and marketing skills which many farmers do not possess.

The result has been that many alternative enterprises have failed. There are, however, many examples of entrepreneurial successes. In areas of the country where tourists predominate in the summer months, many farms provide bed and breakfast and caravan and camping facilities very successfully.

Before embarking on a new venture it is extremely important that a business plan is prepared. This should be carried out in stages to avoid large costly exercises for non viable enterprises. The farmer should initially discuss the idea with such individuals as:

- land agent
- accountant
- bank manager
- farm management consultant.

With this background, and if it is thought that the venture should be investigated further, the farmer should prepare notes with estimates of costs and projected income. At this stage a business plan including an assessment of the market demand and the marketing strategy should be prepared. Many farmers have no experience of marketing and having to find customers. There have been many failed alternative enterprise ventures as a result of the farmer being 'production driven rather than being market led'.

Marketing planning should be one of the first steps in the business plan

58

which is usually considered a very complex subject. The following paragraphs set out a logical approach to marketing planning and it is suggested that these are applied to proposed enterprises that will involve the general public as customers.

Planning model

(a) *The need for the proposed product and service*

Consider the on-going market need for the proposed product or service and its projected life. Some products or services may not have a generic need and their demand may only be temporary, therefore making the venture temporary.

(b) *Market segmentation*

This step is extremely important to enable the market place to be understood. The total market place should be divided into as many groups as possible and the most important ones identified. Examples of some of the bases of segmentation are: income, age, family type, religion, types of organisations or businesses, abroad or domestic.

The following steps should be applied to each of the groups identified above and should be relevant to the product.

(1) *Buying patterns*

The behaviour and buying patterns of each group should be identified. At this stage some ideas may emerge regarding the type, seasonality and location of advertising.

(2) *Size of group*

The size should be measured in terms of the potential usage of the product or service, i.e., potential sales to each group.

(3) *Geographic size and trends*

Identify the potential sales to the groups in geographic areas. Measure any trends within each group.

(4) *Method of distribution*

The method by which products travel to customers should be evaluated. In some instances the products may be sold to wholesalers or agents before being sold to the end user. This step may not be so appropriate when a service is sold or when customers actually visit the farm.

(5) *Evaluate competition*

Investigate as much as possible about the potential competition, look at their strengths and weaknesses and their method of pricing and promotion.

(6) *Re-assess the project*
Based on the information gathered up to this stage a decision will have to be made as to whether the proposed venture is viable and the potential sales identified in the above stages are sufficient.

(7) *Develop marketing strategy*
It is very common to ignore all stages prior to this stage, prepare advertising material, sit back and wait to see what happens. The marketing will be more cost-effective and successful if all the steps are taken.

(8) *Detailed business plan*
Based on the background the business plan can now be prepared to include financial forecasts and both physical and financial targets.

Some examples of alternative enterprises are as follows:

- war games
- bed and breakfast
- turf production or selling grassland for turf
- farm shops
- caravan and camping sites
- clay pigeon shooting, conventional and laser
- holiday cottages
- horse livery
- riding school
- horse trekking
- motor sports
- fishing, coarse and trout
- commercial shoots
- deer stalking.

Chapter 2 – Accounting

2.1 Introduction

Many farming businesses have annual accounts prepared solely to comply with the statutory authorities and they are not used for management and decision making. Farmers generally do not like office work and the responsibilities are often delegated to a self-employed farm secretary who may carry out office duties for several farming businesses in the district. The most important statutory authorities and institutions are:

- Inland Revenue;
- Customs & Excise;
- Department of Social Security;
- Companies House;
- Ministry of Agriculture, Fisheries and Food;
- Bank manager and finance houses to support leasing and hire purchase.

One of the major problems with the preparation of annual accounts that are also meaningful for management purposes is that production cycles often span different financial years. Unless the production cycles are understood by the accountant and the accounts prepared in gross margin format their use can be limited for management and decision making purposes. The recording of physical information and management information is often neglected in farm offices and therefore the information is not available to the accountant to prepare meaningful accounts.

2.2 The role of the accountant

Traditionally many farmers see the role of their accountant as minimising any tax payable and books and records are often presented as late as possible in order to defer any tax bill. This is a lost opportunity for both the farmer and the accountant. Although it is important to perform only the services required by clients, they should be made aware of the annual accounting work carried out and in particular the analytical review and how the presentation of this work can help them interpret the financial results and provide guidance on the management of the business. This results in the accountant being able to add value to both the farming business and the accountant's practice.

2.2.1 The demand for management accounts

There is an increasing awareness by the new generation of farmers, who have often attended an agricultural college, that accounts prepared in management format and in a timely manner can be of considerable use.

Therefore, there is an increasing demand for accounts in gross margin format to itemise the relative margins between the enterprises. It is important for the accountant to respond to this increasing demand and be familiar with the production cycles (**2.5, 4.5.3**) of a farming business and ask for the necessary information to produce meaningful accounts.

2.3 Information required by the accountant

It is recommended that the accountant prepares a list of the books and records required for the preparation of the annual accounts in advance of the year end of the business and presents it to the owners of the business.

Farming businesses have a statutory requirement to maintain certain records and most of these relate to financial recording with the exception of livestock movement records. Records of animal movement are required by the Ministry of Agriculture Fisheries and Food (MAFF) in order to trace animals in the event of notifiable diseases.

2.3.1 Checklist of information required

The following is a checklist that can be drawn up and sent to the owners of a farming business. Equally, for students and farming readers it is an important reminder of the information required by the accountant. The provision of all this information will assist with a timely and economical service.

- Cash book (**4.3.4**) which is usually in the form of an analysed book with a VAT column. Some farming businesses prepare separate VAT books.
- Bank statements covering the year plus the preceding and following months.
- Valuations (**2.13**) itemised into the following categories based on values at the balance sheet date:

(i)   livestock split into age groups to record animals on the herd basis;
(ii)   cultivations and work done on the land;
(iii) forage including tonnes of silage and bales;
(iv)   bought feed;
(v)   seeds itemised in the barn and in the ground;
(vi)   fertilisers itemised in the barn and in the ground split into arable and forage for livestock;
(vii) chemicals for crops itemised in the barn and in the ground;
(viii) crops in store itemised by enterprise, valued at market value and cost of production;
(ix)   fuel, oils and miscellaneous equipment.

- Invoices paid and received cross referenced to the cash book.
- Cheque book and paying in book.
- VAT records.
- Statement of arable area payments and livestock subsidies.
- Cash sales and expenditure (petty cash records).
- Wages records including statutory sick pay, maternity pay.
- List of debtors and creditors.
- Original agreements of HP, lease and contract hire agreements.
- Details of new loans.
- Details of home use of crops for feed and seed.
- Physical records such as cropping areas and livestock movements.

It is advisable to supply forms to be completed by the farmer to assist with obtaining the required information. These can easily be prepared on a computer.

Example 2.1 *Livestock reconciliation form*

Client _____

Balances brought forward	*Cows*	*Youngstock*	*Ewes*	*Lambs*	*Rams*
Date _____					
Purchases					
Sales					
Births					
Deaths					
Transfers in					
Transfers out					
Balance	____	____	____	____	____
Date _____					

63

Example 2.2 *Growing crop valuation form*

Client _____
Valuation of growing crops at _____

Crop	Hectares/ Acres*	Seeds	Ferts	Sprays	Cultivations	Total
Winter wheat						
Winter barley						
Oilseed rape, etc.						
Other 1						
2						
3						
Total	___	___	___	___	___	___

*Delete as appropriate
Please specify other crops in valuation

Example 2.3 *Schedule of live and dead farming stock form*

Client _____
Date _____

Horses	Colour Name	Age	Sex	@ £ each	Total

Cattle
Number | Category | @ £ each
Breeding cows
Heifers over 2 years
etc.

Sheep
Number | Category | @ £ each
Ewes over 3 years
Ewes under 3 years
etc.

Hill sheep
Number | Category | @ £ each
Ewes over 3 years
Ewes under 3 years
etc.

Pigs
Number | Category | @ £ each
Breeding sows with suckers
Breeding sows in farrow
etc.

Poultry			
Number	Category		
Contents of barns			
Hay	In barns and stacks	Tonnes @ £	per tonne
Straw	Wheat	Tonnes @ £	per tonne
	Barley	Tonnes @ £	per tonne
	etc.		
Silage	Clamp	Tonnes @ £	per tonne
	Big bales	Bales @ £	per bale
Crops	Wheat	Tonnes @ £	per tonne
	Barley	Tonnes @ £	per tonne
	etc.		
	Potatoes	Tonnes @ £	per tonne
	Sugar beet	Tonnes @ £	per tonne
Cultivations			
_____	Acres winter wheat	@ £	per acre
_____	Acres winter barley	@ £	per acre
etc.			

Seeds fertilisers and chemicals in the ground from growing crop sheet

Feeding stuffs in store

Seeds, fertilisers and chemicals in store

Grand total _____

To the best of my belief and knowledge the above is an accurate schedule of my/our live and dead farming stock at _____ 19__

Signed _____ Date _____

2.4 Financial Statements

2.4.1 Introduction

The majority of farm businesses are sole traders and partnerships. Where farms are trading as limited companies, the requirements of the Companies Acts, Financial Reporting Standards (FRS), Statements of Standard Accounting Practice (SSAP) and best practice are the main consideration. However the detailed accounts or management accounts may follow principles adopted for sole traders and partnerships.

In improving the usefulness and relevance of the financial statements, it is important to have regard to the practical feasibility and time and cost constraints involved.

2.4.2 **Management accounts**

The remainder of this chapter sets out practical suggestions for improving the usefulness of farm accounts and, where relevant, uses an example set of partnership accounts for a dairy and arable farming business. A traditionally prepared example trading, profit and loss account is shown below and the same full accounts set out in management format are included in Appendix **1**.

Example 2.4 *Alpha Beta Estates-statement of accounts for the year ended 31 March 1998*

Sales		£	£
sales of crops			216,117
sales of livestock			26,970
sales of milk			144,256
grants and subsidies			123,023
sundry receipts			33,197
Total sales			543,563
Cost of sales			
Opening valuation		219,010	
Purchases	seeds and fertilisers	59,385	
	chemicals and sundry	51,091	
	feedstuffs	40,841	
	sundry livestock	8,655	
	sundry crops	9,131	
Closing valuation		(218,863)	
		169,239	169,239
Gross profit			374,324
Less overheads			
wages		74,909	
machinery, motor and contract		27,844	
property costs		24,706	
administration		7,588	
bank interest and charges		9,314	
rent		55,000	
accountancy		3,250	
depreciation		70,741	
fuel and oil		28,385	
profit/loss on sale of assets		(2,129)	
		299,608	299,608
Profit			74,716

2.4.3 Differences between the basic and detailed management accounts

The major differences between the basic and the full management accounts are that in the basic accounts:

- enterprises are not distinguished;
- harvest years are not distinguished;
- stocks are at deemed cost or cost of production (**2.13**);
- valuations have not been analysed and allocated accordingly;
- no adjustment for own use of feed or seed;
- variable costs are not allocated to dairy and arable enterprises;
- stocks and purchases are not analysed, therefore variable cost usage not identified;
- fixed costs are not detailed.

The financial profit of the business is obviously the same in both profit and loss accounts as they have both been prepared along the lines of standard accounting practice. The fundamental difference between them is the layout.

Despite these points there are many farming businesses that will only require basic accounts. A simple farming system on a farm with low output and relatively small effective acreage may have unsophisticated needs well satisfied by the basic form of accounts. More importantly, from the accountant's point of view, there may be little willingness on the part of the farmer client to provide the further necessary information, and a reluctance to meet any further accountancy fees.

However, there are simple and effective changes that can be made to the basic accounts as shown in **2.4** without going into the complexity of the full management accounts in Appendix **1**. These are:

- analysing the opening and closing valuations to distinguish between arable and livestock output;
- allocating the opening and closing valuations of variable costs to the individual cost of sales;
- sub-totalling the fixed costs into the following headings:
  - (i)   labour
  - (ii) power and machinery
  - (iii) property
  - (iv) administration
  - (v) interest and finance.

It will then be possible to analyse some of the key figures for management purposes and compare them with industry standards (**4.8**).

2.5 Accounting for harvests

2.5.1 Introduction

The preparation of annual financial statements for a farming business that grows crops will generally include transactions for more than one harvest. In the basic set of accounts since there is no distinction between harvest years, output includes closing stock and opening stock, both at cost of production. Depending, on the year-end selling policy, it is possible to have between nil and two years' harvests sales in one set of accounts. Output may therefore be affected by more than one year's sales and more than one year's harvest.

2.5.2 Harvests and financial year end

The harvest accounted for in annual financial statements will be based on the crops actually harvested in the period and not when the harvest is sold. For example for combinable crops:

(a)   Years ended from 1 September 1998 to 30 June 1999 will account for the 1998 harvest.
(b)   Annual accounts ending in July 1998 or August 1998 may in fact account for either the 1997 or 1998 harvest depending upon the normal harvesting period on the farm, which will vary depending on the location in the country (**1.13**).

It may be advisable to change the financial year end of farming businesses that have the majority of their income from combinable crops, from July or August to a more appropriate time such as during September through to April.

2.5.3 Root crops

Root crops such as sugar beet and potatoes have different production cycles to combinable crops, being harvested later in the season (**1.14.13, 1.14.14**). Therefore farming businesses with year ends during the period September through to December will end in the period between the combinable crop harvest and the majority of the root crop harvest. In this situation the gross margin of the previous root crop harvest will be accounted for in full management accounts.

Example 2.5 *30 September 1999 year end*

Opening valuation will include:

- 1998 combinable crop harvest in store to be sold.
- 1998 root crop still in the ground valued at cost to date.

During the year the following will occur:

- 1998 combinable crop will be sold termed previous year's harvest.
- 1999 combinable crop will be harvested termed this year's harvest.
- 1998 root crop will be harvested and sold termed this year's harvest.

Closing valuation will include:

- 1999 combinable crop in store to be sold.
- 1999 root crop still in the ground valued at cost to date.

Therefore in this example the valuations and sales will be distinguished to provide the following gross margins:

- 1999 combinable crop harvested in the period.
- 1998 root crop harvested in the period.

2.6 Management accounting for unrealised profit

2.6.1 Introduction

The accounting treatment of stock is set out in the *Statement of Standard Accounting Practice 9 (SSAP 9)*. In order to match costs with associated revenues in the determination of profit, stocks are normally stated at cost, or if lower, at net realisable value. For management accounting purposes it is recommended that open market values or estimated selling prices are used. The difference between the two values is termed the 'unrealised profit'.

2.6.2 Livestock unrealised profit

In order to reflect the true output in management terms from the enterprises in a farming business, trading stocks should be valued at market value or estimated selling price. In practice this is only considered necessary for arable produce and not livestock for the following reasons:

(a) Arable crops follow distinct annual production cycles whereas live-stock enterprises will vary depending upon the system of production (**1.15**).

(b) The selling prices of arable crops are easier to identify, whereas livestock prices will vary depending upon the type and age of animal.

(c) The production animals of livestock enterprises which may be on the herd basis (**2.17**) should not be valued at market value as they are not traded. Any increase or decrease in market value will remain as a valuation in the business and will not be reflected in eventual cash unless the animals are sold.

(d) The most important reason from a practical point of view is that the calculations for unrealised profit in livestock are too time-consuming and therefore the additional time costs are considered to outweigh the benefits.

2.6.3 Arable unrealised profit

In order to calculate the unrealised profit on the arable crops their estimated realisable values are included in the gross output calculation for the harvest. In addition, any opening value of produce for sale will be at estimated realisable value and the subsequent sale of this produce should be identified by the fact that it will be sold prior to the following harvest and the receipts matched to the opening valuation.

The example set of accounts in Appendix **1** details all the unrealised profit adjustments. The closing valuation of wheat at £41,000 in the 1997 harvest included in Appendix **1** note 2 is at market value. The opening values of the previous harvest are also at estimated market value and the subsequent sales allocated to them. These are summarised in note 11 where the difference of cost and estimated realisable value on both the opening and closing stock are combined to show a net decrease of £2,212. This difference is applied to the management income shown in the profit and loss account as one of the adjustments to calculate the financial profit of the business.

2.7 Management accounting for arable area payments and deferred income

The accounting treatment of arable area payments is set out in detail in **2.14**. In order to calculate the true gross margin from the crops of a harvest, the total arable area payments should be included. The basic financial statements in Example 2.4 include a sum for grants and subsidies of £123,023 which is made up as follows:

	£
• livestock subsidies	2,464
• arable area payments and set-aside payments	129,556
• add arable area payments from opening stock	7,116
• less arable area payments deferred on closing stock	16,113
Net credited to the accounting year	123,023

The full management accounts in Appendix **1** include the total arable area payments in each enterprise totalling £129,556, and livestock subsidies of £2,464 in the livestock gross margin. The deferred income adjustments are included in note 11 with the unrealised profit adjustment showing a net figure of deferred arable area payments of £8,997. This figure is applied to the management income in the profit and loss account together with the unrealised profit adjustment to arrive at the financial profit.

2.8 Livestock subsidies

The current livestock subsidies are:

- Beef Special Premium Scheme. (**1.6**)
- Suckler Cow Premium Scheme. (**1.7**)
- Sheep Annual Premium Scheme. (**1.8**)
- Extensification Payments. (**1.9**)
- Hill Livestock Compensatory Allowances. (**1.10**)
- New Slaughter Premium (**1.3.1**)

The first three are paid in stages with advanced payments in the autumn and the balance the following spring. Extensification payments are paid automatically if stocking rates are adhered to. Hill livestock compensatory allowances are usually announced in December with payment the following spring. Coupled with the staggered payments there are quotas, various retention periods that have to be complied with and the final payments may be subject to downscaling depending upon the total amount of claims.

2.8.1 Accounting for livestock subsidies

The Statement of Standard Accounting Practice 4 (SSAP 4) states that the grant should be recognised on an accruals basis in the same period as the related expenditure. In addition a grant should not be recognised until the obligations required have been fulfilled. The whole area becomes very complicated when the points in the last paragraph are taken into account.

The Inland Revenue will accept two methods of accounting for livestock subsidies (*Tax Bulletin Issue 14*, December 1994, p182):

- on receipt, i.e., on a cash basis; or
- at the end of the retention period or in other words when the obligations are fulfilled;

with either one method used consistently. Therefore, in practice, it is suggested that all livestock subsidies are accounted for on a receipts basis as and when they are received.

2.9 Sales of produce to co-operatives

2.9.1 Introduction

A considerable number of arable farmers sell their produce through a marketing co-operative or organisation which can lead to difficulties in understanding the transactions and their associated accounting entries.

The transactions are usually governed by the standard UKASTA (United Kingdom Agricultural Supply Trades Association) contract between the merchant and the farmer.

The co-operative will usually batch crops of the same variety and quality from different owners, therefore making it impossible to identify individual ownership. Stage payments may be made unconnected to actual crop sales.

In most cases the co-operative will act as agent for the farmer, however it will be necessary to look at the contract. Therefore every sale by the co-operative is deemed to be a proportional sale by the farmer. Stage payments in excess of this amount should be included in creditors and not credited against stock.

2.9.2 Accounting treatment

The transactions and crop movements before the year end together with the suggested accounting treatment, may include:

(a) A harvest advance payment paid by the merchant to the farmer prior to the crops being harvested. This is treated as a loan to the business from the merchant which will be repaid when the crops are sold and despatched to the merchant. Any interest element should be charged to fixed costs.

(b) Part or all of the crops sold prior to, or after harvest at an agreed price and delivery date with no crops despatched. Prior to harvest it is not accounted for, after harvest it is included as stock.

(c) Part or all of the stocks despatched to co-operative store sold but no payments received. Include all crops despatched in sales and debtors. Crops not despatched are included in stock.

(d) Part, or all of the stocks despatched to co-operative store with payments received unconnected to actual crop despatched. Include all crops despatched and sold as proportion of total pool in sales and debtors. Crops despatched in excess of total proportional pool sales should be included in stock.

(e) Stage payments should be set off firstly against debtors and any balance should be included in creditors.

2.9.3 Records of transactions with co-operative

It is suggested that a schedule is drawn up along the following lines and retained on file.

Details	Sales	Stocks	Debtors	Creditors
Harvest advances				xxxx
Crops sold not despatched with no payment received		xxxx		
Crops despatched and sold by co-operative as % of pool with no payment received	xxxx		xxxx	
Stage payments to the value of % pool sold	xxxx			
Stage payments in excess of % pool sales				xxxx

2.10 Grants

2.10.1 Introduction

There are a number of grants and subsidies available under numerous schemes. The main bodies and organisations that currently administer the schemes are as follows:

- Ministry of Agriculture Fisheries and Food
- Welsh Office Agriculture Department
- Countryside Commission
- Countryside Council for Wales
- English Nature
- Forest Authority .
- English Heritage
- Rural Development Commission
- Welsh Development Agency
- European Commission

2.10.2 Accounting for grants

Their accounting treatment is set out in *SSAP 4*. The accounting treatment should preferably be consistent with the tax treatment. There are two types of grant: capital grants and grants as compensation for a reduction in income.

2.10.3 Accounting for capital grants

Grants as a contribution towards specific work of a capital nature or a fixed asset should be recognised during the same period as the expenditure to which they relate. The accounting treatment set out in SSAP 4 states that there are two options for accounting for grants towards fixed assets:

(a) The asset should be shown in full. Therefore the grant should not be deducted from costs or the purchase price of the fixed asset but included as deferred income in the balance sheet. The deferred income should be credited to the profit and loss account over the useful life of the asset. Therefore it can be credited in line with the commercial depreciation of the asset. This method discloses the asset and grant in full.

(b) The grant is deducted from the costs or purchase price of the asset. Therefore the net cost of the asset is included in the balance sheet and net depreciation is included in the profit and loss account.

The Companies Act 1985 prohibits the accounting for grants by deducting the amount of the grant from the cost or purchase price of the asset, therefore the former method needs to be adopted for companies. It is advisable to adopt the simpler method of deducting the grant from the value of the asset for sole traders and partnerships.

Some grants are paid for capital work calculated on standard costings with farm staff carrying out the work. In this instance any excess of grant received above costs should be treated as a farming receipt in the year of receipt.

Examples of grants schemes currently available which fund work of a capital nature as a percentage of costs and should be accounted for as such are:

- Parts of Countryside Stewardship Scheme (Tir Cymen in Wales)
- Parts of Environmentally Sensitive Area Scheme
- Farm and Conservation Grant Scheme
- Nature and Landscape Conservation Grants
- Environmentally Sensitive Area Scheme
- Woodland Grant Scheme
- Farm Woodland Premium Scheme.

2.10.4 Accounting for revenue grants

Annual payments are treated as farming income on an accruals basis and should be recorded in *Other* or *Miscellaneous Income* in the annual accounts. As set out in *SSAP 4*, the grant should not be recognised until the conditions for the grant are fully satisfied. Arable area payments and compulsory set-aside payments are not included in this paragraph as they are linked to crop sales and covered in detail in **2.14**.

Examples of grant schemes currently available which provide an annual payment as compensation for a reduction in income:

- Parts of Countryside Stewardship Scheme (Tir Cymen in Wales)
- Parts of Environmentally Sensitive Area Scheme
- Management Agreements for Environmentally Sensitive Areas and Sites of Special Scientific Interest
- Habitat Schemes
- Countryside Access Scheme
- Moorland Scheme
- Nitrate Sensitive Areas
- Farm Woodland Premium Scheme
- Voluntary Set-Aside and Additional Voluntary Set-Aside.

The Woodland Grant Scheme (**6.10**) provides planting grants for the planting of farm woodland and therefore is outside the scope of tax (**5.6.3**). Therefore an adjustment will have to be made in the tax computation when these payments have been included in the annual accounts.

2.11 Fixed assets and depreciation

2.11.1 Introduction

The general accounting principles as set out in the *Statement of Standard Accounting Practice 12 (SSAP 12)* apply to farm accounts. Many farm businesses, even without the land, have substantial capital invested in fixed assets the majority of which consists of machinery.

The accounting treatment of farm machinery is detailed in **2.16** of this chapter. See also 'Machinery Management' in **4.12**.

2.11.2 Fixed asset register

Wherever possible detailed lists of vehicles and machinery should be kept (**2.16.2**). For annual accounting purposes, the presentation of the plant and machinery and other fixed assets should appear in easily identifiable categories, so that the balance sheet notes can easily be traced through to detailed listings in the fixed asset register. For practical purposes the categories should be grouped in similar depreciation rates in order for the same depreciation rate to be applied to the whole category. It is suggested that leased assets are held in a separate group as a reminder of their different treatment for taxation purposes.

A suitable fixed asset analysis might be as follows:

Balance sheet (categories)	Fixed asset register (categories)	Description
Land and buildings	Freehold Leasehold	
Property improvements	Building improvements	Building improvements Drainage New fencing
Fixed equipment	Fixed equipment	Grain storage and drying Conveyors and elevators Milking equipment Silos and slurry stores

Plant and machinery	Cultivation equipment Seed, fertiliser and spray Forage equipment Harvesting and handling General equipment	
	Tractors and combines	Tractors Combine harvester
	Leased assets	Normally tractors and combines
Motor vehicles	Motor vehicles	Cars Farm vehicles
Office equipment	Office equipment	Computers Mobile phones Fax machines

2.11.3 Depreciation rates

Suggested rates of depreciation are as follows:

- Land   nil
- Buildings   5 per cent straight line
- Property improvements   10 per cent straight line
- Fixed equipment   10 per cent straight line
- Plant and machinery   29 per cent reducing balance
- Tractors and combines   15 per cent reducing balance
- Leased assets   15 per cent reducing balance
- Motor vehicles   25 per cent reducing balance
- Office equipment   30 per cent reducing balance

It could be argued that the rate of depreciation on leased assets should reflect the type of asset rather than the fact that they are leased. The prime consideration is to maintain an accurate record of all assets subject to finance leases to ensure that they are correctly accounted for in the tax computation. Therefore it is recommended that they are grouped as a separate category. Most assets that are subject to finance leases will be combine harvesters and tractors where a depreciation rate of 15 per cent is advocated. Therefore the adoption of this method will result in an insignificant difference in the amount of depreciation charged.

2.12 Private proportions

2.12.1 Introduction

In farming businesses personal expenditure, in addition to cash drawings, is often initially paid for by the business bank account. Some of these payments are clearly private, such as school fees and pension payments whilst many can be partly attributed to the business. The proportion is usually based on those allowable for income tax purposes and it is advisable to maintain a consistency with those used for VAT, capital allowances and income tax.

2.12.2 Farmhouses

For sole traders and partnerships the majority of private proportions will relate to the farmhouse which is deemed to be used for running the business in addition to providing living accommodation for the family. It is usual not to define any one specific area of the farmhouse for sole business use but to include a proportion of all expenditure such as heating, lighting and repairs. Historically this has been one-third, however the Inland Revenue now treat each case individually. This expenditure is wholly allowable when incurred by a company, the benefit enjoyed by the director and taxed as such. Expenditure on houses provided for employees is wholly allowable as are lodging allowances for farm workers as amended 1 April 1999 with the introduction of the National Minimum Wage (**5.12.3**).

2.12.3 Other items

Other items of expenditure in a farming business that may be subject to private proportions are:

- motoring expenses
- employment costs for gardeners and gamekeepers
- shoot costs
- horse and dog feed.

2.12.4 Calculating private proportions

It is suggested that the calculations for adjustments for private proportions are made whilst preparing the annual accounts. It is easier to adjust for items incurring VAT in the tax computation whereas other items can be added to drawings and therefore will not give rise to any adjustments in the tax computation.

2.12.5 Self-assessment

Under the new self-assessment rules, costs will need to be recorded in detail, such as records of business mileage and logging of individual business telephone calls, as opposed to stating that a certain percentage of the total costs are incurred for business purposes.

2.13 Farm stock valuations

2.13.1 Introduction

The correct accounting for stock in farming businesses has become increasingly important with the Inland Revenue regularly requiring details of the basis and verification of quantity and value. With the advent of self-assessment, any deviation from accepted practice should be carefully considered. If stock valuations have been incorrectly accounted for, the Inland Revenue can seek adjustment of financial accounts over the preceding six years with the possibility of imposing interest and penalties.

Business Economic Note (BEN) 19 was published in March 1993 by the Inland Revenue as an authoritative statement of acceptable methods of valuing farming stock. The basic principle is that stock is valued at the lower of cost or net realisable etc., which is a standard accounting policy that has not altered.

This principle applies for taxation purposes and in financial statements prepared under the historic cost convention and is not applicable to management accounts where stock may be included at market value or estimated selling price. A compromise may be required for livestock valuations, this is discussed in **2.6.2**.

Farmers normally seek the assistance of an agricultural valuer in the computation of annual stocktaking. However this is not compulsory for any trading medium and some farmers prepare their own valuation. Farmers not using *BEN 19* need to justify their basis of valuation carefully.

In general, actual costs of production should be used unless it is not possible to ascertain them, with reasonable accuracy, from the farmer's records. It can, however, prove difficult to identify actual costs, particularly forage costs in livestock enterprises, and deemed cost is then acceptable.

Stocks can be divided into two distinct areas for the two main farming systems: arable crops and livestock.

2.13.2 Growing and harvested crops – actual costs of production

Actual cost of production should be calculated on the basis set out in *BEN 19*. It is necessary to include direct costs related to the growing of the crop, but overheads or indirect costs are optional and do not have to be included except where they have been included in the past and to omit them would be inconsistent.

The costs which must be included are:

- seeds;
- fertilisers;
- beneficial sprays – this means preventative sprays as opposed to sprays applied to remedy a specific infestation or crop deficiency;
- seasonal licence payments – short-term hire of land to grow a particular crop but not normal farm rents;
- drying;
- storage; and
- employee costs – including director, or contract labour and direct machinery costs incurred on cultivation (e.g., fuel, servicing, rental, spares and the reduction in value due to wear and tear caused by actual usage for the activity concerned), crop working and harvesting.

The costs to be included under the above headings should be based upon the actual expenditure incurred on the farm in question and should be capable of being justified from the farm's own financial records. There are acceptable guides to costings issued annually by the Central Association of Agricultural Valuers. These can be used as a guide to help farmers establish their own costs but should be adjusted to reflect individual circumstances.

Labour costs include paid labour and do not require anything to be included for the notional cost for directors where those directors are paid a salary for their supervisory but not working time.

Where grants and subsidies are received, and these are paid to reduce the costs of items carried forward in stock, then credit must be taken in the profit and loss account. The expenditure is then reduced and an equal reduction should be made in the costs to be carried forward in stock.

2.13.3 Harvested crops – deemed cost

As a reasonable estimate of cost, deemed cost is acceptable if actual costs cannot be readily ascertained. Deemed cost is based on 75 per cent of open market value at the balance sheet date. This will include arable area aid and related set-aside payments where these are treated on a sales basis in the accounts.

2.13.4 By-products

Many mainstream crops will produce by-products such as straw. These should be valued on a cost of production basis (if the main crop is also dealt with on this basis), or at deemed cost.

2.13.5 Co-operatives

Harvested crops which are held by co-operatives should be treated in the same way as any other stock held by the farmer. In this instance, it is necessary to look at the contract between the farmer and the co-operative. The inclusion of stock in the accounts depends on the farmer having legal title to the stock at the balance sheet date. It is important to understand the Inland Revenue views on co-operatives.

In most cases the co-operative acts as agent for the farmer, in which case every sale by the co-operative is deemed to be a proportionate sale by the farmer and should be accounted for as such. Payments made by the co-operative should not be included in sales until the co-operative sells produce to a third party.

Example 2.6 *Sales to a co-operative*

A farmer sends 100 tonnes to a co-operative who hold 1,000 tonnes in a particular pool. The co-operative sells a total of 200 tonnes, which is then treated as being a disposal by the co-operative as agent of 20 tonnes out of the farmer's 100 tonnes. Payments by the co-operative which are not related to sales by them are carried forward as deferred sales. Transactions with a co-operative which acts as a principal, not agent, are disposals by the farming business when title passes.

2.13.6 Residual manurial values

For the purposes of annual stocktaking valuations the Revenue accept that fertilisers applied can be regarded as being exhausted following harvest. The residual manurial calculation, which is normally included in stocktaking valuations, can be dispensed with and any balance previously calculated can either be consigned to the balance sheet or, alternatively, frozen and carried forward indefinitely. On cessation, the difference between opening and closing values would be taken to the profit and loss account.

2.13.7 Dilapidations

Dilapidations which have been included in the past are not an acceptable deduction in computing farm stocks.

2.13.8 Livestock

The same underlying principles apply.

Livestock is included on an animal by animal basis, but it is acceptable to value animals of a similar type and quality on a group basis classified according to age. Livestock costs should be carried forward as follows:

- purchase cost; or
- insemination costs plus additional maternal feed costs in excess of maintenance plus the cost of rearing to the valuation date or maturity if earlier including:
  (i)   feed costs including forage;
  (ii)   vets fees, including drugs;
  (iii) drenches and other medicines;
  (iv)   ringing, castrating and de-horning;
  (v)   supervisory employee or contract labour cost – including such costs as shepherding but excluding directors' managerial time.

2.13.9 Deemed cost valuation (for cattle, sheep and pigs only)

Deemed cost is arrived at by taking a percentage of the open market value of the animal as being equal to the cost of production. It is frequently used due to the difficulty of attributing forage costs to growing animals. Deemed cost should not be used for purchased animals if it less than the original purchase price plus, if the animal was immature when purchased, the costs of rearing from the date of purchase to the valuation date or, if earlier, to maturity. Thus deemed cost applies to home bred or substantially home reared animals only. The percentages in the case of such livestock are:

- cattle   60 per cent of open market value
- sheep and pigs   75 per cent of open market value

The deemed cost method does not apply to any other form of animal except by specific agreement with the Inspector of Taxes. Furthermore, it should not be used where it would not result in a reasonable estimate of cost, e.g., pedigree stock. The Revenue accept that deemed cost be based on open market value at the balance sheet date, or else fixed at the date on which the animal reached maturity for the life of that animal. Whichever method is adopted it must be applied consistently.

2.13.10 Subsidies

Unlike arable subsidies, livestock subsidies are accountable on either an entitlement or a receipt basis (**2.8**).

If proceeding on a receipts basis, the subsidies flow straight into the profit and loss account as they are received and have no direct effect on stocktaking valuations.

If an entitlement basis is being used, then full credit will again be taken at the end of the retention period or other appropriate entitlement date, and the animals again should be valued at market value without further adjustment. It is important to note that deemed cost and also net realisable value calculations may be affected.

2.13.11 Net realisable value

If there is no reasonable expectation of recovering costs on a sale the stock should be included at net realisable value.

The net realisable value for animals was redefined in *BEN 19* and, in particular, it is necessary to differentiate between those animals which are kept for slaughter as opposed to those which are kept for their productive capacity.

Net realisable value is defined as consisting of the sale proceeds that are anticipated after the eventual disposal of the stock in the condition in which the farmer intends to market it. It is important to note that the valuations should be made on the normal commercial basis.

For instance, it is not acceptable to value stock on the basis that it would have been sold in a forced sale on the balance sheet date at its then immature state. Grants and subsidies intended to augment the sale prices of stocks should be included in the net realisable value calculation. For breeding animals, a recognition of the ancillary stream of income from the sale of their progeny less the further cost to be incurred, is needed. Where the proceeds from the sale of the progeny or produce are brought in, then the costs relating to their production and marketing should also be deducted. It is not acceptable to treat the cull value of a breeding sow as being the only future revenue from such an animal as this does not recognise the possible three plus years of piglet production that she could have. The Inland Revenue propose that where there is no ready market for breeding pigs and laying hens, the net realisable value is arrived at by taking the cost price and the expected ultimate cull value and writing the difference between those values off by equal instalments over the animal's expected productive life. Where the animals are not kept for this form of productive cycle then the Revenue will accept that the net realisable value is the open market value as at the balance sheet date.

Example 2.7 *Valuation of pigs*

	£
A maiden gilt purchased for	180
Once it enters the herd it can be valued at its cull value of 55p per kg. If it weighed 110 kg this would make a total value of	60
In reality the sow would be sold after three years' breeding as a fat sow weighing 220 kg at 55p per kg	120

Therefore, the correct treatment is to write down the difference between the £180 and £120, i.e., £60 over the three year working life of the sow.

2.13.12 Unweaned youngstock

Where there is a cost to be carried forward which includes unweaned youngstock then the normal unit of value would be mothers and progeny as couples or normal units as marketed. This is distorted where the mother is on the herd basis and there is no market in the unweaned progeny, for example, unweaned lambs. In this instance it is suggested that the costs which are carried forward are those arrived at by taking the detailed schedule of costs as opposed to a percentage of perhaps an orphan price which might be artificially inflated by sentiment.

2.13.13 The herd basis

A farmer who has livestock which forms part of a 'production herd' can elect for the herd basis to apply to that herd and if he does so, then that basis will apply instead of the trading stock basis (ICTA 1988, Sch. 5 para 1(2)).

A production herd accounted for on the herd basis is treated to a large degree as a fixed asset for tax purposes and need not be valued for stocktaking purposes. Reconciliations should, however, be maintained to establish transfers in and out of the herd, distinguishing between home bred and bought in animals.

2.14 Accounting for arable area payments

2.14.1 Introduction

The Arable Area Payments Scheme allows area payments to farmers growing eligible crops on eligible land. An additional requirement is that a certain percentage of the eligible land must be set aside and left fallow or grow a non-food crop (see **1.10**). Some businesses have more than the minimum requirement of set-aside land and receive payments, however, it is only the payments on the minimum requirement that need to be allocated to stock to calculate deferred income and stock-deemed values.

The Inland Revenue will accept the arable area payments and the set-aside payments as subsidies towards the selling price which should be recognised as income at the time the crop is sold.

The set-aside payments cause difficulty with this method of accounting as there is a choice of either not growing a crop or growing a non-food crop. If a non-food crop is grown the payment should be treated in the same way as the area payments for cereals, oilseeds and proteins. If no crop is grown the payment should be treated as an additional subsidy towards the other crops and allocated between them on an acreage basis.

The area payments should be credited, and profit taken, in the accounts for the period in which the sale of the crop takes place.

No allocation of area or set-aside payment is made to by-product sales such as straw.

Credit for the area payment and the set-aside payment for home produced crops used for livestock feed or for seed should be taken when the feed is consumed or the seed planted.

Harvested crops unsold at the year end should be valued at the lower of cost and net realisable value (see **2.13**). Farmers using the 'deemed cost' method (see **2.13**) as an estimate of cost for year end valuation purposes should add the area payment plus an appropriate proportion of the set-aside payment to the market value before applying the 25 per cent reduction to arrive at 'deemed cost'.

The accounting and taxation treatment of area payments will therefore vary, depending upon the financial year end of the business and the marketing policy for the crops.

Where a crop has been sold before the year end, the area payment and the set-aside payment should be brought into the accounts as a debtor if it has not been received by the year end.

Where area payments and the set-aside payments are received before the crop is sold, and the crop is in stock at the year end, they should be carried forward as deferred income.

Area Payments	Crop	Accounting treatment of area payments
Not received	Sold	Debtor
Not received	Not sold	Debtor, but take out as deferred income
Received	Sold	Include in sales
Received	Not sold	Take out as deferred income

To avoid any misunderstanding with the Inland Revenue, it may be appropriate to disclose the accounting policy adopted.

Example 2.8 *Letter informing Inland Revenue of accounting policy*

Arable area payments

Area payments relating to cereals, oilseeds and protein crops are treated as a subsidy towards the selling price.

Set-aside payments are treated as a subsidy towards the selling price of non-food crops grown on set-aside land or, if no such crops have been grown, as an additional subsidy towards the selling price of cereals, oilseeds and protein crops allocated on an acreage basis.

Stock is valued using the deemed cost method. Relevant area and set-aside payments are added to the market value of the crop before deducting 25 per cent to arrive at deemed cost.

Example 2.9 *Illustrating the accounting and valuation calculations on a deemed cost basis – 30 September year end.*

1 *Arable area 160 hectares*

	Yield t/ha	Total yield tonnes	Market value / tonne £	Total market value £
Set-aside 10 per cent	16			
Wheat	90	7.2	648	75	48,600
Beans	24	3.5	84	77	6,468
OSR	30	3.0	90	130	11,700
	160				66,768

Stock at 30 September:

Wheat	345
Beans	45
OSR	40

2 *Allocation of crop area payment to crops in store*

$$\frac{\text{Tonnes in store}}{\text{Tonnes harvested}} \times \text{crop area payment}$$

	Wheat	Beans	Oilseed rape	Total
Tonnes in store	345	45	40	
Tonnes harvested	648	84	90	
Stores as a percentage	53%	53%	44%	
Crop area payment	21,320	8,212	6,538	36,070
Allocated to stores	11,300	4,352	2,877	18,529

3 *Allocation of set-aside payment to crops in store*

	Wheat	Beans	Oilseed rape	Total
Hectares	90	24	30	144
Percentage cropped area	63%	17%	20%	100%
Set-aside allocation	3,025	816	960	4,801
Tonnes in store	345	45	40	430
Tonnes harvested	648	84	90	822
Stores as percentage	53%	53%	44%	
Allocation to crops in store	1,603	432	422	2,457

The accounting entries required as a result of the above calculations are as follows:

1 *Area payments and set-aside not received at 30 September*

	£
Wheat	21,320
Beans	8,212
OSR	6,538
Set aside	4,801
Total	40,871
Debit debtors	40,871
Credit output	40,871

2 *Deferred income*

Area payment plus set-aside allocated to crops in store

	Area payment	Set-aside payment	Deferred income
Wheat	11,300	1,603	12,903
Beans	4,352	432	4,784
OSR	2,877	422	3,299
Total	24,060	2,793	20,986
Debit profit & loss account			20,986
Credit creditors			20,986

3 *Closing valuation and provision for unrealised profit*

	Wheat	Beans	OSR	Total
Market value	25,875	3,465	5,200	34,540
Area payment	11,300	4,352	2,877	18,529
Set-aside	1,603	432	422	2,457
Total	38,778	8,249	8,499	55,526
Deemed cost at 75%	29,084	6,187	6,374	41,645
Unrealised profit/(loss)	(3,209)	(2,722)	(1,174)	(7,105)

Debit closing valuation in balance sheet – deemed cost   41,645
Credit closing valuation in gross margin – market value   34,540
Credit provision for unrealised profit/(loss) – P & L account 7,105

4 *Profit & loss account*

Sales	32,228
Area payments and set-aside payment	40,871
Closing valuation at selling price	34,540
Output	107,639
Variable costs say	(35,580)
Gross margin	72,059
Total fixed costs (say)	60,000
Management profit	12,059
Deferred income	(20,986)
Provision for unrealised (profit)/loss	7,105
Financial profit for taxation purposes	1,822

NB: for illustrative purposes the profit from the previous harvest realised in the accounts has been excluded.

Balance sheet entries

Valuation	41,645
Debtor – area payment and set-aside	40,871
Creditors – deferred income	20,986

For 31 December year end the situation is similar except that the area and set-aside payment should have been received apart from oilseed rape second instalment, and will be reflected in the balance sheet through the bank account, rather than being shown as a debtor.

The above example uses the deemed cost method in the valuation of crops in store at the end of the year. Farmers with records which enable the calculation of actual cost of production (see **2.13**) will normally result in a lower valuation and a deferral of the tax liability.

2.15 Accounting for joint ventures

2.15.1 Introduction

There has been a substantial increase in joint ventures in the agricultural industry over the past few years. The number of arrangements has increased as a result of several factors:

(a) prior to the introduction of Farm Business Tenancies (**6.3**), land-lords wishing to retain vacant possession and avoid a further lifetime tenancy after a previous tenancy had ceased;

(b)   farmers retiring from active farming but wishing to retain vacant possession of the farm land;

(c)   farmers in financial difficulties and achieving poor technical performance attempting to make their business viable by realising working capital and raising the technical performance of the business;

(d)   farmers pooling their machinery and possibly labour to reduce their costs.

There has been a substantial increase in demand by farmers wishing to take on additional land by a joint venture: offering their machinery, labour and management expertise and thereby spreading their fixed costs over a greater area without capital expenditure in more land.

In general, joint ventures have been constructed in order to avoid the formation of a partnership and a tenancy and to ensure that the land-owner is considered by the Inland Revenue to be trading and not in receipt of rental income. The risk of the formation of a lifetime tenancy has disappeared with the introduction of the Farm Business Tenancy in September 1995. However, the taxation and potential partnership con-siderations still exist (**6.3**).

2.15.2 Types of joint ventures

Although there are a multitude of possible joint venture arrangements, broadly they fall into the following categories:

- share farming;
- contract farming or contract management arrangements;
- partnerships to manage machinery syndicates;
- limited company as a vehicle to pool machinery and possibly labour.

Many large farming companies enter into farming partnerships with landowners introducing equity into arrangements. Alternatively, some-times a limited company is formed with the landowner and the farming company having equal shares. Care must be taken when a limited company is formed to farm the land so that:

(a)   the previous farming partnership or limited company will cease to trade and any trading losses brought forward may be lost; and

(b)   should the previous business be run through a limited company it may be treated as an investment company as a result of it not trading, merely owning a 50 per cent share in the new limited company.

Farming partnerships are considered in **6.8** and the remainder of **2.15** will discuss accounting for contract farming and share farming arrangements.

2.15.3 Share farming

In a share farming agreement the landowner and the farming operator agree to split the sale proceeds in a particular ratio based on the relative values of their contribution to the venture. Examples of the contributions are as follows:

- landowner provides:
  (i) land and buildings;
  (ii) house;
  (iii) fixed equipment such as grain bins or milking parlours;
  (iv) major property repairs;
  (v) working capital in the form of a share of variable costs; and
  (vi) a share in the livestock.
- share farmer provides:
  (i) labour;
  (ii) machinery;
  (iii) management;
  (iv) working capital in the form of a share of variable costs; and
  (v) a share in the livestock.

The share farming agreement should ensure that the two businesses are separate with their own VAT accounting and tax assessments. Care should be taken to ensure that the arrangement is not construed as a partnership, otherwise the parties would have joint and several liabilities for each other's debts.

No tenancy is created provided the operator does not enjoy exclusive possession of any part of the land and buildings.

It is not normally necessary to produce a set of accounts for a share farming venture as both parties' return is their proportion of output rather than being linked to a profit figure (see example below).

2.15.4 Contract farming

A contract farming arrangement is essentially a landowner using the services of a contractor or another farmer to farm the land. The owner supplies variable costs of seeds, fertilisers and sprays for growing the crops; the contracting farmer supplies labour, machinery and management. The contractor will receive a set fee for the services provided and a bonus as a percentage of the calculated surplus from the venture. The arrangement is suitable for both livestock and cropping enterprises.

Contract farming agreements are centred around a memorandum joint venture account, which is an arithmetical calculation to establish how much the contractor should be paid for the services.

It is often advisable in a contract farming arrangement to set up a separate bank account in the landowner's name with all transactions relating to the agreement going through the account. This will also automatically provide the interest calculation on working capital as the account becomes overdrawn to fund variable costs. The funding of the variable costs in cropping arrangements can be provided by the contracting farmer. In this instance, the contracting farmer is providing an interest free loan to the landowner as the legal title to the crops always remains with the landowner.

A correctly drawn up agreement should aim to enable the landowner to carry on the trade of farming and provide a reasonable return for both parties.

The following is a simple example of a 400 acre arable farm with a 31 March year end. Example contract farming and share farming arrangements are shown with the appropriate accounting entries.

Example 2.10 *Profit and loss account 31 March 1998*

	£ per Acre	£ Total
Gross margin	230	92,000
Overheads:		
labour	35	14,000
power and machinery	95	38,000
property	15	6,000
administration	26	10,400
finance costs	40	16,000
Total fixed costs	211	84,400
Profit	19	7,600

Balance Sheet 31 March 1998

Fixed assets:		
land at cost		400,000
machinery		150,000
Current assets:		
valuations tillages at £40 per acre	16,000	
variable costs at £50 per acre	20,000	
debtors	2,000	
Current liabilities:		
bank overdraft	100,000	
leasing and HP	20,000	
trade creditors	2,000	
		(84,000)
Net assets		466,000
Capital account		466,000
Capital employed		466,000

2.15.5 A typical contract farming arrangement

In this example it is assumed that the landowning farmer enters into a contract farming arrangement with the contractor funding the variable costs on an interest free loan basis until harvest proceeds are sold in the autumn. The funding of the variable costs is not common in these arrangements but included in example **2.11** to indicate the accounting entries.

Example 2.11 *Memorandum account*

		£ per Acre
Gross margin		230
Fixed costs agreed		
insurance of crops		4
drying – electricity		6
contractor's fee payable at harvest		80
Harvest surplus		140
Landowner's retention		100
Divisible surplus		40
Landowner	20%	8
Contractor	80%	32
Total landowner		108
Total contractor		112

The annual accounts for a year ended 31 March and the associated balance sheet will be drawn up part of the way through the growing season. Therefore the following items will be reflected in the accounts:

(a) The interest free loan made by the contractor to the landowner to the same value as the variable cost expenditure to date.
(b) The cultivation work carried out by the contractor on the land. This valuation will be the property of the landowner with a corresponding amount in creditors owing to the contractor.

The following profit and loss account and balance sheet reflects an ongoing situation based on the memorandum account.

Example 2.12 *Profit and loss account 31 March 1999 – contract farmed*

	£ per Acre	£ Total
Gross margin	230	92,000
Overheads:		
labour	0	0
power and machinery	20	8,000
contract	112	44,800
property	15	6,000
administration	26	10,400
finance costs	0	0
Total fixed costs	173	69,200
Profit	57	22,800

Balance sheet 31 March 1999 – contract farmed

Fixed assets:			
land at cost			400,000
machinery			20,000
Current assets:			
valuations	tillages at £40 per acre	16,000	
	variable costs at £50 per acre	20,000	
debtors		2,000	
cash at bank		10,000	
Current liabilities:			
bank overdraft		0	
leasing and HP		0	
trade creditors		2,000	
contractor	tillages at £40 per acre	16,000	
contractor	variable costs at £50 per acre	20,000	
			46,000
net assets			430,000
capital account			430,000
capital employed			430,000

Example 2.13 *A typical share farming agreement*

	Total	Land owner	Share farmer
Section 1			
Land 400 acres at rental value £60	24,000	24,000	
House			
Buildings	2,500	2,500	
Fixed machinery maintenance	1,000	1,000	
Machinery depreciation	20,000		20,000
Machinery running costs	8,000		8,000
Management	5,000	2,000	3,000
Telephone and office	800		800
Insurance of standing crops	1,000	1,000	
Totals	62,300	30,500	31,800
Percent Share	100%	49%	51%
Section 2 (based on above percentages)			
Variable costs	36,000	17,640	18,360
Crop drying costs	2,000	980	1,020
Insurance of crops in store	1,000	490	510
Total costs	101,300	49,610	51,690
Section 3 based on above percentages			
Crop sales and subsidies	128,000	62,720	65,280
Surplus	36,700	13,110	13,590

The annual accounts to be drawn up for the landowning share farmer will only include a proportion of gross margin and will exclude the items of the overheads paid for by the share farmer.

The growing crops will be the property of the landowner whilst in the ground but the cultivations carried out by the share farmer up to the end of March will have been carried out by the share farmer's own labour and machinery, the value of tillages will also be the property of the landowner at this stage with a corresponding amount owing to the share farmer.

Example 2.14 *Profit and loss account 31 March 1999 – share farmed*

	£ per Acre	£ Total
Gross margin at 49 per cent	113	45,200
Overheads:		
labour	0	0
power and machinery £8,000		
less £1,020 crop drying	17	6,980
contract		0
property	15	6,000
administration less £510 insurance	25	9,890
finance costs	0	0
Total fixed costs	57	22,870
Profit	56	22,330

Balance sheet 31 March 1999 – share farmed

Fixed assets:			
land at cost			400,000
machinery			20,000
Current assets:			
valuations	tillages at £40 per acre	16,000	
	variable costs at £50 per acre	20,000	
debtors		2,000	
cash at bank		200	
Current liabilities:			
bank overdraft		0	
leasing and HP		0	
trade creditors		2,000	
contractor	tillages at £40 per acre	16,000	
contractor	variable costs at £50 per acre		
	at 51%	10,200	
			10,000
Net assets			430,000
Capital account			430,000
Capital employed			430,000

2.15.6 Accounting considerations

Businesses with financial year ends prior to the calculation of a memorandum account will not know how much to provide for the amount owing to the contracting farmer for the final profit share. There are two options available:

(a) delay the preparation of the final accounts until the creditor is known, this will depend upon the time delay involved; or
(b) include an estimated amount for the profit share which will have to be adjusted the following year in the contract charge.

Many contract farming arrangements include an annual valuation of grain for sale, variable costs and cultivations in September. Unless the financial year end of the business is at the same time as the valuation it has no practical use or relevance to the preparation of the annual accounts.

The total remuneration of the contractor consists of supplying the following services:

- labour
- machinery
- management.

However, the total amount is normally invoiced as contracting fees plus VAT. Should it be considered necessary to more accurately account for the services provided, it is suggested that the total contracting fees paid to the contractor be split as follows:

- £70 per acre allocated to power and machinery contract;
- £30 per acre allocated to labour contract;
- the remainder allocated to professional management fees.

Conversely the fees received by the contracting farmer can be accounted for in the same manner.

2.16 Accounting for farm machinery

2.16.1 Introduction

Machinery costs are by far the most complex to account for out of all the fixed costs. The use of financial organisations other than banks to fund machinery is commonplace and the different types of finance agreements are numerous with the arrangements available ever changing. The accounting and tax treatment of payments under these arrangements are also complex. The method of accounting can reflect the level of costs shown in the annual accounts and can lead to misleading interpretation for management purposes. It is assumed that the reader is familiar with

SSAP 21 which governs the accounting treatment of assets used and purchased under leased and hire agreements.

Total power and machinery costs are usually in the region of £80 to £90 per acre on arable farms and up to £150 per acre on specialist dairy units. Extensive livestock businesses will have cost well below these. These costs are normally made up of:

- depreciation   50 per cent
- repairs and spares   20 per cent
- power   18 per cent
- contractors   6 per cent
- licences and insurance   6 per cent.

The capital tied up in machinery on a combinable crop farm is usually in the region of £180 per acre and at a depreciation rate of 18 per cent the annual charge on the £180 is £32 per acre. In addition, if the business borrows money the interest charge on the £180 at 9 per cent will be £16 per acre. Conventional accounting methods do not reflect the capital tied up in machinery, instead being a general charge on the business if the capital is borrowed and therefore may understate the true cost of machinery.

The method of accounting for farm machinery varies with the legal status of the machine which in practice is generally governed by the method of funding. The taxation treatment of machinery is detailed in **5.7**.

2.16.2 Outright purchase

The asset is added at purchase price to the fixed assets in the balance sheet. Should a grant be available on the purchase price the grant should be treated in accordance with *SSAP 4*. (**2.10.3**)

Farmers retain machinery for differing periods depending upon the type of machine and it is therefore advisable to use the reducing balance method of depreciation rather than the straight line method in order for the annual depreciation charge and the balance in fixed assets to reflect the actual position as near as possible. The following reducing balance depreciation rates will reflect the average drop in machinery value over the normal useful lives of the different categories:

- combine harvesters   15 per cent
- tractors and self propelled machines   15 per cent
- general machinery with working parts   20 per cent

- cars and vehicles   25 per cent
- office equipment   30 per cent

The resultant written down values will generally reflect the trade-in prices achieved when the item is replaced.

A list of machinery per client should be maintained as a fixed asset register and brought forward in the accounts file. When sold, an item is taken out of the fixed asset register at its written down value and any difference between this value and the selling price should be shown separately as a profit or loss on sale or disposal of fixed assets. It is common for this balance to be amalgamated with the depreciation figure in the annual accounts which makes it difficult to interpret the accounts for management performance and comparisons, this practice is therefore not recommended. The fixed asset register, which lends itself to being maintained on a spreadsheet model, should be shown to the client every year to confirm the assets and movements shown.

A depreciation rate that does not reflect the true drop in value of a category of machinery will result in a distortion of profits from year to year and a large balance shown as a profit or loss on disposal.

Example 2.15 *Showing the use of different depreciation rates*

The example shows two depreciation rates. The average reduction in market value of a tractor over a period of years is 15 per cent per annum. The 25 per cent depreciation rate will overstate the depreciation charge in the accounts over the four years and show a profit on its eventual sale of £3,340. This will understate profit for four years and understate it in the fifth year making the accounts difficult to interpret for management purposes.

Tractor purchase price		£25,000
Depreciation rate reducing balance	15%	25%
Written down values within fixed assets in balance sheet		
end of year1	21,250	18,750
end of year 2	18,063	14,062
end of year 3	15,353	10,547
end of year 4	13,050	7,910
Sale price	13,250	13,250
Profit on sale	200	5,340

2.16.3 Hire purchase

Hire purchase is also referred to as Lease Purchase or Deferred Purchase. The asset becomes the legal property of the purchaser or hirer when the final payment is made.

The capital value of assets acquired under hire purchase agreements are accounted for as additions to fixed assets in the period in which they are acquired.

Any interest element of the repayments can be calculated by the sum of digits method or on a straight line basis for the length of the agreement and charged to the profit and loss account as overheads of the business.

The liability owing to the finance company is included in the balance sheet as a creditor, split into:

- amount owing within 12 months; and
- amount owing later than 12 months from the balance sheet date.

2.16.4 Conditional sale

Sometimes called plant purchase. The legal title to the asset vests with the purchaser from the outset and is therefore not subject to the terms of a hire purchase agreement. These were originally available to allow grants to be paid which required ownership of the asset. The accounting treatment is the same as hire purchase.

2.16.5 Finance leases

The lessee cannot obtain legal ownership of the asset, however, the lessee has obligations that are substantially similar to those of an outright purchaser. Finance leases should be distinguished from operating leases (**2.26.5**) as defined in *SSAP 21*.

Historically, particularly in the financial statements of unincorporated farming businesses, the asset was not shown in fixed assets. This was generally called 'off balance sheet finance' as the corresponding liability owing to the finance company was not included as a creditor in the balance sheet. The leasing payments were included in the overheads of the business on a cash basis often termed 'hire of machinery'. This method of accounting was unsatisfactory as it did not represent the true position of the business and in particular it was difficult for lenders such as bank managers to make objective assessments. For accounting periods beginning on or after 1 July 1984 assets acquired under finance lease agreements should be recorded in the balance sheet in fixed assets and the liability to pay future rentals included in creditors. The rental payments are split into a capital and an interest element. The interest is included in overheads and the capital element reduces the liability. When sold the asset is deducted from fixed assets at its written down value and any difference between this value and selling price is shown separately as a profit or loss on sale in the profit and loss account.

Secondary payments that can be as high as one per cent of the original purchase price are normally accounted for as they fall due in fixed costs.

2.16.6 Contract hire or operating leases

An increasing amount of the larger items of machinery such as the larger tractors and combine harvesters are acquired on farms under these arrangements.

In simple terms the agreement is constructed as a lease arrangement with low rentals, usually including a maintenance element, during the period of hire and a large balloon rental as the final payment. The final payment is subject to a separate repurchase agreement or undertaking by the supplying dealer or in some cases the finance company itself. Therefore, the final payment is made by a third party and the farmer has no value in the machine at the termination of the agreement.

The accounting treatment of operating leases follows the old rules of finance leases where the rentals are accounted for when they fall due. These are included in the fixed costs of the business usually in 'machinery hire'. The asset is not included in the balance sheet and no liability exists.

2.16.7 VAT

All items of machinery are subject to VAT. The VAT is payable on the capital cost of the asset when acquired by means of a hire purchase or conditional sale agreement. VAT is charged on the rentals on finance and operating leases, and this is the simplest method of distinguishing between the methods of funding and adopting the appropriate accounting treatment. The VAT on machinery including leasing and hire purchase is discussed in **5.17.9**.

2.16.8 Commercial considerations

Many manufacturers of agricultural machinery subsidise the interest charged by finance companies in order to make the purchase of their equipment more attractive. This can be a relatively cheap source of borrowed money. The subsidy is usually packaged by the finance company and advertised widely. Care must be taken as most of the advertised interest rates are flat rates expressed as a fixed percentage per annum of the capital cost irrespective of capital repayment structure. Therefore the annual percentage rate (APR), which is not published for leasing agreements, may be considerably more.

Consideration should be given to the option of finance lease versus hire purchase regarding the secondary rental charged with finance leases. This can be particularly relevant for assets that will be retained in the business for a considerable length of time. The assets should generally be hire purchased in order to avoid paying secondary rentals for several years.

Cars that are partly used for private purposes should be hire purchased in order to avoid the 50 per cent add back of the VAT element on the rentals. However, in theory, the lease rentals should be cheaper than hire purchase because the leasing company will have recovered the VAT on the purchase of the car.

The tax and accounting position of clients can be significantly influenced by the facts of each case and these should be determined as precisely as possible during the audit and accounting work. A brief checklist that should be considered is listed below.

- Ensure that the type of agreement has been correctly identified. If unsure contact the finance company.
- If the agreement is a lease did it commence prior to 12 April 1991?
- Have any rebates of rentals for disposed leased assets been received?
- Were any assets acquired on hire purchase not used in the period?
- Is the agreement a conditional sale?
- Were any cars acquired on lease with a capital cost exceeding £12,000?
- Have the maintenance elements of rentals of lease agreements been identified?
- Have claims for input VAT been correctly made?

Discounts on new machines can be considerable and these can be partly hidden by a high trade-in value. Therefore, depending upon the status of the machine traded in and the method of funding the new machine, it may be important to ensure that the agreement documentation shows the most beneficial values.

Historically only fixed interest agreements have been offered. However more sophisticated packages are now available but not widely advertised. These include variable rates with fixed payments, the length of the agreement being the variable. Fixed and variable EURO hire purchase and lease agreements are available.

Clients should be encouraged to contact their accountant when they are considering the purchase and trade-in of larger items of machinery.

2.17 Accounting for the herd basis

The taxation aspects of the herd basis are discussed in (**5.10**), including brief notes on the operation of the herd basis (**5.10.7**). The following is a summary of the accounting entries required. No particular form of accounting records are required. It is generally sufficient if livestock numbers and costs can be adequately reconciled between the beginning and end of the year. The cost of the herd is maintained as a separate asset and carried forward in the balance sheet as a herd account.

2.17.1 Initial cost of the herd

The initial cost of the purchase of the animals or their value at the date of election form the basis of the herd account Their cost is not included in the profit and loss account as a cost nor in the valuation of trading stock:

	£
80 cows purchased or transferred at £600	48,000

Once the herd account has been established, the initial cost of each of the animals becomes the herd basis cost of that animal or its replacement.

Accounting entries will depend upon whether:

- the animal is a permanent addition or reduction to the herd, therefore permanently increasing or decreasing the size of the herd; or
- the animal is a replacement for an animal in the herd or, when sold, the animal is replaced by another animal.

2.17.2 Temporary increase or decrease

There is provision for a period of up to 12 months to elapse between selling or the death of an animal and another animal replacing it. Likewise, when an animal is added to the herd 12 months may elapse before the animal it replaces is sold. In this situation the first temporary addition or reduction is held in suspense until the second animal is added or sold. This period can be extended by negotiation with the Revenue, particularly if replacements are normally home reared and insufficient animals are available at a particular time.

2.17.3 Home bred animals reaching maturity and added to the herd increasing the herd size

When an animal reaches maturity (**5.10.3**) the cost of rearing the animal should be included as a trading receipt and the herd account debited with the same amount. The effect of crediting the profit and loss account with the cost of production of the animals will be to cancel out the actual costs of rearing them. Most farmers do not keep sufficiently detailed records to identify the actual cost of production, therefore the deemed cost (**2.13.9**) value is normally used.

Example 2.16 *Home bred heifers transferred to the herd account increasing the herd size*

		£
80 cows at £600		48,000
15 heifers at £500 market value at 60%		4,500
Herd basis cost carried forward:		
80 animals at £600	48,000	
15 animals at £300	4,500	
		52,500
Credit profit and loss account		4,500

2.17.4 Mature animals purchased and added to the herd

The cost of the additional animals is not included in the profit and loss account but debited directly to the herd account.

Example 2.17 *Mature animals added to the herd increasing the herd size*

Herd basis cost brought forward:		
80 animals at £600		
15 animals at £300		
		52,500
5 animals purchased at £700		3,500
Herd basis cost carried forward:		
80 animals at £600	48,000	
15 animals at £300	4,500	
5 animals at £700	3,500	
		56,000

2.17.5 Immature animals purchased and later transferred to the herd

The animals are initially included in trading stock and transferred to the herd when they become 'mature', at their purchase price plus their cost of rearing to the time of transfer.

2.17.6 Animal sold from herd and not replaced

If the animal will be replaced within the following 12 months, the sale proceeds can be held in 'suspense' until it is replaced (**2.17.2**). When the sale of the animal does not constitute, when added to others sold in a 12 month period, a substantial reduction in herd numbers (more than 20 per cent), the resulting profit or loss with reference to its herd basis cost is included in the profit and loss account. When the animal sold was a replacement and therefore cannot be individually identified (**2.17.7**), its actual cost will not have been recorded in the herd capital account, but included in the profit and loss account at the time of introduction. Therefore, the herd basis cost of the animal sold will be one of the original animals in the herd. See **2.17.9** below on identification of individual animals.

Example 2.18 *Animal sold and not replaced reducing the herd size*

	£	£
Herd basis cost brought forward:		
80 animals at £600	48,000	
15 animals at £300	4,500	
5 animals at £700	3,500	
		56,000
Sale of cull animal reducing herd size		300
Cost of one of original animals		600
Loss charged to profit and loss account		300
Herd basis cost brought forward:		
79 animals at £600	47,400	
15 animals at £300	4,500	
5 animals at £700	3,500	
		55,400

2.17.7 Animal sold from herd and replaced by another animal of the same quality

The cost of the purchased animal is charged to the profit and loss account and the sale proceeds of the culled animal is credited to the profit and loss account. The net cost of replacement is therefore allowed as a cost in the profit and loss account and 'the herd basis cost' of the old animal becomes the 'herd basis cost' of the new animal. The herd capital account is therefore not adjusted.

Where the replacement animal is home produced, the cost of rearing will already have been charged against profits in the form of feed, vet and medicines and forage costs throughout the life of the animal. In this instance, therefore, no charge is made to the profit and loss account for the home bred replacement animal, the only entry being the inclusion of the sale proceeds of the animal sold in the profit and loss account.

Example 2.19 Herd animal replaced by another purchased animal of the same quality	
Sale of cull animal at £300	300
Purchase of replacement animal at £800	700
Difference charged to profit and loss account	400
No adjustment to herd account	

Example 2.20 Herd animal replaced by another home bred animal of the same quality	
Sale of cull animal at £300 credited to profit and loss account	300
No adjustment to herd account	

2.17.8 Replacement with an animal of superior quality

If the new animal is a better quality than the animal it replaces, the net cost of replacement is restricted to the amount it would have cost to replace with an animal of the same quality. The additional cost representing the improvement element should be added to the herd capital account and not charged to the profit and loss account.

Example 2.21 *Replacing an animal with another animal of superior quality*

	£
Sale of cull animal	300
Purchase of replacement animal	2,000
A replacement of the same quality would have cost	700
The improvement element is therefore	1,300
Sale proceeds credited to profit and loss account	300
Restricted cost of replacement animal in profit and loss account	700
Restricted net cost charged to profit and loss account	400
The herd basis cost of the cull animal	600
Improvement element	1,300
Herd basis cost of the new animal	1,900

The herd basis cost carried forward therefore becomes:

Herd basis cost brought forward from Example 2.18:

79 animals at £600	47,400	
15 animals at £300	4,500	
5 animals at £700	3,500	
		55,400

Herd basis cost carried forward:

78 animals at £600	47,400	
15 animals at £300	4,500	
5 animals at £700	3,500	
1 animal at £1,900	1,900	
		57,300

What constitutes an improvement in quality is a matter of judgement and in practice, unless the improvement is substantial, no adjustment is normally made.

2.17.9 Identification of animals

The identification of individual animals, or groups of animals with the same base cost, will be required in the following circumstances:

- where there is a permanent reduction in herd numbers; and
- where an animal is replaced with another animal of superior quality.

In practice, particularly in larger herds or flocks, where many of the replacements are home bred and reared, the identification of individual animals will be very difficult. When the herd basis records are insufficient to identify individual animals and, in the absence of any evidence to the contrary, the Revenue will accept a ' first in, first out' (FIFO) basis as a method of calculating the profit element over and above the herd basis cost.

As the original animals, and subsequently their replacements, in the herd capital account are likely to have the lowest base cost, the FIFO basis adopted by the Revenue when animals cannot be identified, will have the effect of reducing the amount charged as a deduction in the profit and loss account and the herd capital account balance carried forward will be correspondingly higher.

Herd basis cost brought forward:	£	£
78 animals at £600	47,400	
15 animals at £300	4,500	
5 animals at £700	3,500	
1 animal at £1,900	1,900	
		57,300
Unidentified cull animal sold and not replaced		300
Cost of one of original animals on FIFO basis		600
Loss charged to profit and loss account		300

If the cull animal sold is identified as one of the original five purchased animals or their subsequent replacements at a higher cost of £700, the loss charged to the profit and loss account becomes £400. In this instance the herd capital account carried forward is £100 less than when the cost of one of the original animals transferred to the herd capital account, at £600, is used.

Therefore care must be taken to ensure that detailed records are maintained to ensure that individual animals or batches of animals can be identified when required. The overall aim therefore is to reduce the herd capital account by the highest value animals to obtain a higher charge in the profit and loss account.

2.18 Accounting for euros

There has been considerable debate within the agricultural and allied industries regarding the use of the euro as a currency and the benefits and disadvantages to individual farming businesses (**6.14**). Whilst the UK remains outside EMU the euro is a foreign currency and the standard accounting procedures for foreign transactions should be used.

In simple terms purchases in euros outside the EMU should be converted to sterling at the exchange rate on the date of the purchase invoice. Any subsequent change in exchange rate between the invoice date and the actual payment in euros should be recorded as a foreign exchange gain or loss and recorded in the profit and loss account.

There is at least one farming computer accounting software package that has a euro transaction module and others are likely to be available in the near future. If a manual system is used it is advisable to maintain the records of euro transactions in a separate cashbook or ledger detailing the euro amount and date of invoice, the sterling equivalent at the prevailing exchange rate, the subsequent amount and date of payment in euros and sterling.

Customs and Excise require all euro invoices to show the sterling equivalent of the net supply and the VAT element and these amounts need to be recorded in the euro transaction cashbook. The exchange rate for the VAT element can be one of three:

- the market rate on the invoice date;
- a monthly rate publisheed by C & E;
- a commercial rate used by the business with the permission of the local VAT Business Advice Centre.

Details of borrowing in euros are included in **6.14**.

Chapter 3 – Auditing and reporting

3.1 Introduction

This chapter assumes that the reader is familiar with the Auditing Standards issued by the Auditing Practitioners Board. It is not intended to be a specific auditing reference but covers the application of auditing concepts to a farming business. Reference is made to both 'financial statements' and 'annual accounts' in this chapter. Financial statements are the statutory accounts in Companies Act format whereas annual accounts are the management accounts.

Most farming companies are family owned businesses that have been incorporated for tax planning purposes. Many are relatively small businesses and are often unable to disincorporate because of potential capital gains tax on assets within the company. If they are in the definition of a 'small company' they may benefit from some of the exemptions from an audit.

3.1.1 Financial statements and management accounts

Many farming businesses do not prepare their own management accounts (**2.2**, **4.1**) but rely on their accountant and auditor to provide this information. Therefore management accounts are usually prepared for the client in addition to statutory accounts. It is advisable for them to be prepared at the same time when the analytical review and verification procedures can be applied to both. An audit approach that is balance sheet based, together with an analytical review, is usually the most cost effective in determining completeness and accuracy of the figures. This approach also enables the auditor to comment on any commercial aspects of the business, therefore offering better value for money.

3.2 When an audit or report is required

All limited and unlimited farming companies require an audit unless they satisfy the following conditions for exemption :

Size:
- qualify as a 'small company' under section 247 of the Companies Act;
- have a balance sheet total not exceeding £1.4 million;

- have an annual turnover not exceeding £350,000 to be exempt completely from audit.

Status:
- not a plc throughout the year.

Holders of ten per cent or more in aggregate of the issued share capital or of any class have the right to lodge a notice with the company up to one month before the year end, calling for an audit to be carried out in relation to that year's financial statements.

Companies that are exempt from having their accounts audited are also exempt from the requirements to appoint auditors.

3.2.1 Accountants report

Companies eligible for exemption from audit and whose turnover fell between £90,000 and £350,000 used to have to appoint a reporting accountant to provide a report, which took the place of the audit report for filing purposes. This is no longer required.

3.3 The role of the auditor

When preparing the financial statements for a farming business, certain verification procedures should be carried out to ensure that:

- the information shown properly represents the trading activities of the business during the period covered; and
- that the balance sheet reflects the true position of the business at the balance sheet date.

In many farming businesses the financial statements need to be relevant to the management needs of the business as well as to the requirements of taxation. The management accounts are usually included as management information in addition to the financial statements.

The auditors of a farming business trading as a company, however, require a greater degree of external evidence to support company financial statements, and make more systematic reference to invoices and other data and contact the bank to verify balances. It is not usual to contact debtors and creditors to verify balances, but to use procedures to verify suppliers statements and after date cash receipts. The role of the auditor is to give an opinion on the financial statements as distinct from the actual preparation of the financial statements and management accounts. However, in practice in farming businesses, most accountants will undertake both roles at the same time. In addition, the auditor has an obligation to ensure that any contingent liabilities, capital comitt-ments or any other material items that may have a potential impact on the company are disclosed. It is common for the statutory books of the farming company to not be up to date, for example the actual and beneficial ownership of shares may not have been recorded. The full history of share ownership and movements is required for effective tax planning.

3.4 Planning and approach

3.4.1 Introduction

The overall approach to the audit and verification of the farm accounts varies with the specific circumstances of each business and the quantity and quality of available management information. It is essential to determine the type of farm, as defined by the relative contributions of the range of enterprises (**1.13**), for example, a specialist dairy farm as opposed to an extensive arable farm. The problems likely to be asso-ciated with a particular financial year end and the enterprises should be considered. The year end procedure investigates the work going on before and after the balance-sheet date. This must be known so that appropriate consideration can be given to stock valuation, cut-off tests and the number and stage of production cycles for crops and livestock covered by the accounts.

3.4.2 Enterprises and land use

The land usage and cropping records for the harvest years covered by the accounts should be available and summarised for the working file. Full descriptions of the crop and livestock enterprises should be sought. Some of the crops that can easily be confused are winter and spring sown crops, vining peas and dry peas. The relative returns of crops vary significantly, therefore the auditor must be clear about the precise enterprises on the farm.

3.4.3 Farm records

Some farms may have detailed physical records of the major inputs, stocks and outputs of crops and livestock. Where these are fully recon-ciled to the financial statements they may be used extensively to provide audit evidence. However, on the majority of farms, detailed control accounts will not be available. Enquiry should be made of the physical records maintained, since they may not be seen by the farmer client to be relevant to the accountant's and auditor's work. It may be possible to carry out some reconciliation work with the physical records.

The adequacy of the physical and financial records should be considered in deciding upon the audit and verification work necessary.

3.4.4 Requirements of the client

The requirements of the client should also be carefully considered. In most cases, the annual financial statements prepared by the accountant are the only financial management information available to the farmer. Therefore the preparation of the financial statements, management accounts and the audit are dealt with as one process: the work being verified and audited as the annual financial statements are being prepared.

3.4.5 Computers

Many farmers now have some form of on-farm computerised accounting system. Consideration should be given to the integrity and applicability of the system in use, as well as the skill of the operator, before reliance is placed on any information provided. This is particularly relevant where a non-standard package is used (**4.4**) such as a spreadsheet-based program designed by the farmer.

3.4.6 Permanent information

The permanent information file (PIF) which should be updated annually, should record descriptions and details of the land farmed, the production cycles of the enterprises, the marketing policy, labour and machinery employed and summarised information on past performance. The permanent information may be maintained under the following headings:

- personnel and management;
- business organisation;
- type of business and enterprises;
- land holdings;
- material purchase and sale arrangements via co-operatives or major merchants; and
- summary of the key economic statistics over the previous five years.

3.5 Analytical review

3.5.1 Introduction

After the detailed audit and verification work is completed and the special factors affecting each farm have been taken into account, further verification of the transactions and balances in the farm accounts may be carried out through the analytical review.

The more carefully the farm financial statements have been prepared and presented, the more useful this review will be. The amount of review work done depends upon the responsibility of the accountant, whether or not he is carrying out an audit and the use to which the analytical review might be put in providing a financial review of the business for the client and the preparation of management accounts.

The amount of audit evidence likely to be available from the analytical review must be considered in each individual case before the work is commenced.

In the case of audit and verification of farming businesses of limited size, the analytical review can be used as an initial common sense review. Questions that arise can then lead to detailed tests that allow the auditor to satisfy his criteria and find the records a true and fair representation.

3.5.2 First stage – comparison of balance sheets

The first stage of the analytical review involves a comparison of the opening and closing balance sheets in financial and, where appropriate, physical terms. The review should cover the following:

Balance sheet item	*Point for review*
Fixed assets	Investment levels Changes of machinery and vehicles Effect on repairs and maintenance Land holding and buildings Changes in capacity Reasons for change
Stocks	Numbers and quantities of livestock, crops and stores Marketing policy Cost of financing Reasons for change Unit valuations
Debtors	Seasonal selling factors Reasons for change
Creditors	Trading and capital items Reasons for change
Bank and finance creditors	Reasons for changes Dependence upon short term finance Gearing levels
Capital employed	Reasons for changes Balance of employment between fixed and working capital Tenants capital and landlord capital per acre.

3.5.3 Second stage – review of results

The second stage of the analytical review is a review of the results of the farm business for the period and should include :

- farm gross margin;
- farm fixed costs;
- finance charges;
- rental equivalent;
- farm profit;
- individual gross margins;
- fixed costs:
  (i)   labour

(ii) power and machinery
(iii) property
(iv) administration
(v)   finance.

Before reviewing these figures it is essential to establish the basis on which they have been determined. In particular, gross margins make little comparative sense unless they include closing stocks at market value and are shown separately for each harvest year.

Ideally, all of the above figures should be expressed per hectare or acre for the current and two previous years.

Although gross margins are normally adjusted to take account of harvest years, no such adjustment is necessary with farm fixed costs. When reviewing farm fixed cost levels, the effect of early and late seasons should be taken into account, since this factor can be important in understanding variations from year to year, particularly the amount of work carried out on the land on arable farms which will be reflected in the tillage valuations. A detailed review of the fixed costs should consider the following:

(a) labour:
    (i)   casual labour controls
    (ii) cost of employee benefits
    (iii) changes in wage rates from the Agricultural Wages Board
(b) power and machinery:
    (i)   fuel usage and price changes
    (ii) repair levels
    (iii) depreciation charges and policy
(c) property:
    (i)   rental reviews
    (ii) property repair levels – capital or trading
    (iii) insurance
(d) administration:
    (i)   postal and telephone charges
    (ii) costs of secretarial help
    (iii) professional adviser's fees – relating to capital or trading

3.5.4 Third stage – detailed performance

The third stage of the analytical review looks at the detailed performance behind the financial figures above. This review should include:

- crop yields;

- livestock yields – milk fatstock, egg production;
- breeding performance of livestock;
- variable costs of crops per acre;
- variable costs of livestock per head;
- conversion of feed into meat;
- rate of growth of fattening stock.

3.5.5 Fourth stage – comparison with budgets and management information

The final stage of the analytical review might involve a comparison of the budgets and cashflows in the farm business with the out-turn shown by the final accounts. Further, any detailed management accounts for the whole farm or for a specific enterprise should be reconciled as appropriate.

In many farm businesses it is useful to consider the likely profit and taxable profit prior to the financial year end. This may be done by a detailed analysis of transactions from available information and by preparing a projected balance sheet.

Some analytical review work may be done at this stage, but there may be particular problems of interpretation where detailed information is incomplete and the draft accounts are made up to some date other than the normal balance sheet date.

3.6 Yields and output analysis

The livestock enterprises and crops grown need to be established and the timing of normal marketing of the produce and animals established (see **1.13** to **1.15**). In many arable businesses depending upon the crops grown and the financial year end of the business, the sales within a financial year may include some of the produce from the same crop (e.g., wheat, barley, etc.) from two different harvest years. In addition, different crops are harvested at different times of the year. This is particularly relevant when a mixture of combinable and root crops are grown (see **2.5**).

The principles of initial harvest estimation of physical quantities will be examined for a number of common crops.

3.6.1 Cereal sales

The auditor should establish the earliest point at which sale quantities are measured. Although it is possible to estimate yields of cereals in the harvest field by measuring amounts combine harvested, it is usual to estimate quantities either in the trailer or in the barn. It is now possible to weigh cereals discharged from the combine harvester to the trailer or in the trailer itself. More commonly, harvest yields are measured by:

- sales to date from the relevant harvest;
- grain in store in bins or grain stores within buildings; or
- own use for feed or seed.

It must be remembered that reference should be made to the moisture content of the grain when assessing weight. A professional valuer should be able to determine the weight of corn from its capacity. The estimated yields determined by the farmer or the valuer might be compared with one or more of the following:

- yields per farm budgets;
- previous yields on the same farm;
- other clients' yields;
- yields published by university surveys; and
- MAFF yield estimates for the region.

The reason for yield variations should be sought. Variances might occur through seasonal factors, disease, varietal changes or similar reasons. The treatment of levies and weighbridge charges should be ascertained. These are usually deducted from the total shown on the self-billing invoice provided by the grain merchant.

3.6.2 Potato sales

Yields are normally estimated for potatoes stored in loose heaps, bulk stores in barns or specialised, atmospherically controlled stores. Estimated yields determined by the farmer or valuer might be compared with comparative yields from sources quoted in Appendix **3**.

3.6.3 Sugar beet sales

These may be originally estimated by test harvesting in the field and then by heap in clamps or on the field. Quantities are finally determined by weighing at the British Sugar Corporation factory, where readings for dirt weight, top weight and sugar percentage are also made. Quantities may also be compared with transport records.

3.6.4 Peas, beans, oilseed rape and herbage seed

Apart from vining peas which are not normally weighed until arrival at the factory, these crops are harvested by a combine harvester, and the harvest yield estimates follow the principles laid down for cereals.

Example 3.1 *Analytical review of harvest yields*

In the analytical review section, it will be seen that harvest yield figures are normally determined and subsequently checked as in the following table.

	Crop 1 tonnes	Crop 2 tonnes	Crop 3 tonnes
Previous year harvest			
Opening stock at the start of the financial year	98	270	120
Own use for feeds or seeds	(12)	–	(50)
Sales of the crop	(100)	(250)	(70)
Surplus/(Deficit)	14	(20)	–
Current year harvest			
Sales of the crop	150	230	70
Own use for feeds or seeds	20	10	50
Closing stocks at the end of the financial year	80	120	30
Estimated yield	250	360	150
Current year hectares grown	50	12	40
Estimated yield tonnes per hectare	5	30	35

It can be seen that disposal of the previous year harvest is clearly shown, whilst the components of the current year yield are compared with the acreage grown of each crop.

These yield estimates should be compared with the yield determined in the harvest field, the barn or on despatch, and significant variances investigated. Actual yield may occur through further drying or cleaning and deterioration in store. The peak stocks at harvest should be compared with the total storage capacity and sales. The auditor should also be aware of the effect of moisture content on the yield weight.

3.6.5 Livestock reconciliation

The numbers of livestock sales and stocks are normally verified by a numbers reconciliation (**2.3.1**). Numbers of livestock at the balance sheet date are provided either by the farmer or a professional valuer. In either case it is necessary to prepare a schedule to reconcile the opening and closing figures. It is often valuable to request the farmer to prepare the reconciliation. Not only is this likely to save detailed work, but it is also valuable for the farmer to have an appreciation of the verification procedures.

Information regarding purchases and sales should be available from the invoices and contract notes. Numbers of births and deaths must be provided by the farmer. If more than one kind of livestock is kept, a numbers reconciliation must be carried out for each kind of animal by enterprise type.

Animals are often kept for a number of purposes. Here the numbers reconciliation must distinguish between the principal categories and account for any transfer from one to the other. The reconciliation for a dairy herd with young dairy replacements and beef animals might be as in Example 3.2.

Example 3.2 *Livestock reconciliation*			
	Dairy herd	*Calves, beef animals and dairy cattle replacements*	*Total*
Number at previous balance sheet date	100	200	300
Purchases	–	30	30
Sales	(20)	(150)	(170)
Births	90	105	195
Deaths	(5)	(20)	(25)
Transfers in	25	90	115
Transfers out	(90)	(25)	(115)
Number at current balance sheet date	100	230	330

In preparing the numbers reconciliation, it is important to identify what has happened to each animal from one balance sheet date to another. This identifies movements in and out of each herd as the young replacements become part of the dairy herd and as calves become part of the beef enterprise.

Physical records of livestock births, deaths, sales and purchases may be available from more than one source on the farm. Tracking down precisely the correct information has always been difficult but has improved considerably in the past two years as a result of the increased amount of record keeping required to conform with livestock subsidy requirements. The method of accounting for deaths in particular will need to be discussed and agreed with the farmer. When an animal is born dead it must either be recorded as a birth and a death or ignored.

Verification of sales prices can be done by reference to contracts, orders, self-billing invoices, sales invoices and published market prices in weekly agricultural magazines.

3.6.6 Forward contracts

The sales quantities and valuation basis should be compared with any forward contract commitments. Such contracts might be for the whole or part of a particular crop or group of livestock and be at an agreed price or related to market movement. Crop forward contracts in particular have become increasingly popular, often incorporating an option premium for a minimum price.

Where the price likely to be obtainable for produce has been hedged through a future contract, then it should be established whether all margin calls have been met and whether any stop loss arrangements have been made. Any potential material exposure to price movements may require disclosure as a contingent liability.

3.6.7 Grants, subsidies, set-aside payments

A careful review should be made of the farmer's entitlement to grants, subsidies and set-aside payments, bearing in mind the farm's cropping and capital investments during the period. The auditor should ensure that these forms of income are applied to sales/debtors in the correct year (**2.7**, **2.8**, **3.10**). When grants are capital in nature (**2.10.3**), they should be included as deferred income in the balance sheet in accordance with standard accounting practice (*SSAP 4*).

3.7 Purchases

Audit evidence may be obtained from a review of stocks, purchases and usage in physical and financial terms. Usage of seeds, fertilisers, sprays and foodstuffs may be expressed per acre in determining gross margins as a means of comparison (**3.7.1**).

It is common for purchase commitments to be entered into for major inputs such as fertilisers and feeds. It may not be practicable, for example, in the case of liquid fertiliser, to take delivery of the total commitment by the balance-sheet date, therefore cut-off tests should be applied. Price verification should be carried out by reference to orders, invoices and contracts.

3.7.1 Variable costs usage accounts and own usage of produce

Usage accounts should be prepared for all major variable costs including seeds, fertilisers, sprays and feeds. These can be prepared either in physical quantities or the value of stocks. It is usually more efficient to initially prepare a usage account based on the value of stocks and, if there is a material discrepancy, a physical account should be prepared.

Example 3.3 *Usage account for March year end*			
	Seeds	*Fertilisers*	*Sprays*
Value of stock at previous balance sheet date:			
in ground	4,700	5,000	6,000
in barn	(–)	500	1,000
Cash payments	3,700	8,300	11,900
Own use of crop produce as seed	1,000	–	–
Opening creditors	(600)	(500)	(500)
Closing creditors	500	700	600
Value of stock at current balance sheet date:			
in ground	(4,600)	(5,000)	(6,000)
in barn	(–)	(500)	(1,000)
Used in the harvest period	4,700	8,500	12,000
Hectares of crop grown	100	100	100
Usage £ per hectare	47	85	120

The usage per hectare can be compared with industry standards. Care must be taken in the value of own grown produce used as seeds as shown in Example 3.3. This should be valued at the cost of production per tonne plus dressing costs, but in practice the same price per tonne as the crop sold from that harvest plus any dressing costs is used.

3.8 Fixed assets

Verification of existence may rely upon a combination of physical inspection when attending the stocktaking and any valuer's listing which may be prepared at the time of the annual valuation of stocks. In practice, the valuer will not list any machinery during routine stock-taking, and the auditor will have to use the fixed asset register from the audit file to confirm accuracy with the farmer whilst at the farm premises.

A substantial level of new investment in most farm businesses requires judgement in justifying whether such investment is revenue or capital. For all significant farming businesses, a capitalisation policy should be established and routinely followed.

It has become common for machinery and vehicles to be acquired using various forms of instalment finance (**2.16**). This may be leasing, hire purchase or a credit sale arrangement. An increasing number of larger machines such as combine harvesters and larger tractors are hired under contract hire agreements or short-term hire arrangements and care must be taken to account for them in accordance with *SSAP 21* (**2.16.4**, **2.16.5**).

In some farm businesses, certain fixed assets, such as land, which are commonly used by the business are not included in the farm balance sheet, being owned directly by the shareholders and directors of the company and possibly a rent paid to them. Alternatively, the farming business may occupy the land as a tenant, with the land owned outside the owners of the business.

Capital allowances are available when the payment for farm machinery becomes due, even when delivery is delayed. Where the custom of the trade is for a payment to be made on account on placing the order, in practice, the Revenue normally accepts that the whole of the purchase price may be capitalised as at the date of the payment on account. In theory the capital allowances available are restricted to the proportion of capital paid on account compared with the total purchase price. This is discussed in detail in **5.7.8**.

3.9 Stocks

Farming clients may employ the services of an independent valuer to list and value stocks at the balance-sheet date. The accountant must decide whether the valuer's certificate has sufficient detail, and if not, what other work must be carried out. As an absolute minimum, it is considered that the auditor should carry out cut-off tests, livestock numbers reconciliation, cost and yield comparisons and balance sheet comparisons. Although not common, the auditor may wish to consider whether he should attend the stocktaking with the valuer in order to observe how the existence and valuation of stocks are established. It is not normal for the valuer to verify title to any of the stocks, merely to list and value them, therefore the auditor will have to apply tests, in particular cut-off tests, to verify ownership. When the auditor relies on the valuer to supply stock values, the auditor has the responsibility to assess the competence and independence of the valuer. In addition, the auditor must be satisfied that the valuer has actually visited the farm and seen the stocks and not merely taken details over the telephone from the farmer. It may be necessary to ascertain the date the valuer attended the farm as in some areas there may be several farms with the same year end and it may not be possible for the valuer to attend them all.

On-farm physical records of livestock numbers, stock of seed, fertiliser, sprays, feedstuffs and produce should be reviewed to assess the adequacy of the data for audit evidence purposes. An increasing number of arable farms maintain crop records manually or on a computer and these might be used by the valuer to produce a valuation.

The basis of valuation of stocks on farm is reviewed in **2.13**.

3.10 Purchased stores

This includes seeds, fertilisers, sprays, feedstuffs, machinery spares and fuel at their bought in cost. Cut-off tests, in conjunction with those for purchases and creditors, should be carried out to verify that stock is correctly included and valued. The valuation is normally on the FIFO basis. Major inputs should be reconciled through stocks, purchases and usage.

Quantities in stock should be reviewed in relation to storage capacity available. There are likely to be limits to the total storage available in the case of liquid fertilisers and any material, such as those feedstuffs which are stored loose in bulk hoppers. Fertiliser and feed in bags may normally be stored without quantity limits in practice. Sprays, although almost always in containers, are normally only stored in specific secured storage areas.

Where the balance-sheet date is during a busy season of application of farm inputs, the auditor should be particularly careful about the cut-off between purchased stores and the work in progress in tillages and cultivations. In particular, the distinction between applied stocks, which are also in creditors, and those which were paid for by the year end often cause difficulty, particularly when the stocks are purchased on credit arrangements commonly called 'harvest plans'.

Where substantial stocks of machinery spares are carried, the auditor must consider whether appropriate checks are made to eliminate obsolete, slow-moving and redundant stocks. Where farm equipment is continually updated, spares may more easily become redundant. Obsolescence should also be considered in relation to seeds, fertilisers and sprays. Barn records and crop records may be maintained for this category of stock and their usefulness should be considered in controlling stocks and providing audit evidence.

3.11 Growing crops

This has two principal cost components: the variable costs of seeds, fertilisers and chemicals and the work done in cultivating, and applying these on to the land.

3.11.1 Variable costs

The variable cost element will not usually be allocated to specific crops. The transfers from stocks should be specifically allocated by crop or group of fields in the case of seed. Further specification may be possible through the variety of particular crops grown. Most allocations of seeds are from specific purchases and a test check of rates of seed application may be made.

3.11.2 Cultivations and work done

Work done, whether determined by reference to published contract costs or specifically priced by the valuer, should be the subject of reasonableness tests. This may follow the time sequence of operations for cereals:

- seedbed preparation:
    (i)   ploughing
    (ii)   heavy cultivations
    (iii)   light cultivations
- sowing seeds:
    (i)   drilling
- post seeding:
    (i)   rolling.

Some of these operations may be performed more than once or not at all and may take place in a different order. However, drilling, with the allocation of seed costs, clearly cannot take place before some seedbed preparation operations. The importance of understanding the specific crop production techniques on the client farm cannot be overemphasised, in view of the importance of interpreting what work the auditor might reasonably expect to have been done by the balance-sheet date. Normally, the seasonal nature of arable farming, the growing of autumn sown and spring sown crops and varying rates of set-aside requirements means that material changes in the valuation can be explained in terms of changes in cropping, acreages and the weather.

3.12 Harvested crops

Existence should be verified by reference back to harvest yield estimates and the disposal of the crop to the balance sheet date. Depending upon

126

the actual balance sheet date and the timing of sales, it may be possible to determine the stocks by after-date sales and own usage. Particularly where stocks are stored loose, the potential error in measurement decreases as the quantity itself decreases.

Care should be taken to review sales to co-operatives and forward sales to merchants, since the physical movement of crops from the farm may not follow the sales made (**2.9**).

3.13 Livestock and production herds

A professional valuer will usually count, categorise and value livestock for balance-sheet purposes at cost. The auditor should consider what further work he wishes to carry out to satisfy himself that livestock are correctly stated. The livestock reconciliation should provide the basic data around which the audit and verification tests are performed. The reconciliations should be supported by ledger account details or separate schedules showing the specific animals purchased and sold. In the case of production herds, whether or not on the herd basis, lists of those animals should be available for inspection. The auditor should prepare or review schedules of transfers in and out of the herd and between other livestock categories.

For all production livestock, the numbers born and reared in relation to the number of breeding females should be determined. These figures may be compared with previous years, other clients, published information and farm budgets. They should also be discussed with the client.

Number of young weaned per breeding female per annum on average is:

* cattle   one calf per cow or heifer every year;
* sheep   hill areas one lamb per ewe; in lowland areas up to 1.75 lambs per ewe. Some breeds can lamb 3 times in two years;
* pigs   average 9 piglets per litter, 2.25 litters per annum totalling 20 to 24 piglets per annum per sow or gilt.

The actual production figures obtained on individual farms will vary considerably depending upon the management and husbandry, geographical location and breed.

A particular problem for the auditor is distinguishing between various categories of livestock even where he does attend the stocktake. This problem of recognition may be lessened by seeking client help on categorising livestock in the numbers reconciliation, or by attending the livestock count with an independent valuer. Mature and immature livestock may be distinguished through the maintenance of adequate livestock records. Where kept these should show the date of birth of the young by sex, weight at various ages, milk production and breeding information.

3.14 Hay, straw and silage

The valuation of these items may be substantial depending upon the balance sheet date. Stock levels should be broadly the same from year to year. Quantities in store should be compared with any limitations of storage capacity. In particular, silage may be stored in a silo or clamp of known total volume. The quantity in store can also be compared with likely usage levels. The unit value applied to these items is normally derived from standards provided by independent valuers, since the identification of the actual costs in the production process is difficult. Hay and silage are crops usually produced specifically for feed although big bale silage wrapped in plastic and hay are sometimes sold. Home-produced straw is a by-product from the arable cropping and is used for bedding and feeding. A considerable amount of straw is sold by arable farming businesses in the eastern part of the country to dealers who supply livestock farmers in the western part of the country.

3.15 Own usage

Apart from the usage of livestock for personal consumption, arable crops may be variously used for animal feedstuffs and seed. These animal feedstuffs may be for private consumption for game and horses as well as for farm consumption. In the absence of detailed records, the client may have to provide reasonable estimates of quantities taken from the arable output and applied as private consumption or as livestock costs.

3.16 Debtors

The standard verification tests of after-date receipts, cut-off tests through stock records related back to harvest estimates and self billed despatch and invoice information, may be applied to verify debtors in the farm balance sheet.

The cut-off tests carried out may be detailed using the crop records, barn records and the schedules supporting the livestock reconciliation.

Sales of harvested crops to co-operatives (**2.9**) should be carefully reviewed. The cashflow for the ensuing period may provide further audit evidence.

3.17 Creditors

After-date payments, cut-off tests and statement reconciliations may be used in the verification of creditors. The review of purchased stocks and the levels of fixed cost expenditure should also provide further evidence of the reasonableness of creditor levels. Where the client prepares an updated cashflow on a regular basis, this may provide further information.

The farm business may have finance creditor commitments for leasing, hire purchase or instalment credit arrangements, particularly for machinery and seeds, fertilisers, chemicals and feeds. Facilities are widely used for credit arrangements for the purchase of the variable costs for cropping with repayments up to 18 months later. This situation can cause difficulties in reconciling the outstanding creditor to the stock purchased, particularly when the balance sheet date is at a busy time of the year such as the autumn when crops are sown. The contracts should be reviewed and the presentation considered. It may be valuable to relate this review to the work on verifying the bank transactions, since the only evidence of contracts entered into might be provided by the bank statements showing direct debit or standing order payments. The asset or stock financed by these arrangements should be traced into the balance sheet and/or trading account.

Farm merchants and co-operatives provide advances against crops being grown (**2.9**) and committed to them by contract. The client should be requested to provide details of all such arrangements.

3.18 Bank and cash

Any unusual items from the verification work on bank transactions and balances should be carefully reviewed. Standing orders and direct debits may provide evidence of the existence of finance commitments.

Although the volume of cash transactions on farms has fallen significantly in recent years, some farm businesses may sell material volumes of produce for cash. The system of control over cash receipts, and in particular stocks and sales, should be carefully reviewed by the auditor. Potatoes, other vegetables, fruit and eggs are commonly sold for cash, either at the farm gate or through a farm shop. Livestock sold at auction may be sold for cash, however, the Revenue have been targeting these and the practice has considerably reduced.

3.19 Trade investments

Agricultural co-operatives obtain finance through two principal sources:

- initial share capital subscribed by farmer members; and
- trading bonuses to members which are frequently capitalised as loan or share capital.

Any interest or dividends declared on these investments held by the farmer-member may in itself be capitalised in further loan or share capital. Confirmation of the changes in these investments should be sought directly from the farming co-operative.

3.20 Joint ventures

Particular audit and verification difficulties may occur with these business arrangements (**2.15**) not least due to the lack of control over stocks, legal title to stocks and work done and charges incurred by one party on behalf of others. A common problem is that the memorandum account on many contract management agreements on arable enterprises are not finalised until a considerable time after the harvest period and the balance sheet date. It can often therefore be difficult to verify the amounts owing to the contractor for the work done. The amount of verification work required will depend upon the amounts.

Chapter 4 – Financial management practices

4.1 Introduction

The degree of financial management in farming businesses varies considerably from the basic statutory requirements to sophisticated computerised systems. In many businesses these functions are carried out by the farmer or one of the family. An increasing number of businesses now employ self-employed farm secretaries who visit farms periodically. The frequency of visits will depend upon the work required but usually range from weekly (on larger businesses) to monthly or quarterly visits to calculate the VAT on smaller farms.

4.2 Statutory requirements

There has been an increasing need to comply with regulations in the farming industry. This has been extended recently to the identification of animals for BSE.

The most important of the statutory requirements are:

(a) The movement of animals in the event of notifiable diseases should be maintained in a separate book. These details also required for retention periods for subsidies.

(b) Integrated Administrative and Control System (IACS) applies to the subsidies and headage payments available (**1.6**). In order to apply for the subsidies available apart from sheep headage payments under the Sheep Annual Premium Scheme, a farming business has to submit details of all the land farmed by a specified date in May every year. The availability of the subsidies are dependent on the farmer supplying the required information by the due date. Because of the accuracy of this information it is recommended that the accountant requests a copy of this form for the permanent file. A national computerised database has now been established based on this information.

(c) VAT records do not have to be maintained in any particular way, however, the relevant information must be efficiently available and maintained for six years.

(d) The Department of Social Security require records of employees' and employers' national insurance contributions to be maintained and the correct amount to be paid monthly along with the tax deducted. Employers also have an obligation to pay and record statutory sick pay and maternity pay.

(e) Limited Companies are required under s237(2) of the Companies Act 1996 to maintain proper accounting records.

(f) The Inland Revenue require all businesses to maintain financial records for five years from the filing date of the self-assessment form, therefore in practice up to seven years.

(g) Computerised national Cattle Tracing System (CTS) which commenced on 28 September 1998 (**1.6**).

4.3 Record keeping and accounting systems

4.3.1 Introduction

The management of the business depends upon the ability of the farmer to make decisions and the more up-to-date the information that is available the more informed the decision and the less risk involved. The recording of physical and financial information has increased considerably over the past few years.

4.3.2 The farm office

Most farm offices are located in one of the rooms in the farmhouse and are therefore well suited to housing computers and conducive to a comfortable working environment. Many larger farming businesses have offices which have usually been converted and refurbished from an agricultural building separate from the farmhouse. In particular, businesses that have large intensive or specialised enterprises such as dairy, poultry or pig enterprises will usually have an office near the location of the animals. This may be a separate office from the main office where the enterprise manager will maintain records of the animals. Many smaller family farms will not have a specific office; the business being conducted in the domestic rooms of the farmhouse.

4.3.3 Dealing with paperwork

A methodical system is required to deal with the increasing amount of paperwork. There are many farming businesses that have no method of dealing with incoming paperwork, maintaining them for processing and storing them once processed. This is an area where the accountant can advise clients on the methods of handling and storing information with the eventual benefit of better information available for preparing the annual accounts (**2.3**).

4.3.4 Analysed cash book

A fully analysed cash book incorporating VAT recording is sufficient for many farming businesses. In many instances one book is used with receipts being recorded at the back of the book and expenses at the front. To ensure an efficient system is maintained the following points should be considered:

(a) The headings in the analysis columns should be discussed with the accountant to ensure compatibility.
(b) Each transaction should be allocated a sequential number and the relevant invoice cross-referenced.
(c) Sufficient detail should be included in order for the accountant to analyse the payments. This is particularly relevant to expenditure such as telephone and electricity where there may be a number of invoices relating to different locations. It is advisable to make notes alongside the payment and receipt entries in the analysis columns in the cashbook.
(d) Contra receipts and payments should be fully entered and analysed, some may include VAT.
(e) The cashbook should be totalled on a monthly basis and reconciled to the bank statement.

The monthly totals from the analysed cash book can be used to monitor budgeted cash flow for the period.

4.3.5 Bank reconciliation and bank statements

Many analysed cash books prepared by farming businesses are not reconciled to the monthly bank statement which inevitably incurs time and costs by the accountant. Each column in the cash book should be totalled on a monthly basis and reconciled to the bank statement by including unpresented cheques. Many farming businesses pay invoices in the last few days of a month which inevitably results in a large number of the cheques being unpaid at the end of the month. This results in a greater number of entries required in the bank reconciliation every month. It may be advisable to pay all invoices on the first of the month, however, this may delay the timing of VAT being claimed, particularly if the business accounts for VAT on a monthly basis as opposed to quarterly.

4.3.6 Petty cash book

As in all businesses it is advisable to maintain a petty cash book.

4.3.7 Sales and purchase ledgers

Farm computer systems have introduced the use of sales and purchase ledgers to farming businesses. This inevitably produces a greater amount of sophistication and complexity which in turn requires a greater degree of control and organisation in the farm office which may not be available in every situation. The benefits of using sales and purchase ledgers are that because most farming businesses are net reclaimers of VAT, the VAT may be claimed earlier on the invoice date rather than when the invoice is paid. In addition, a true position of debtors and creditors can be shown at any point in time.

The maximum turnover for the cash accounting scheme is currently £350,000. Many farming businesses have reached this threshold in the last few years and may not have adjusted their accounting system accordingly. This is particularly important in businesses that carry out work subject to standard rated VAT, for example contracting work.

4.3.8 Invoices

All invoices should be maintained in date order and cross-referenced to the transactions in the cash book or the accounting system on a computer system.

4.3.9 Contra entries

There are several transactions in farming businesses that include contra charges. Most farm produce is zero-rated for VAT, however, the contra entries against these are usually vatable at the standard rate and therefore need to be accounted for. Examples of the most common transactions are:

- milk sales with transport costs;
- grain sales with weighbridge charges; and
- livestock sales with commission charges.

Most of these will be recorded on self-billing invoices prepared on behalf of the farm by the purchaser.

Machinery purchases and sales will normally be two transactions subject to VAT at the standard rate. The transactions can become complicated when the items of machinery are subject to leasing or hire purchase agreements.

4.4 Computerisation

4.4.1 Introduction

The ability of computers to generate management and accounting information from raw data has advanced farm business management over the past few years. As a result of the decrease in the price of computers and the specialist software available, an increasing number of farm businesses now use a computer system. There are several functions that a computer can perform in the farm office.

4.4.2 Accounts packages which can be split into three levels

- simple cashbook;
- extended cashbook incorporating enterprise reporting;
- double-entry system on a trading basis with stock records and extensive reports.

There are several companies who have developed specialist farming accounting packages. However, many farming businesses have purchased standard non-farming packages and are using them successfully.

The following features have been incorporated in the specialist accounting packages and may not necessarily be available in other packages.

(a) The ability to record contra transactions without having to move through several screens and menus between the sales and purchase ledgers. As contra transactions are common in commodity sales it can be a laborious task entering the transactions in different parts of the program. This problem has been overcome in some programs by the use of windows and multi-tasking, where it is possible to have the sales and the purchase ledgers on the screen at the same time.

(b) All specialist farm programs have integrated sales, purchase and nominal ledgers; therefore, when a transaction is entered in either the sales or purchase ledger, the nominal, and possibly the stock records, are updated at the same time. This avoids having to update the ledgers at the end of every month.

(c) Double-entry systems with stock records and balance-sheets have the facility to record births and deaths which is the creation and deletion of assets without purchasing or selling them.

(d) Some of the programs available are able to report transactions on a cash or a trading basis when the ledgers are being used on a double-entry or trading basis. This provides the facility to report ongoing debtors and creditors as well as cash movements and may be important for monitoring the business (**4.7**).

(e) A recent development is a link between accounting programs and field records programs. This reduces the number of transactions required to be entered. For example, when stock such as fertiliser is purchased through the accounts package it can be automatically recorded in the field records program as stock and allocated out at a later date.

(f) At least one agricultural computer accounts program has facilities for a Eurobank account with the ability to convert to sterling through adjustable exchange rates.

Some farming businesses are running cash book programs developed from spreadsheets very successfully, however, these normally take up considerable time to develop by the individual and are prone to incorporate errors.

4.4.3 Crop records

These are very common and record the physical and financial data involved with the growing of crops. In addition, most have the facility to maintain stock records and movements of chemicals and to record and cost cultivations for the end of year valuation. To carry out the function of producing cultivation costs for the year end the program must have the facility to produce reports on a periodic date basis.

For example, a 31 March year end will be half-way through the production cycle and a facility in the program will be required to record and total all cultivations between two date ranges such as from the end of the previous harvest to the 31 March.

Some of the crop records programs have developed mapping facilities to enable the information for each field to be shown as a colour-coded map.

4.4.4 Animal records

Specialist and intensive enterprises lend themselves most to computerisation. There are several programs that have been specifically developed for dairy cows and pigs. During recent years database-type programs have been developed for beef and sheep where family history needs to be recorded, and in particular for pedigree animals.

4.4.5 Spreadsheets

Spreadsheets are being used extensively for business management and some farmers have developed an interest in their application for many purposes such as accounting and VAT, crop records and livestock recording. Their main use is for budgeting and the preparation of cashflows.

4.4.6 Links with accountants

Many accountancy firms have copies of the main accounts packages and therefore are able to use the data discs and print out the accountant's audit trail to prepare the annual accounts. The latest technique is an electronic link between the accountant's own accounts preparation software and the leading agricultural programs. This enables the farmer to provide a disc containing all of the transactions so that the accountant can download the data into the office accounts preparation software. In future years it is likely that farming businesses will be able to send their financial information via a modem to their accountant.

4.4.7 Bureau system

A bureau system is a very useful entry into the use of computers. This can be achieved in several ways:

(a) The completion of specialised computer input sheets, which are then posted to the provider of the service where the information is recorded on a computer and posted back to the farm.
(b) Some farm secretaries have portable or laptop computers which they transport to various farming businesses to carry out the work.

4.4.8 Justifying a computer system

The ability to generate information is not sufficient to justify a computer system. The benefit is realised when the information is put to good use. Therefore it is important to receive adequate training for the operation of the software to enable full use to be made of it. The benefits of the different software programs are:

(a) Crop records and animal records such as dairy and pig programs have the most potential to obtain a return on the capital cost of a system. The amortised capital cost can be compared with the increase in margin per animal or per acre.
(b) Spreadsheet programs are relatively cheap to purchase and in many instances are available with the computer. Their use in some businesses can easily be justified when they are used for budgeting and cash flow planning, including supplying information to the bank (**4.10**).

(c) Accounts programs when used on a simple cash based system to replace an analysed cashbook may save some time in adding columns every month but it may be difficult to identify any increase in profitability as a result of using such a program. There is an argument that simple farming businesses should continue to maintain a manual-analysed cashbook. When the program is used to record actual transactions against pre-entered cash flow budgets the benefits will begin to show.

Therefore the use of computer programs purely for recording data, such as an analysed cash book, will be difficult to justify. The more use that is made from the data produced the easier it is to justify the capital expenditure.

4.5 Funding the farm business

4.5.1 Introduction

Farming as a business is very capital intensive and in addition has many special factors. Of prime importance is the high cost of land in comparison with its earning capacity, the cost of quota to enable the production of various commodities and the relatively long term nature of production cycles. The capital associated with a farming business will vary considerably depending upon the type of enterprises. They can be considered as:

- fixed or long-term capital;
- medium-term capital;
- short-term or working capital.

4.5.2 Fixed and medium-term capital

The fixed capital of a farming business is also termed landlord's capital or long term capital, it comprises:

- land and farmhouses;
- buildings and fixed plant.

The general increased profitability in most farming enterprises in recent years resulted in an increase in the value of agricultural land and subsequently the considerable reduction in profitability has resulted in a general decline in land values. However, local demand in some areas has maintained values at or near peak values.

Medium-term capital comprises:

- breeding livestock;
- machinery and plant; and
- production quota.

Example 4.1 *Fixed and medium term capital on a 150 acre dairy farm with 100 milking cows*

	£
Land and buildings at £2,500 per acre	375,000
Farmhouse	100,000
Milk quota at 6,000 litres per cow at 33 pence	198,000
100 dairy cows at £500 per cow	50,000
Other replacement stock say	15,000
Plant and machinery at £300 per acre	45,000
Total	783,000
Total per acre	5,220

Example 4.2 *Fixed and medium term capital on 500 acre arable farm*

	£
Land and buildings at £2,500 per acre	1,250,000
Farmhouse	100,000
Plant and machinery at £200 per acre	100,000
Total capital	1,450,000
Total per acre	2,900

Example 4.3 *Fixed and medium term capital on 600 acre upland stock farm*

	£
Land and buildings at £1,500 per acre	900,000
Farmhouse	80,000
50 suckler cows and replacements at £500	25,000
Suckler cow quota at £120	6,000
1,000 sheep and replacements at £75	75,000
Sheep quota at £20	20,000
Plant and machinery at £100 per acre	60,000
Total	1,166,000
Total per acre	1,943

The above are merely examples to provide an indication of the amount of capital employed. The actual amounts will vary considerably depending upon the general profitability of the enterprise concerned, the land type and the geographic region.

4.5.3 Working capital requirements

The production cycle of enterprises varies considerably, ranging from a few months, extending to in excess of 12 months. In some instances the following production cycle may need to be funded before any receipts have occurred from the previous cycle. The only accurate method of calculating the working capital requirements of a range of enterprises is to complete a cash flow projection for the complete business for at least a full production cycle. This is particularly important in a start up situation as a project may appear to be profitable but it may not be feasible because of the working capital that may need to be borrowed to fund the production cycle.

Examples of working capital are:

- the purchase of trading livestock;
- costs of production including feed, vet and medicines;
- arable costs including seed, fertilisers and sprays; and
- ongoing overheads such as labour, machinery running costs, rent, interest and drawings.

Crop production cycles
Most combinable crops are sown in the autumn, harvested the following late summer and sold up to the following late spring. Some varieties are drilled in the spring and harvested the following late summer or early autumn, for example spring beans or spring barley. The working capital requirement will be for a shorter period and in general will be less per acre.

The following are examples of how the length and direct costs of production cycles vary between different crops. The costs exclude overhead costs of the business.

Example 4.4 *Production cycle costs*

Crop	Drilled	Harvested	Cost £ per acre	Months
Winter wheat	Oct	August	100	11
Spring barley	March	August	70	6
Sugar beet	March	November	230	9

Example 4.5 *Winter wheat production cycle*

The following example calculates the working capital requirements of one acre of winter wheat which is sold in November following the harvest. At present most area payments are received in December, with oilseed rape area payments received in September and April.

The working capital calculations are based on the following harvest budget and for simplicity assume a start-up situation, therefore the 1996 harvest is the first harvest. Under current costs and prices the result is a cash deficit.

	£ per acre
Crop sales: 3 tonnes at £78 per tonne	234
Area payments	96
Less:	
seeds	25
fertilisers	35
sprays	40
overheads at £15 per acre per month	180
drawings, tax and capital at £5 per acre per month	60
Net cash deficit	(10)

141

	Month incurred	Cost per acre 1998 harvest Cash in/(out) (£ per acre)	Cost per acre 1999 harvest Cash in/(out) (£ per acre)	Cumulative cost per acre Cash in/(out) (£ per acre)
Seeds	Oct	(25)		
Fertilisers	Oct–Dec	(15)		
Sprays	Oct–Dec	(15)		(55)
Overheads	Oct–Dec	(45)		
Drawings	Oct–Dec	(15)		(115)
Fertilisers	Jan–May	(20)		
Sprays	Jan–May	(25)		(160)
Overheads	Jan–Sept	(135)		
Drawings	Jan–Sept	(45)		
Cumulative net costs at Sept 1998				(340)
Seeds	Oct		(25)	
Fertilisers	Oct–Nov		(15)	
Sprays	Oct–Nov		(15)	(395)
Overheads	Oct–Nov		(30)	
Drawings	Oct–Nov		(10)	(435)
Crop sale 3 tonnes at £78	Nov	234		
Overheads	Dec		(15)	(201)
Drawings	Dec		(5)	
Area payments	Dec	96		
Cumulative net working capital		(10)	(115)	(125)

The crop is sold 14 months after it was drilled and the arable area payment is received 15 months after it was drilled. As the crop has an annual cycle, the additional three months of overheads and drawings (Oct to Dec) are allocated to the following year's crop. On an ongoing basis the above production cycle will overlap with the previous harvest to produce, on average, an annual cash surplus of £29. The crop will normally be available for sale in August at the earliest with cash payment in September. Historically, crops sold later after harvest were expected to achieve a higher price per tonne than those sold early. This is no longer the case. The actual timing of sale will vary between August and June or July the following year and if the crop is sold towards the latter part of this period it will increase the working capital substantially. Therefore the timing of the sale of the crop can have a dramatic effect on the working capital requirement.

The example indicates a peak working capital requirement per acre in the region of £435 prior to the sale of the crop. On a typical medium-sized arable farm of 500 acres this will total £217,500. Traditionally arable farms have peak borrowing requirements immediately prior to harvest, during the months of June to September.

The Agenda 2000 proposals include the delay of the payment of arable area payments to the period 1 January to 31 March. This will not increase the peak working capital but will increase the working capital requirement in the additional three months of January, February and March.

Livestock production cycles

The working capital requirements of livestock enterprises will vary considerably depending upon the enterprise. The following are examples of the length of production cycles and direct costs, but excluding the fixed costs or overheads. The value of the cows in dairy herds and beef suckler herds are not treated as working capital but as medium-term capital (**4.5.2**).

(a)   *Dairy*

Milk production from dairy cows is based upon an annual lactation with a monthly income from milk sales. Therefore the working capital requirement will normally be negligible but will depend upon the amount of direct costs such as fertiliser and feed that is purchased and paid for in advance of being used or consumed.

(b)   *Beef cows producing calf*

The gestation period for a cow is nine months and the calf, once weaned, is either sold or transferred to another enterprise at around seven months of age, making a total of 16 months. The cow will, on average, produce a calf every year with the previous calf weaned three months prior to the next one being born. The previous calf will be sold or transferred after being weaned. Working capital of around £150 is incurred in maintaining the cow and rearing the calf until sold or transferred.

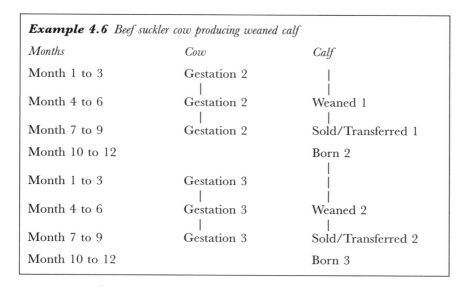

Example 4.6 *Beef suckler cow producing weaned calf*

Months	*Cow*	*Calf*
Month 1 to 3	Gestation 2	
Month 4 to 6	Gestation 2	Weaned 1
Month 7 to 9	Gestation 2	Sold/Transferred 1
Month 10 to 12		Born 2
Month 1 to 3	Gestation 3	
Month 4 to 6	Gestation 3	Weaned 2
Month 7 to 9	Gestation 3	Sold/Transferred 2
Month 10 to 12		Born 3

(c) *Other beef systems*
There are numerous systems of beef production varying in length from around three months up to 24 months depending upon the age of the animal purchased or transferred. The costs include the purchase of calves and stores and exclude forage costs.

Example 4.7 *Beef production cycle costs*

	Direct costs excluding overheads (£ per head)	Time in months
Fattening purchased stores	330–380	6 to 7
Fattening purchased calves	380–415	18 to 20
Fattening purchased calves	316–400	22 to 24
Indoor fattening barley beef	415–430	3
Indoor fattening silage beef	340–380	3

(d) *Fat lamb production*
The gestation period of a sheep is approximately five months and the lambs are sold fat at around 12 weeks of age. Normally one lamb crop will be produced every year.

Example 4.8 *Sheep production cycle costs*

	Direct costs excluding overheads (£ per head)	Time in months
Spring lamb production	32	8

4.5.4 Expansion

Many farming businesses have, or are considering, expansion with the aid of a farm business tenancy or a contract management agreement (**6.3**). A farm business tenancy will require all the working capital whereas in a contract management agreement the landowner usually provides the working capital for seeds, fertilisers, and sprays whilst the contract farmer provides the capital for machinery fuel and labour (**2.15**). The requirement of additional working capital should be fully assessed and agreed with the bank manager when considering expansion.

The rent for farm business tenancies is normally payable in advance as opposed to in arrears for traditional tenancies. This has a significant effect on the working capital requirements for expansion. The following example shows the additional capital required to farm an additional 400 acres on a farm business tenancy at an annual rent of £100 per acre. It is assumed that current labour and machinery can cater for the additional acreage.

Example 4.9 *Capital required for arable enterprise on farm business tenancy of 400 acres*

		£ per acre	£ total 400 acres Cumulative
September	rent 6 months in advance	50	20,000
September	seeds	25	30,000
September to April	fertilisers	35	44,000
September to June	chemicals	40	60,000
March	rent 6 months in advance	50	80,000
September	rent second year 6 months in advance	50	100,000
September	seeds for 2000 harvest	25	110,000
September to November	Fertilisers and chemicals	30	122,000
Total working capital prior to crop sales in November		305	122,000

Therefore a considerable amount of additional working capital is required. Tenant farmers in particular may have difficulty in borrowing sufficient capital from one source. Based on the low margins currently available in many enterprises relative to the large amount of capital required, serious consideration should be given to any expansion plans with the additional risks to the core business fully assessed.

4.5.5 Summary

Therefore most farming businesses will have a mixture of enterprises all with different and overlapping production cycles. The key points relating to the efficient management of working capital in a farming business are:

(a) The preparation of a cashflow projection for the whole business is the only accurate method of calculating the working capital requirements (**4.7.3**). This is essential if the working capital is borrowed.

(b) A budget may be profitable but may not be feasible if the plan

145

requires a large amount of borrowed working capital. Gross margin budgets do not take account of the timing of production cycles.

(c) The shorter the production cycle the quicker the money is turned over and the margin made. This reduces the risk and is important from a lender's point of view.

(d) Many enterprises offer flexibility in the time of sale. In particular, many crops are stored on farms for several months after harvest in order to attempt to obtain the highest price. If the working capital is borrowed it will incur interest and an assessment will need to be made to compare the interest accruing with the expectation of a higher selling price.

4.6 Sources of capital

4.6.1 Introduction

Agriculture is considered to be a very safe industry to lend money to. The main reason is that around 80 per cent of holdings are owner occupied and the stability in land value provides security for the lender. However, the substantial premium price paid for land in addition to the value represented by its productive capacity often presents particular financing difficulties. The profitability of farming businesses usually represents around 3 per cent to 5 per cent of the land value. Current land values are relatively high although there has been a reduction of up to 25 per cent during 1998 in some areas.

(a) The profit achieved from arable enterprises has reduced by around 50 per cent in the last two years down to around £50 per acre from around £120 to £150 per acre before rent and finance charges. Land values are in the region of £2,500 per acre. Land values in the past few years have been in the region of £2,000 per acre when profits were in the region of £80 per acre. However, at present, residential values are maintaining the value of commercial land. The remaining 20 per cent of the holdings in England and Wales are wholly or mainly rented and these businesses obviously are not able to benefit from the asset values of owning land.

(b) Land subject to a tenancy prior to 1 September 1995, and therefore allowing at least lifetime security to the tenant, will have a rental yield in the region of three per cent to six per cent. Therefore land with a vacant possession value of £2,500 per acre will have a tenanted value of around 50 per cent to 60 per cent of this at £1,200 to £1,500 per acre with a rent subject to a three year review of around £48 to £60 per acre. Rentals that have been reviewed in the past three years will probably have been set at a higher rate than this, being based on the productive capacity at the time, therefore causing some difficulties to tenants during 1999. Therefore land cannot be self-financing and the purchase of land will have to be subject to the following criteria:

(i)   When a complete farm is purchased a substantial amount of private funds will have to be invested at a relatively low return in order for the business to be viable (**4.5.2** and **6.6**).

(ii) Additional land may be purchased using borrowed funds, with the cost of borrowing spread over a relatively large existing acreage. Therefore, the existing business will assist the funding of the additional land.

The economic price of land is discussed in detail in **6.6**.

There are many sources of capital available to the farming industry. Because of the relatively low return on the land value and the complexity of the working capital many of the high street clearing banks have specialist agricultural departments and staff that deal solely with the agricultural industry. Many banks have specialist subsidiaries that deal solely with agriculture.

4.6.2 Type and length of borrowing

The basic principles are that the length of borrowed funds should match the economic life of the asset being funded. Again, as discussed in the above paragraphs on the types of capital in a farming business, the borrowing can be defined as:

(a)   Long-term borrowing for the purchase of land, property and buildings should be in the form of a long-term loan up to 20 to 25 years.

(b)   Medium-term borrowing should be used for funding production herds, buildings, plant and machinery, irrigation reservoirs and facilities or other medium-term diversification projects such as fishing lakes, holiday accommodation or tourist attractions.

(c)   Short-term finance should be used for funding working capital production cycles as discussed in **4.5.3**.

4.6.3 Long-term bank loans

The availability of long-term loans to purchase land or replace existing borrowings has become very competitive, with some lenders willing to lend funds in some situations at base rate for an initial short period of up to two years. These facilities are similar to the competitive nature of the standard mortgages in the domestic housing market where substantial cash back arrangements are available. The amount of the loan will normally be limited to half to two-thirds of the value of the land and a first or second charge will be required. Some lenders have developed specialist packages to suit individual requirements, for example:

(a) The borrowing for land purchase can be split into two loans of different lengths; a medium term loan of say five to eight years together with a long-term 20 year loan. The relative amounts of each can be flexible to suit the individual circumstances. This will have the effect of making a substantial reduction in the amount borrowed in the early years which may be particularly relevant during periods of high levels of profitability.
(b) The loan repayments can be fixed during the term of the loan but the length of the loan will vary as interest rates change.
(c) A combination of fixed and variable interest rates or the ability to fix the interest rate of a variable-rate loan at any stage.
(d) Loans with capital repayment holidays for an initial short period.

It is important to negotiate the following when setting up a loan:

(a) The margin above base rate on variable loans usually between one per cent to three per cent.
(b) The initial set up administration fee, usually up to one per cent.
(c) A valuation may be required in some circumstances by a specified valuer. Most banks have a list of their preferred valuers. It may be possible to negotiate that a local valuer be appointed at possibly lower cost.

4.6.4 Agricultural Mortgage Corporation (AMC)

The AMC has been the traditional source of long-term funds to the agricultural industry. It is now owned by Lloyds TSB Bank but still operates independently. Loans of up to 40 years are available on a first charge at fixed or variable interest rates on an annuity or interest only basis. The AMC operates through a network of land agents that are able to discuss proposals and complete the application forms. Charges are one per cent of the advance.

4.6.5 Personal funds and family loans

A substantial amount of farm businesses are funded from personal funds and family loans. Most capital investments require a substantial amount of personal funds in addition to borrowed capital.

4.6.6 Overdraft

The overdraft facility offered by all the clearing banks is the main form of borrowing to the industry. Although in principle overdraft facilities should only be used for funding production cycles, in many farming businesses the overdraft represents long-term or hard-core borrowing. The overdraft is usually negotiated annually directly with the bank manager when a maximum facility will be put into place. This will be important on arable and beef and sheep farms where the production cycles dictate that the majority of the income will be received during a relatively short period; the overdraft will therefore be required to fund the production cycles prior to receipt of the income.

The following should be negotiated when arranging an overdraft facility:

(a) The margin over base rate which will range from one per cent up to 3 per cent or 4 per cent for less profitable businesses. The bank will therefore charge a margin subject to the risk. The risk is usually assessed on a point system following internal bank guidelines.
(b) The annual arrangement fee which is usually in the region of one per cent of the facility but varies considerably.
(c) Quarterly or periodic fees.
(d) Commission received by the bank for any life insurance or any other commission-based products arranged by them.
(e) Facilities such as maximum and minimum interest rates.
(f) Specific criteria laid down in perceived high risk situations. These may include the sale of land if certain parameters are not adhered to, such as requiring more working capital than the agreed level, or, if the profit as shown in the annual accounts is below a certain amount, over a two-year consecutive period.

Most banks take a commercial view and assess their total return from the specific customer or in some cases the family connection when more than one customer. Therefore, the above may be negotiated as a package where a reduction in the margin charged may be accompanied by a rise in the periodic or arrangement fees. It is therefore recommended that the accountant or other business adviser is involved in negotiating with the lender when substantial fees are involved.

4.6.7 Point of sale finance

These provide funds for farming input costs such as feed, seeds, fertilisers, sprays, fuels and sometimes livestock. The finance is usually arranged directly through the agricultural supplier who acts as an agent for a finance house. The main facilities are arranged through Growcash, a subsidiary of National Westminster Bank, and Masterloan, a subsidiary of Barclays Bank, although many others exist. Some facilities are linked directly to specific goods where the manufacturer subsidises the interest charged. Most of these loans are designed to be repaid within a 12 month period to coincide with production cycles, however, facilities exist for repayment to be delayed for up to 18 months. The interest can be either fixed or variable. There is a danger that through the use of these facilities for periods of up to 18 months, the farm business may enter into credit arrangements beyond the prudent borrowing limit. It can be difficult to account for these facilities in terms of allocation of costs to enterprises and the correct accounting for the cut off at the end of the financial year (**3.7**).

This form of finance can usually be arranged without the need for detailed management accounts and budgets to support the application which makes the arrangement easy and possibly attractive. Unless the interest rate is attractive, this form of borrowing is used to replace funds which a bank manager may be reluctant to provide through an overdraft facility. A bank reference is usually required.

4.6.8 Harvest advances

These are supplied by the merchant, up to a specified percentage of the potential value of the crop which is agreed to be sold to the merchant at a specified date. In practice this form of borrowing is used when the business requires a greater amount of working capital than is available from the bank in the form of an overdraft. The merchant deducts the capital and interest charges from the value of the grain and pays the farmer the net balance.

4.6.9 Hire purchase, conditional sale and leasing

These facilities are discussed in **2.16**, and have become increasingly popular over the past few years for financing and acquiring machinery. The amount of capital involved in machinery in the agricultural industry makes this area of lending attractive to financial institutions. Many of the manufacturers have formed joint ventures with financial institutions to provide financial packages where the manufacturer subsidises the interest, therefore providing a relatively cheap form of borrowing short- to medium-term capital.

The legal structure of hire purchase, conditional sale and leasing vary considerably, however, in practice, they all represent the means of obtaining machinery and equipment. Careful consideration should be given to the method used depending upon each individual business (**2.16** and **5.7.8**).

4.6.10 Contract hire

The machine is hired for a specified period ranging from a few months to several years. Contract hire has grown in popularity for larger items such as combines and larger tractors because in most cases:

(a) a replacement machine is offered within 24 hours if the original machine breaks down;
(b) none of the business' capital is utilised in the machine, reducing the requirement for medium term working capital; and
(c) rental payments normally include servicing and repairs enabling the business to budget accurately.

4.6.11 Pension schemes (see also 6.7)

Most insurance companies operating pension schemes permit a proportion of the premiums that have been paid to be borrowed back to finance the farming business. These loan back arrangements are usually completely independent from the personal pension fund and are simply a loan at a commercial interest rate from the insurance company.

A proportion of the fund from a self-administered scheme (6.7) can be lent back to the business at a commercial rate and for a recognised commercial purpose of a capital nature. The loan is usually restricted to 25 per cent in the first two years of setting up the scheme and 50 per cent thereafter. The interest is paid into the fund.

It is normally possible for a self-administered scheme to purchase assets owned by the company which has the effect of releasing the capital in the fund back to the company. All transactions have to be on a commercial basis and a commercial rent paid to the pension scheme by the company for the use of the asset.

The use of pension funds are further discussed in 6.7.

4.6.12 Sale and leaseback

As discussed in previous paragraphs owner occupiers have substantial investment in farm land which yields a relatively low return. In some situations in the past where the farming business is facing cash shortages, the sale and leaseback arrangement has been a method whereby the business has managed to raise capital at the expense of the obligation to pay future rentals and has managed to continue trading. The capital released to the tenant may enable the business to expand. Over the past few years few sale and leaseback transactions have been arranged. With

151

the introduction of the Farm Business Tenancy there may be renewed interest in sale and leaseback arrangements.

4.6.13 Commercial considerations

(a) As discussed the provision of finance by lenders to the agricultural industry is becoming increasingly competitive, however, it is important for the individual farming business not to be continuously chasing cheaper sources of borrowing. The rapport with the individual representing the lender is of prime importance as there may come a time when capital may be required in a situation where the lender is taking a risk and therefore a long-term successful relationship with the lender will be essential.

(b') Assets are valued for IHT purposes net of any mortgages, therefore consideration should be given to the structure of borrowings against a first charge on assets subject to APR. If at all possible assets not eligible for APR should be charged against borrowings to make full use of the relief (**5.16.11**).

(c) When assessing the cost of borrowing and the impact on an existing business it is important to take account of the capital repayments in addition to the interest in the assessment. In cash flow terms the business will have to fund both interest and capital. The amount of annual capital repayments will depend upon the length of the loan, for example, the repayments per £1,000 borrowed at an interest rate of 7.65 per cent.

Example 4.10 *Total cash cost of borrowing*

	£ per annum
Interest payable	76.5
Interest and capital on annuity basis 25 years	90.04
Interest and capital on annuity basis 10 years	143.99

The different repayments are all per £1,000 per annum at the same interest rate, but differ significantly in terms of annual cash repayments and therefore can have a significant impact on the assessment of the viability of the business.

4.7 Profit and cash flow budgets

4.7.1 Introduction

These are the main method of budgeting, monitoring and controlling farming businesses and are used extensively. Farm businesses are most logically thought of as combinations of enterprises. An enterprise is a division or department of the total business usually identified by the type of product. A conventional format has been developed to record each enterprise in the form of a gross margin which consists of the sales from the enterprise and the associated costs that will vary with the size of enterprise; these are commonly known as 'variable costs' or 'input costs'. The costs that do not vary with the size of the enterprise will be the 'fixed costs' or the 'overheads' of the business. An example of gross margin accounting is included in the annual accounts in Appendix **1**. Ideally a budget for a farming business should contain the following:

- enterprise gross margins;
- profit projection – trading or cash format;
- cash flow budget – monthly or quarterly;
- reconciliation between profit and net cash movement; and
- opening and closing balance sheets.

In practice the amount of information required will be governed by the size of business, the purpose of the budgets, the amount of borrowing and the circumstances under which the budgets are required. A large farming business that is overborrowed with a bank requiring information, will require all of the items listed above, whereas a farming business with minimal borrowings may only require a cash flow budget to indicate cash surpluses and to monitor monthly actuals against budget. The profit projection can be either a full trading and profit and loss account or simply an annualised cash budget, being the totals from the cash flow budget.

4.7.2 Common problems encountered with profit and cash flow budgets

Banks and other lending institutions often require profit and cash flow budgets to be prepared on an annual basis to support lending. Some of the main problems encountered with the preparation of these budgets are:

(a) Often only a cash flow projection is produced without any support-ing gross margins or trading budgets. A cash flow projection over a 12 month period can be completely misleading, particularly in a period of change in the business. A net cash inflow as a result of the timing of sales or from the sale of capital or extraordinary items can hide an underlying trading loss. On the other hand an annual cash outflow can hide a profitable business for similar reasons.

(b) Items relating to opening stock, debtors and creditors are often omitted from the cash flow.

(c) The format of the cash flow budget may be difficult to understand, containing a mixture of trading and non-trading transactions. (**4.7.6** and Example 4.13).

(d) It can be difficult to reconcile the gross margin budget and the annual cash flow projection. The main reason for this is that gross margins record enterprises over their production cycles and do not necessarily take time into account. Therefore enterprises that do not have annual cycles such as some beef fattening systems which can vary from three months to 18 to 24 months (**4.5.3**) may not coincide with an annual cash flow (**4.7.3**).

(e) Gross margin calculations may contain valuation differences which are not cash items.

(f) Taxation and planned machinery replacement are commonly left out of budgets.

(g) Where a farm business has both livestock and arable enterprises, it is common to find that a proportion of the arable output is used as a livestock input. For example, barley produced and recorded in the barley enterprise gross margin may be fed to a livestock enterprise. It is important that a transfer is made between the different enterprises to reflect the true performance of each enterprise. The barley should be credited to the barley enterprise and as a cost to the livestock enterprise at its commercial value. These transactions will not appear in the cash flow and will not have an overall effect on profit.

(h) Where there are a number of livestock enterprises there are often transfers of livestock between them, for example, the transfer of heifers from a herd replacement enterprise to a dairy herd and the transfer of calves from a dairy herd to a beef enterprise.

(i) If the farm business is registered for VAT it is recommended that VAT is ignored in the cash flow budget because this will, in normal circumstances, net out to nil over a period of time. However, the budget may understate the working capital requirements if the business reclaims VAT on a quarterly basis and large transactions such as machinery or fertiliser are purchased at the beginning of a quarter period. Care should be taken with VAT on exempt items such as property and land transactions that, subject to certain criteria included in the partial exemption rules, may not be reclaimed until the end of the VAT year.

154

4.7.3 Preparing a cashflow budget

It is assumed that the reader is familiar with the general principles of cash flow budget preparation and the following are problems often encountered when preparing a cash flow budget for a farming business:

(a) When the closing balance sheet forming part of the annual accounts of the previous period is used as a basis for opening stocks, they will be at cost of production rather than market value and therefore the subsequent cash receipts will normally be greater than the valuation.

(b) Own use of grain for seed or feed should not appear in the cash flow.

(c) The cash receipt for milk sales will not be received until the latter part of the month after delivery.

(d) Assets acquired under finance leases may be capitalised in the trading budget and the actual payments will need to be included in the cash flow.

(e) Only the interest portion of hire purchase payments will appear in the trading budget; the capital repayments will also need to be included in the cash flow.

(f) All cash flow budgets ending after September for arable businesses will need to contain variable costs for the following harvest. These costs may not be included in the trading account. To account for these correctly they should be included in the usage account calculations as closing stock (**3.7.1**).

(g) Trading livestock purchased towards the end of the cash flow period may not be included in the gross margin in the trading budget. To account for these correctly they should be included in closing valuation in the gross margin at market value.

4.7.4 Reconciliation between profit and cashflow budgets

It is recommended that a reconciliation between the profit forecast and the cash flow is prepared along the lines of a funds flow statement in order to check the accuracy. In its simplest form this may be as follows:

Example 4.11 *Funds flow statement*

	£
Total farm profit	XXXX
Add depreciation	XXXX
Adjust for: debtors movement	XXXX
creditors movement	XXXX
valuation movement	XXXX
Deduct: capital purchases	XXXX
private expenditure and tax	XXXX
loan repayments	XXXX
Add: capital sales	XXXX
new loans	XXXX
capital introduced	XXXX
Reconciliation to net annual cash movement	XXXX

An example funds flow statement is included on pages 21 and 22 of Appendix **1**.

4.7.5 Allocation of forage costs to different enterprises

In farming businesses that have several livestock enterprises it may be difficult to allocate forage costs such as fertiliser or grass seed to individual enterprises. However, when budgets are being prepared which may form a basis for enterprise planning it may be important to allocate them. The method most commonly used is the 'grazing livestock unit' (GLU), often referred to as 'livestock units' (LU). The forage needs of each type of livestock, averaged over the whole of the year, are expressed by reference to the forage needs of a single dairy cow. Therefore a single dairy cow is one LU, whereas a lowland breeding ewe is 0.11 LU. The total livestock in a farming business can therefore be expressed in their LU equivalents and the forage costs apportioned accordingly, for example:

Example 4.12 *Forage costs allocation*

Enterprise	LU	Total LU
60 beef cows	0.75	45
60 young beef cattle	0.65	39
1000 sheep	0.11	110

The relative forage requirements can therefore be calculated:

Cattle enterprise	84	43%
Sheep enterprise	110	57%

Therefore if the annual fertiliser costs are £2,500 they can be allocated:

Cattle enterprise	£2,500 at 43%	£1,075
Sheep enterprise	£2,500 at 57%	£1,425

4.7.6 Format of cash flow budgets

It must be remembered that a cash flow budget is not only prepared to quantify the working capital requirement but also for the lender to assess the business and for the budget to be monitored effectively. It is therefore recommended that the budget is prepared along the lines of the following format:

Example 4.13 *Cash-flow budget format*

Receipts
Sales enterprise 1	X
Sales enterprise 2	X
etc	
sub total	XX
variable costs under various categories	
sub total	XX
Total gross margins	XXX
Sundry income	X
Fixed costs detailed as appropriate	X
Total farm trading cash flow	XXXX
Capital sales	X
Capital expenditure	X
Private	X
Loans	X
Net cash flow	XXXX
Opening balance	X
Closing balance	XXXX

This format will be consistent with the gross margin budget and easier to reconcile to it as set out in **4.7.3**. It will highlight the trading cash flow and the non-trading items. It should also be consistent with most farming computer programs that may be used to monitor the budget.

4.7.7 Timing of gross margin budgets and cash flow budgets

Ideally the budget should fulfil two criteria:

(a) It should coincide with the financial year end of the business enabling it to be monitored efficiently.
(b) It should ideally coincide with production cycles of the main enterprises. This may not be a problem with a dairy enterprise which has an annual cycle split into months. Arable enterprises may not be straightforward where, for example, a September 1996 year end will detail the 1996 arable gross margins in the profit forecast,

whereas the cashflow budget will probably only contain the sales from the 1995 harvest.

It may be necessary to prepare a cash flow budget for a few initial months up to the start of the next financial year and at that stage begin the 12 month cash flow budget.

The length of the budgets will depend upon the circumstances:

(a) 12 months when the working capital requirements need calculating and the budget requires monitoring.
(b) 24 months when a change is being introduced into the business. The first 12 months will usually cover the period of change and the second 12 months should be a normal trading period under the new system.
(c) Over 24 months when the period of change is likely to last longer than 12 months. This will usually be the case in a start up situation on a new farm.

4.7.8 Monitoring budgets

The preparation of periodic profit and loss accounts, other than for annual accounting periods, is not recommended for most farming businesses because a profit is not realised until a sale is made at the end of a production cycle. Therefore periodic profit and loss accounts will require periodic revaluation of stocks which is considered too time-consuming relative to the benefit.

The most efficient method of monitoring a farming business is to:

● prepare a trading budget reconciled with opening and closing balance sheets;
● prepare a cash flow budget based on the trading budget;
● monitor the monthly cash movements.

The weakness of this method, which may only be applicable to some situations with high borrowing, is that debtors and particularly creditors will not be monitored. Therefore the ongoing net cash flow may be better than budget at the expense of a build up of creditors. The practical options of overcoming this are:

(a) Monitor a cash flow budget in detail and periodically list debtors and creditors manually. This may be possible and adequate for smaller farming businesses, in particular where a computer is not being used on the farm.

(b) Some of the specialist farming computer programs have the facility to report on a cash and trading basis. Therefore the cashflow can be monitored, and a debtor and creditor list produced on a periodic basis.

Where an on-farm computer is used and transactions recorded on a trading or double-entry basis it is possible to prepare a trading-flow rather than a cash flow budget and monitor the income and expenditure transactions on the computer. It will be possible but difficult to reconcile this to the bank statement by the debtor and creditor reports from the computer.

4.7.9 Cash flow variance report

It is recommended that the terms 'Better / (Worse)' are used instead of the traditional 'Variance' which assists in the interpretation of the report. For example:

Example 4.14 *Terms used in cash flow variance reports*

	Actual	Budget	Better/(Worse)
Sales	12,500	15,000	(2,500)
Purchases	6,000	7,000	1,000
Net cash flow	6,500	8,000	(1,500)

4.7.10 Discounted cash flows

Discounting techniques are generally used by consultants rather than farmers themselves, the work being carried out on spreadsheets. As in general business, discounting is used for investment appraisal and can be applied to the following situations:

(a) Comparison of different methods of funding machinery. The cost of leasing, hire purchase and contract hire net of tax can be compared over a specific number of years and the resultant net cash flows discounted to net present values for comparison.
(b) A comparison of leasing versus purchase of milk quota net of tax over a specified number of years with the resultant net cash flows discounted to net present values.
(c) Discounting techniques are used extensively in forestry and farm woodland calculations whereby the net present value of farm woodland, including the grants (**6.10**) versus commercial farming, can be compared.

160

4.7.11 Commercial considerations of using gross margins

The gross margin system of accounting has several weaknesses that need to be taken into consideration:

(a) Because time is ignored they may be misleading when used for comparing between enterprises, for example, comparing winter barley, which has an annual production cycle, with 18-month beef enterprise.
(b) Gross margins are often used for farm planning purposes without taking account of fixed costs and the possible change in fixed costs as a result of a change in enterprise mix. They may therefore provide a false indication of the profitability of the business.

4.7.12 Partial budgets

A partial budget is often used to identify the effect of relatively minor changes in the farming business. Rather than prepare a full profit forecast for the business only the items that change are included, therefore calculating the net change in profit as a result of a change in enterprises.

As most enterprises use land, the expansion of one enterprise will be at the expense of another. This will obviously not apply to intensive enterprises such as indoor pigs and poultry.

Examples of when a partial budget can be used are as follows:

(a) increase in number of dairy cows with a tighter stocking rate or with a reduction in a beef or sheep enterprise;
(b) buying a combine harvester versus using a contractor;
(c) increasing a sheep flock versus a decrease in a beef enterprise;
(d) renting or contract farming additional land.

There are several methods of calculating a partial budget, as follows:

(a) on a trading basis, therefore including such items as depreciation and interest on additional capital. This will assess the change in profit;
(b) on a cash basis only, therefore calculating the change in the net cash movement;
(c) use gross margins to record the changes;
(d) detail out all of the components of the gross margins involved in the assessment.

Example 4.15 *The use of a partial budget*

Increase in cow numbers versus a reduction in wheat acreage.
Assumptions:

- 10 additional cows purchased
- 12 acres of land
- Additional quota to be leased

Additional profit	£	*Reduction in profit*	£
Gross margin 10 cows after forage costs	7,500	Gross margin 12 acres wheat net of set-aside	3,000
Costs saved		*Extra costs*	
Fuel and machinery repairs on 12 acres at £20	240	50,000 litres milk quota at 7 pence	3,500
		Interest on additional capital 10 cows at 600 at 8%	480
	7,740		6,980
Net reduction in profit			760
	7,740		7,740

4.8 Financial performance measures

4.8.1 Introduction

There are a large number of measures available but only a small number are applicable and used in practice to assess the viability and performance of a farming business. Many of them require detailed adjustments of annual accounts or financial statements and are therefore less likely to be used.

4.8.2 Rental equivalent

This is the most common measurement and is widely used by lending institutions to provide a measure of the ability to service borrowing commitments or in general to assess the ability of the business to fund existing commitments.

Two assessments are made:

- rental equivalent per acre; and
- total rental equivalent as a percentage of gross output.

The calculation in theory is based on:

- rent and rates;
- overdraft and loan interest; and
- lease and hire purchase interest.

In practice rates are not generally included in the calculation as they are not usually significant.

An increasing number of lenders now include capital repayments in the calculation based on the points made in **4.6.13** above, as the assessment is based on the ability of the business to generate sufficient cash to repay future commitments. It is suggested that current interest rates should be adjusted to the medium-term average interest rates unless they are fixed. In order to keep the calculation as simple as possible, capital commitments should not be included but taken account of in the overall assessment.

The assessment is not a precise calculation but a general indicator and several other factors will need to be taken into consideration such as:

- the technical ability of the farmer;
- past financial and technical performance;
- how long existing commitments will last; and
- the date of the next rent review.

The criteria for the rental equivalent calculation as a general guideline are:

(a)	Rental equivalent per acre:

        Arable combinable crops   less than £60 per acre
        Dairy   less than £110 per acre
        Beef and sheep   less than £40 per acre

(b)   Rental equivalent as percentage of gross output:
        All farm types:

− less than 10%	strong
− 10% to 15%	safe
− 15% to 20%	careful management
− over 20%	weak may require reorganising

Example 4.16 *Rental equivalent calculation on 500 acre arable farm*

	£
Current rent	30,000
Current rates per annum	1,500
Overdraft average per annum at 3% over base	50,000
Bank loan on grain store 10 years 3% over base	10,000
Annual leasing and HP payments	10,000

The suggested calculation is therefore:

	£ Total per annum	£ per acre
Current rent	30,000	60
Current rates per annum	1,500	3
Overdraft interest adjusted to medium term average of 12%	6,000	12
Bank loan interest adjusted to 12%	1,200	2
Annual leasing and HP interest at 10%	1,000	2
Totals	39,700	79
Total gross output	200,000	
Rental equivalent as percentage	20%	

Therefore this business is considered to be weak and vulnerable and the assessment of the technical ability and business management skills of the farmer will be of paramount importance.

Example 4.17 *Rental equivalent calculations on annual accounts in Appendix 1*

An example rental equivalent per acre, excluding rates, is shown on page 19 of Appendix **1**. In this example only the rent and finance charges are used for the calculation.

The rental equivalent as a percentage of gross output in the example accounts in Appendix **1** can be calculated as follows:

	£
Rent	55,000
General rates	2,344
Finance costs	7,647
Total	64,991

Gross output of the business	
Dairy	133,281
Followers	21,264
Barley	69,692
Wheat	197,024
Beans	15,304
Oilseed rape	82,957
Industrial oilseed rape	15,409
Set-aside	
Other income	10,750
Total	545,681

$$\frac{64,991}{545,681} \times 100 = 11.9\%$$

Therefore this is considered to be a reasonably strong business.

4.8.3 Profit and fixed costs per acre

A comparison of profit, before rent and finance charges, with similar businesses is a useful comparison to measure farming performance.

A comparison of the key items that make up the profit with similar farms on a per acre basis is:

- Gross margins with outputs at market values
- Sundry income
- Labour costs – paid labour only, including full time and casuals
- Machinery costs split into: depreciation
  repairs and spares
  other machinery costs
- Property costs excluding rent
- Administration costs including secretarial and bookkeeper wages
- Drawings per acre

The comparison of the above income and costs per acre with either industry standard figures or with similar clients will quickly provide an indication of any strengths and weaknesses. An example of the profit and fixed costs per acre is shown on page 18 of Appendix **1**.

4.8.4 Farmer's balance sheet

This is a term to describe a schedule drawn up by the banks and other lending institutions. It is a statement of net worth of the owners of the farm business using realistic market valuations of assets based on the date it is prepared. It often involves a realistic estimate of farm stocks, a review of debtor and creditor positions and a fixed asset valuation. The schedule is used extensively by lending institutions to form a picture of the trend in net worth from year to year.

4.8.5 Balance sheet ratios

Most balance sheet ratios used in general businesses can be applied to a farming business, however, they are not widely used.

4.8.6 Return on tenant's capital

It is considered that one of the key measures of financial efficiency in the farm business is the return on total tenant's capital employed. Many of the larger farming institutions and companies employ this method to monitor performance. It is normally defined as:

- management and investment income expressed as a percentage of tenant's capital.

To obtain the management and investment income the following adjustments need to be made to the financial profit figure as shown in the annual accounts:

Example 4.18 *Adjustments to calculate management and investment income*

	£
Financial profit	XXXX
Add back interest and finance charges	XXXX
Deduct:	
estimated value of unpaid manual labour	(XXXX)
estimated rent for owner-occupiers	(XXXX)
Adjust for deferred income	(XXXX)
Adjust for (profit)/loss on asset sales	(XXXX)
Revalue stock from cost to market value	(XXXX)
Management and investment income	XXXX

To obtain the total tenant's capital, the following adjustments will need to be made to the annual farm balance sheet:

Example 4.19 *Adjustments to calculate tenant's capital*

	£
Net worth of year end balance sheet	XXXX
Deduct:	
landlord's capital	XXXX
Add:	
revaluation of all tenant's capital to market value	XXXX
all borrowings	XXXX
Total tenant's capital employed	XXXX

Example 4.20 *Return on tenant's capital on the accounts in Appendix 1*

		£
(a)	Financial profit (page 1)	74,716
	Add back interest and finance charges (page 1)	7,647
	Deduct estimate of unpaid manual labour	
	2 men at £15,000	(30,000)
	Rent already included	
	Adjust deferred income (page 1)	8,997
	Adjust (profit)/loss on asset sales (page 1)	(2,129)
	Revalue stock from cost to market value (page 1)	(2,212)
	Management and investment income	57,019
(b)	Tenant's capital	
	Net worth shown as current accounts (page 2)	616,302
	Deduct landlord's capital (page 2)	(38,124)
	Add revaluation of stock to market value	
	livestock £56,855 at 60% (page 14, note 10)	37,903
	produce £42,835 at 75% (page 14, note 10)	14,278
	borrowings deferred income (page 2)	16,113
	leasing and HP (page 2)	26,539
	loans (page 2)	38,791
	Tenant's capital	711,802

Return on tenant's capital

$$\frac{57,019}{711,802} \times 100$$

8%

167

A comparison of return on tenant's capital can be obtained from the regional surveys carried out by the Agricultural Economic Units.

4.8.7 Cost per unit of production

This efficiency measure is a relatively new concept applied to farming businesses. It has come about as a result of:

(a) the shortcomings of the gross margin system of recording which are discussed later in this chapter;
(b) the possibility of having to produce agricultural products at world market prices;
(c) the advent of decoupling subsidies and general support from production will possibly lead to a greater fluctuation in prices for agricultural products within the EU.

The total costs expressed per unit of production enables the break even price to be determined and then compared with the market price. The method lends itself particularly to businesses that have one predominate enterprise, such as pure arable or pure dairy farming businesses, and can be difficult to calculate with a range of different enterprises that have common overheads.

Example 4.21 *Cost of production per litre of milk on 150 acre dairy farm with 100 dairy cows.*

Average yield in litres per cow per annum   5,750
It is assumed that the value of calves and cull cows equals the cost of replacements.

	£ Total per cow	Pence per litre
Variable costs including forage	385	6.7
Fixed costs per acre of £240	360	6.3
Total	745	13.0
Milk price net of transport costs		19.0
Profit per litre to fund drawings, tax and reinvestment		6.0

This efficiency measure can be particularly useful to calculate the break even cost of leasing additional milk quota.

Example 4.22 *Cost of production per tonne of wheat on 500 acre arable farm*

The requirement of set-aside for most of the combinable crops complicates this calculation.

Average yield of wheat in tonnes per acre   3.0

	£ total per acre	£ per tonne
Variable costs £100 per productive acre	100	33
Fixed costs £180 total allocated to 90% of area	200	67
Total cost	300	100
Wheat price net		78
Arable area payment subsidy	96	33
Set aside payment £122 on 10% of land	13	4
Profit per tonne to fund drawings, tax and reinvestment		15

Similar calculations can be prepared for kilograms (live weight or dead weight) of beef or lamb sales per acre.

4.8.8 Net worth

The net worth of a business calculated from the balance sheet included in the annual accounts may show a misleading figure because fixed assets, particularly land, will be stated at cost and possibly well below current value. In addition trading stocks will be at cost rather than current value. In practice net worth can be used to evaluate a business as follows:

- to monitor the long-term trend of net worth as shown in annual accounts on a consistent basis over a number of years; and
- to calculate net worth based on the farmer's balance sheet (**4.8.4**).

4.8.9 Capital budgets

Capital budgets are increasingly being used to manage and plan the expenditure and reinvestment in machinery. An example is included in **4.12.6**. Ideally two capital budgets are required:

(a) The initial budget is prepared to identify the investment required, including the timing of replacement, and to assess the overall investment in machinery in the business over a number of years.

(b) The second stage is to restate the net change over costs per annum in anticipated cash flow to include leasing, hire purchase and contract hire instalments. This will provide the net cash flow per annum to include in a cash flow projection for the whole business.

4.9 Farm viability

4.9.1 Introduction

It can be seen from earlier paragraphs in this chapter that a farming business requires a substantial amount of capital to fund the fixed- and medium-term assets and to fund the production cycles of the enterprises. In addition, they require a high level of technical input in order to achieve the production performance required. In contrast to other businesses, a farmer normally has to perform all of the functions of management and inevitably there are many individuals that do not possess the necessary skills in all disciplines to achieve the required performance.

4.9.2 Component of viability

Viability can be considered at a total farm business level or at enterprise or project level. It has three components:

(a) Profitability is based on the gross margins and projected profit and loss account.
(b) Feasibility relates to the cash flow and the working capital required to achieve the projected profit. If the working capital has to be borrowed the requirements may be for more, or a longer period, than the lender is prepared to advance, therefore the projected profit is not feasible.
(c) Worthwhileness is the return on the capital employed. In general a relatively low return on total capital employed, including land, is accepted in the agricultural industry. The return on tenant's capital is considerably higher as discussed in paragraph **4.8.6**. There are several methods of calculating worthwhileness:
(i)   internal rate of return or discounted yield, being the interest on the total capital the project can sustain to break even; or
(ii) return on marginal capital being the return on the additional capital required for the change in the business.

4.9.3 Insolvency

The most common problem that farming businesses face is lack of working capital. Insolvency is defined either as an excess of liabilities over assets, or alternatively as an inability to pay debts as they fall due. The bank may be willing to continue support without calling in its lending in order to fund production cycles on the basis that sale proceeds will repay the required amount of the borrowing. Assets may exceed liabilities, but the business may still be insolvent if most of the assets comprise land and buildings.

4.9.4 Warning signs of insolvency

Insolvency does not often occur suddenly and there are usually a number of warning signs:

- seasonal borrowing requirements in the form of an overdraft reach the maximum limit;
- the bank is unwilling to extend overdraft facilities;
- the bank wishes to take out an agricultural charge under the Agricultural Credits Act 1928 (**4.9.5**);
- an annual cash deficit;
- increased borrowings from various sources;
- longer periods of credit taken from suppliers;
- bank wishing to restructure borrowings by moving part of the hard-core overdraft to a loan with structured repayments;
- increasing rental equivalent (**4.8.2**);
- experimental and unplanned diversification;
- lack of control over the records and paperwork.

The fact that a business is insolvent according to the definitions does not necessarily result in formal insolvency proceedings. There are many courses of action a farmer can take to help restore the business. Professional assistance will normally be required.

One of the most important considerations is to identify why the business has reached the vulnerable position. If the reason or reasons can be identified they will be important in considering options for the future. For example:

- a disease in one of the livestock enterprises;
- unseasonal weather affecting production;
- the embarking of a non-profit-making new enterprise, being a traditional farming enterprise or a diversification project;
- below average performance in one or more of the enterprises;
- lack of technical ability of the farmer;
- lack of managerial control over the records and paperwork of the farm;

- personal problems of the farmer such as death of member of the family.

The options available to the farmer should take the above reasons into account and might include:

- selling parcels of land either for agricultural production or as small plots adjoining gardens;
- employ technical assistance in the form of an agronomist or livestock consultant;
- cease unprofitable enterprises;
- sell machinery to raise capital and use contractors (although in most situations at this stage the machinery will be funded by credit agreements to around the value of the machinery);
- sell dairy herd and sell or lease out quota;
- introduce share farmer to dairy enterprise;
- contract management agreement on whole farm or arable enterprises; or
- let land out on a Farm Business Tenancy or grass keep arrangements.

4.9.5 Charges required by lenders to farming businesses

(a) The fixed charge or mortgage is the most common and relates to specific and defined assets, normally including land, houses and buildings. Lenders normally require all adults who live in a farmhouse charged to it to sign an agreement stating that they will vacate the property if the bank wish to repossess to sell with vacant possession.

(b) A debenture may be required when a farm trades as a company which will comprise a fixed and floating charge. A floating charge usually encompasses all the tenant's capital (**4.8.6**) and cannot normally be granted by an individual apart from an agricultural charge.

(c) Agricultural charge under the Agricultural Credits Act 1928 provides for farmers trading as unincorporated businesses to grant fixed and floating charges on their tenant's capital. For example:

    (i) fixed charge over growing crops, livestock, plant and machinery, all replacement livestock or progeny; or

    (ii) floating charge over all other farming stock and agricultural assets including rights to compensation.

The holder of an agricultural charge may appoint a receiver whose task it will be to take possession of the charged assets and realise them in order to repay the lender.

4.10 Reporting to the bank manager

4.10.1 Introduction

Many sectors of the agricultural industry are in deep crisis, with substantial reductions in commodity and livestock prices during 1997 and 1998. This will result in increased borrowing requirements in many businesses, usually in the form of an overdraft. In this situation it is extremely important for the owners and managers of farming businesses to work closely with their banks regarding the working capital they require to borrow.

Most of the major banks employ agricultural specialists who oversee their farming customers either directly or through the local branch manager. All proposals and problems above certain limits will be referred to the agricultural specialist who will have a knowledge of the industry.

The same principles as with any business apply to farming businesses; one of the most common problems quoted by banks is the lack of effective communication and information provided by the farmer. Most farming businesses apart from dairy farms will have seasonal funding requirements and when this is borrowed it is normally in the form of an overdraft. This is usually arranged annually in advance based on either a cash flow projection or on the cash flow pattern from the previous season.

4.10.2 Communication

Early communication with a bank manager is vital during periods of low profitability and annual cash deficits. The suggested course of action to gain the confidence of the bank manager is:

- invite the bank manager to visit the farm to see the enterprises;
- ensure the annual accounts are prepared on time and the bank have a copy as soon as possible;
- prepare a realistic cashflow projection, or have one prepared by a farm secretary, accountant or adviser: unrealistic figures will lose confidence;
- make a case for additional borrowing, backed by past records and enterprise details;
- ensure that a request for additional funding is made well in advance of the requirement;
- negotiate with the bank manager on a commercial basis regarding fees, charges and interest rates.

In situations where there has been a lack of communication and information available, the amount of information requested by the bank will depend upon:

- the amount borrowed;
- the history of profitability and annual net cash movements of the business;
- the degree of confidence that the manager has in the ability of the farmer in terms of technical ability and business management skills.

The information normally required by a bank or lender as it becomes increasingly concerned is as follows:

- a copy of the annual accounts for the business to be able to calculate key indicators such as rental equivalent (**4.8.2**). In some instances these may not be available until considerable time after the year end of the business which may cause concern to the bank;
- a farmer's balance sheet (**4.8.4**);
- a cashflow forecast for the business for the following year;
- a cashflow forecast and profit projection reconciled to opening and closing balance sheets;
- periodic variance reports between actual and projected cash movements;
- periodic lists of debtors and creditors.

4.10.3 Statement of affairs

Farm accounts are normally prepared on the basis that the business will continue trading as a going concern. The balance sheets will record the position of the business at a given moment in time, recording the assets and liabilities in order of long-term or short-term. Many assets will be recorded at cost or book value. A farmer's balance sheet (**4.8.4**) will be the first step in restating the assets at estimated realisable values. A statement of affairs will show assets at their estimated realisable value, identify the assets charged to the bank and also state liabilities in their order of priority applied by law in the event of a formal insolvency.

Examples of the differences that may occur in the values stated in a balance sheet and in a statement of affairs:

(a) The value of land and property will normally be at its original cost in a balance sheet and is therefore often understated. It will not reflect any prospects for development.

(b) Production herds may be on the herd basis (**2.17**) and their value understated.

(c) Trading livestock and produce will be valued at actual or deemed cost of production and possibly understated although it is possible for realisable value to be less in a depressed market.

(d) The market value of plant and machinery will often be less than the book value recorded in the balance sheet.

(e) Quotas, apart from those that have been purchased, will not normally be shown in the balance sheet. In the case of milk quota this figure could be substantial, however care must be taken to avoid duplicating quota value with land value.

(f) Tenants' improvements such as buildings may have been capitalised and included in the balance sheet. Their realisable value may be considerably lower.

(g) On a tenanted farm the landlord may have claims against the tenant in respect of dilapidations.

(h) Commodity stocks and possibly equipment are normally included in the accounts without reference to the fact that legal title may not have passed if the sale was subject to a reservation of title as it is assumed that the business will continue trading. In the case of a formal insolvency, stocks that are not legally owned cannot be included as assets.

(i) Additional liabilities may arise if the business ceases, such as redundancy payments.

(j) Assets subject to hire purchase and leasing agreements will be the property of the hirer. When trading ceases and capital assets sold the tax position will need to be re-assessed.

4.11 Gross margin, enterprise accounting and annual accounts

4.11.1 Introduction

The gross margin system of enterprise accounting is widely used in farming businesses to budget, monitor and record the margin achieved from individual enterprises. In addition, the annual accounts are often used to assess the actual performance of the business. This section looks at the difference between the gross margin system of budgeting and enterprise recording and the annual accounts prepared along the lines of standard accounting practice. The preparation of gross margin budgets is discussed in **4.7**. The interaction of gross margins and annual accounts can occur in the following situations:

(a) Potential lenders assessing proposals put forward by farmers or their advisers. In this situation the lender may have assessed and accepted the proposal in management gross margin format and will normally have the annual accounts to monitor the performance.

(b) Farmers planning the reorganisation of their businesses.

(c) Accountants who are requested to assist farmers in preparing proposals that may be used to support funding requirements or to comment on proposals.

(d) Farm management advisers who are employed to advise and monitor businesses and possibly report to a lender.

4.11.2 The gross margin system and annual accounts

Annual accounts are produced primarily for taxation purposes, however, when prepared in management format they can also fulfill an important role in the management of the farming business. The main differences between gross margins and annual accounts are the time-scale and the valuation of stock

4.11.3 Time scales

There are two aspects of time scales:

(a) Gross margin budgets for some enterprises will cover a period longer or shorter than the 12 month period covered by the annual accounts. Therefore the margin per enterprise, as shown in the gross margin budget, will not be fully reflected in the annual accounts. It will, on average, be either greater or less than the gross margin. Examples of such enterprises are:
   (i) beef animals that are kept for periods up to 24 to 30 months before slaughter;
   (ii) dairy herd replacements that are bred from the dairy cows and retained on the farm. These will normally calve from around two years old upwards;
   (iii) beef animals retained for short periods say three to six months and if more than one batch is kept in a 12 month period;
   (iv) more than one crop of vegetables grown on a piece of land in a 12 month period, commonly referred to as 'double cropping'.
   The exception to this is when an enterprise having a longer than 12 month production cycle has, on average, an annual throughput. The most common example of this is a dairy herd replacement enterprise that provides a constant number of heifers every year for a dairy herd. In any 12 month period there will be calves, young heifers and in-calf heifers, and their costs and output in a 12 month

period will reflect the same costs for a single batch of animals over a two year period.

(b) The gross margins may represent enterprises with annual production cycles, but the annual accounts may not coincide with the production cycle. For example:

(i) Gross margins representing combinable crops will cover a period up to the harvest and sale of the crop whereas the year end of the business may fall in March, between two harvests. Therefore the gross margin will be accounted for in two sets of annual accounts.

(ii) A 12 month beef system may fall partly in one set of annual accounts and partly in the following year.

When there is a constant level of production there is no significant difference between a gross margin budget and the annual accounts, for example, dairy and pig enterprises.

4.11.4 Stock valuation

Stock in annual accounts will normally be valued at cost in accordance with *BEN 19* apart from some instances when the unrealised profit may be calculated on arable crops as shown in the example accounts in Appendix **1**. It is considered too time consuming and therefore costly to calculate unrealised profit on livestock enterprises, and therefore this will lead to distortions between gross margins and the results in the annual accounts.

Production herds or flocks will normally be included in the annual accounts on the herd basis (**2.17**). Trading stock will be valued at actual or deemed cost. For example, cattle have a deemed cost at 60 per cent of market value. Therefore any movement in valuation over a 12 month period will be at 60 per cent of the movement at market value used in gross margin budgets.

Example 4.23 *Difference in valuation movement in gross margins and annual accounts.*

	Gross margin market value		Annual accounts deemed cost 60%	
	£	£ Total	£	£ Total
Opening value 8 beef cattle	400	3,200	240	1,920
Closing value 10 beef cattle	400	4,000	240	2,400
Movement in valuation		800		480

Therefore the annual accounts in this example will show an increase in valuation of £320 less than the gross margin budget. When budgeting, care must be taken not to use valuations from balance sheets as opening valuations, and to calculate closing valuations at market value.

Example 4.24 *Accounting for beef enterprise in gross margin terms and for annual accounts*

Gross margin budget 18 month beef system

Sale of fat animal	450
Headage payment (first 90 male animals)	84
Less purchased calf in autumn	100
Gross output	434
Variable costs including forage	240
Gross margin	194

Reconciliation with annual accounts with 31 March year end

Month		Gross margin	Annual accounts	Cumulative cash
October	calf purchase	(100)	(100)	(100)
Nov–March	variable costs	(48)	(48)	(48)
31 March	value of animal	280	160	
Year 1	margin	132	12	(148)

At this stage the actual margin made to date in management terms is £132. The annual accounts show a margin of £12 because the animal is valued at costs to date of £148 plus direct labour costs of £12. If costs have not been recorded, the animal can be valued at deemed cost of 60% of £280, being £168. (**2.13.6**). The cumulative cash cost is £148 excluding the direct labour which is a general overhead in the business.

	opening valuation	(280)	(160)	
April–March	costs	(192)	(192)	(340)
	headage payment	84	84	84
31 March	value of animal	440	382	
Year 2	margin	52	114	(256)

The margin made in the 12 month period in management terms is £52. In the annual accounts, the headage payments have been accounted for on a cash receipts basis. The value of £382 in the annual accounts is still at cost to date of £352 plus direct labour costs of £30 therefore showing a margin of £114. Cumulative cash cost is £256.

April	opening valuation	(440)	(382)	
	sale of fat animal	450	450	450
Year 3	margin	10	68	
Total margin		194	194	194

In management terms the actual margin in the third year is £10 per head.

The annual accounts now account for the balance of the margin from the enterprise as a result of the sale of the animal.

(a) The above example is based on one animal. Where a number of animals are involved the difference in the margins over time may be substantial, which could be very important if the business is being closely monitored. If a large number of batches are being fattened over a time period, with animals being sold periodically, the individual animals will be accounted for as in the example, but the overall margin in the gross margin and the annual accounts will be similar.

(b) The gross margin is a budget based on an 18 month beef system. However, because of the timing, it is accounted for in three different periods of annual accounts.

(c) The total margin is the same in the gross margin and the annual accounts.

(d) The accounting concept of valuing trading stock at cost until sold delays the taxable profit and therefore the tax that may be charged on the profit.

Example 4.25 *Accounting for arable enterprise in gross margin terms and in the annual accounts.*

Gross margin budget winter wheat

	£ per acre
Crop output 3 tonnes at £78	234
Arable area payments	96
Gross output	330
Variable costs	100
Gross margin	230

The gross margin is based on selling the wheat as follows:

	£
One tonne in September after harvest	73
Two tonnes February at £80.5	261

Reconciliation with annual accounts with 30 September year end

Month		Gross margin £ per acre	Annual accounts £ per acre	Cumulative cash £ per acre
Oct–Sept	variable costs	(100)	(100)	(100)
30 September	value of 2 tonnes	146	140	
	sale 1 tonne	73	73	73
	area payments debtor	96	96	
	deferred area payments		(64)	
Year 1	margin	215	145	(27)

The actual margin made to date in management terms is £215. At this stage the annual accounts show a margin based on the sale of one tonne out of the three and one third of the area payments. The valuation of £140 is based on total costs per acre of £100 variable costs and £110 direct labour and machinery costs (**2.13.2**) allocated to two tonnes out of the three produced from the acre. The cumulative cash position is a shortfall of £27.

Oct	Opening valuation	(146)	(140)	(27)
Oct	Opening area payments		64	
Dec	Area payments received			96
Feb	Sale 2 tonnes at £80.5	161	161	161
Year 2	Margin	15	85	313
Total Margin		230	230	230

The margin made in the 12 month period is £15, being the additional margin for storing the grain until February.
The margin accounted for in the annual accounts is £85.
The cumulative cash surplus for the year is £313, including a cash deficit of £27 from the previous year, giving a cumulative cash surplus of £230 equal to the margin.

Therefore it can be seen from both the examples that the true margin in management terms, the contribution to profit as shown in the annual accounts and the cash flow can differ widely over a time period because of the differing accounting techniques used. It is important for all individuals who assist in the management decisions and are involved in monitoring farming businesses to understand that profit can deviate because of accounting techniques, and not necessarily because of the level of production and performance of the enterprise.

4.12 Machinery management

4.12.1 Introduction

Machinery costs represent approximately 30 per cent of the costs of production per tonne of winter wheat and the capital tied up in machinery is around £200 per acre on many arable farms compared to around £90 to £100 per acre in variable costs. Therefore if total farm costs are to be reduced and margins maintained or improved, machinery is one of the main areas for attention when assessing future profitability.

4.12.2 Peak work loads

Most of the total annual labour and machinery costs are incurred over short periods. On arable farms this period ranges from harvest in July to drilling in October, a period of around 16 weeks. Similarly with livestock enterprises, silage and hay making equipment is only used for a few weeks. Assuming technical management to be in order, the most profitable businesses are those efficient in the use of labour and machinery during the peak periods.

Traditionally farm planning has involved the use of gross margins to maximise the total farm gross margin with labour and machinery calculated to match the requirements of the enterprises chosen. On arable farms where around 30 per cent of the total cost of production per tonne comprises machinery costs, it may be more profitable to use lower gross margin enterprises and concentrate on minimising peak workloads rather than maximising total farm gross margin. This becomes increasingly important the lower crop prices are, as the gearing effect of yield times price has less of an impact on the profit. In practice a balance of the two will optimise profit.

The key to cost management is planning the use of labour and machinery during the peak workload periods; this is the autumn on most arable farms. Work rates and timing of operations should be calculated to identify opportunities for economies and efficient use of resources. Different crop rotations demand different requirements on labour and machinery; each crop having a different autumn and spring peak work load. By reducing the peak demands the total labour and machinery requirements of the business are reduced. For example, the use of one large combine rather than two smaller ones will free up a key machinery operator to carry out cultivation work.

4.12.3 Economies and diseconomies of scale

One of the most popular methods of reducing fixed costs is to expand, spreading the costs over a larger area or an increased number of stock. Many businesses have expanded using contract management and share farming agreements (**2.15**), and in most situations this has been very successful. However, there comes a point in every farming business when an additional item, or larger item of machinery will be required to cope with more land. Depending upon individual circumstances it is highly likely that total fixed costs will increase at this point until further expansion takes place. Machinery costs per acre reduce as acreage increases but increase as additional or larger items are purchased. It is very important for every business to consider their position in this respect when considering expansion. The set-aside requirement (**1.11.7**) effectively increases the overhead costs on the productive acreage and in practice has resulted in spare capacity for effective expansion in many cases. The autumn peak workload can effectively be reduced by twice the set-aside percentage by cultivating the previous year's set-aside early and leaving the following year's set-aside as natural regeneration.

4.12.4 Joint ventures

Instead of an individual farming business expanding to reduce machinery costs per acre or per head, it may be more beneficial to share machinery with another farmer or to use existing machinery on other farms. As a result of the current downturn in the profitability of many enterprises many farming businesses are considering pooling their machinery and labour in order to gain economies. There are several methods of achieving this:

*(a) **Machinery syndicates, partnerships and companies***
Two or more farmers share in the ownership of a machine that is used for a specific operation, for example, a forage harvester. Farming businesses can pool all of their machinery and possibly labour, treat them as a cost centre and contract out the operations to each business.

*(b) **Contract management agreements or share farming agreements***
These benefit both parties to the extent that they both enjoy the benefits of the economies of scale achieved.

*(c) **Neighbouring agreements***
Adjoining farmers agree to carry out work for each other at agreed

rates, therefore individuals do not need to have a full complement of machinery.

(d) *Machinery rings*

Members of the ring carry out work for each other at published agreed rates. Two per cent commission is paid by both parties to cover the costs of administration by a full-time or part-time ring manager. Members do not rely on one contractor, as the ring manager has all the members at his disposal. As the work is carried out by the owner of the machine, the ring manager can ensure that only skilled operators are used.

(e) *Contractors*

An increasing number of arable farmers now use a contractor to carry out all operations, therefore benefiting from the economies of scale achieved by the contractor. Timeliness of operations can be a problem, but where the contractor relies on one farmer for a major part of income the joint venture is usually successful. The total costs charged by contractors for whole farm contracts vary depending upon the crops grown, but on combinable crops, are usually in the range of £80 to £100 per acre.

4.12.5 Management of machinery can be broken down into four stages

1. Capital budgeting;
2. Costing of main items;
3. Replacement options;
4. Funding decisions.

4.12.6 Capital budgeting

The timing of replacement of machines needs to be planned by farmers to ensure they do not run into cash problems in the future. Preparing a forward capital budget can avoid the need to replace several items in one year with an adverse effect on cash flow. The capital budget should span the life of most of the machines in the business, this is usually about eight years, and should include all mainline machines. The total planned expenditure, less any projected trade-in value over that period, divided by the total number of years will give the 'average annual net change-over cost'. This should equal target depreciation plus inflation. A typical figure for target depreciation on a farm of mainly combinable crops might be £35 per acre. A higher figure indicates possible over-expenditure on machinery.

Some of the main benefits of a capital budget are that it:

183

- forces the farmer to realistically judge the long-term demands placed on the business;
- alerts the farmer to large expenses in the future, therefore enabling them to be planned and evened out;
- alerts the farmer to the possible future borrowing needs of the business;
- allows time to look at the alternatives of using and acquiring machines and to plan their funding to suit cash flow.

Example 4.26 *A capital budget in £*

		Years							
		1	*2*	*3*	*4*	*5*	*6*	*7*	*8*
Item	*Age*								
Combine	5	70,000							
4WD tractor	4				25,000				
2WD tractor	7			15,000					
Sprayer	6		7,000						
Drill	1								11,000
Vehicle	2					15,000			
Total new values		70,000	7,000	15,000	25,000				11,000
Trade-in values		25,000	3,000	6,000	7,000	3,000	0	0	1,250
Net change over cost		45,000	4,000	9,000	18,000	12,000	0	0	9,750

Total planned net expenditure over 8 years	97,750
Divided by number of years	8
Average annual net change over cost	12,219
Farm size in acres	450
Average annual change over cost per acre	27

The above net change over cost may not necessarily reflect the actual annual cash costs of funding the machinery as most of the larger items are usually funded by short- to medium-term finance arrangements.

4.12.7 Costing of main-line machinery

The annual cost of an individual machine needs to be calculated and this consists of fixed and variable costs. The fixed costs include interest on the average capital tied up in the machine, average depreciation over its useful life and insurance. The sum of these figures gives a total annual cost that a business is locked into irrespective of the acreage or hours worked. The more work the machine carries out the lower these costs become on a per acre or per hour basis.

The variable costs include labour, fuel and repairs and these costs are directly related to the amount of work carried out by the machine.

Example 4.27 *Machinery costing of 120 horsepower four-wheel drive tractor*

		£		
Purchase price after discount, before trade in value		30,000		
Selling price after five years		10,000		
Average value		20,000		
Interest on average value at 8%		1,600		
Average depreciation over five years		4,000		
Insurance at £15 per £1,000 on average value		300		
Total annual fixed costs		5,900		
Hours worked annually	400		600	900
Fixed cost £ per hour	14.75		9.83	6.55

At this stage these costs per hour can be compared with the hiring of a tractor over a peak work load period.

Operating costs per hour			
• Labour cost per hour	6.00	6.00	6.00
• Fuel	1.65	1.65	1.65
• Spares and repairs			
Level of use	Low	Medium	High
As % of new price	3.0%	5.0%	8.0%
Cost £ per hour	2.30	2.50	2.70
Total operating costs per hour	9.95	9.72	10.35
Total fixed and operating costs per hour	24.70	19.55	16.90

These costs per hour can be compared with a contractor who supplies the tractor and the labour. Equally a contractor can use this method of costing to calculate:

• the number of hours or acres that the machine will need to be worked to cover costs and produce a profit;

- the amount that will need to be charged per hour or per acre; and
- the capital cost of the machine.

Some items of machinery such as a combine harvester will need to be calculated on a per acre basis.

In order to cost machinery accurately and plan their replacement, access to realistic information is required. Machinery costs can vary considerably depending on the soil type, and therefore costings based on industry averages may not be accurate for an individual business. The annual repair costs relating to an individual machine can be monitored and the machine can be replaced when the costs become too high.

4.12.8 Replacement options

For each potential replacement machine all options need to be considered:

- retain for another year;
- short-term hire;
- contractor or machinery ring;
- joint ownership with neighbour; or
- purchase – new or second hand.

4.12.9 Funding decisions

If the decision is made to purchase another machine, funding the net change-over cost will have to be considered. Machinery is accounted for via depreciation. This writes-off a piece of equipment over a number of years based on its purchase price. Depreciation is not a cash item and so could be treated as a fund which builds up and should, in theory, pay for replacing the item at the end of its useful life. However, in practice, it is not sufficient since there is no allowance for inflation and improvements in technology. For this reason an additional source of capital may be needed, either profits or additional borrowings.

4.12.10 Funding options

These include:

- cash;
- overdraft;
- loan;
- finance lease;
- hire purchase;
- conditional sale; and
- contract hire or operating lease.

In commercial terms these arrangements are often very similar in total cost but they differ significantly in their tax treatment (**5.7.8**). Farming clients should therefore be encouraged to contact their accountants prior to completing a machinery purchase.

Chapter 5 – Taxation

5.1 Introduction

Farming as a business is subject to tax as set out in s53 ICTA 1988 where it states that profits from farming are treated as a trade and in broad terms defined as the commercial occupation of land for the purposes of husbandry. Farming businesses have become increasingly diverse in the derivation of their income over the years and this, coupled with the special nature and problems of the trade, has resulted in a number of special provisions and reliefs and specific tax legislation, some of which have been introduced to take account of the wider interpretation of the definition of farming as a trade.

Specific details of the taxation law are considered outside the scope of this book, as they are generally fully available and used by accountants in general practice. The purpose of this Chapter is to draw attention to and comment briefly upon the application of tax legislation and the specific provisions that apply to the trade of farming.

Farming is a way of life rather than a business to many farmers where the personal and family life are intermingled with the actual trade of farming. In addition, the income and expenditure can vary enormously from one year to the next depending upon the weather, livestock and crop diseases, timeliness of operations, the timing of selling of produce and stock and several other factors. For example, it is theoretically possible for an arable farm to sell the output of between zero and two full harvests in any given financial year.

All of these factors emphasise the importance of producing meaningful management accounts and budgets identifying production cycles, in order to appreciate the sensitivity of taxable profits and future tax liabilities and advise accordingly. Farming is very capital intensive with an increasing amount of machinery, at the expense of labour, being used. The acquisition of machinery has historically been partly tax-driven which can lead to a distortion of taxable profits (**2.16**).

In order to carry out effective tax planning an appreciation of all of these factors is required together with the aspirations and personal wishes of the family. Up-to-date information on asset ownership and values, liabilities, tenancies with third parties or within the family, partnership agreements and wills are all required for effective capital tax planning.

This chapter contains the changes announced in the Budget on 9 March 1999 and are subject to them becoming legislstion in the ensuing Finance Act.

5.2 Trading profits

The strict interpretation of farming needs to be flexible as the number of activities which remain peripheral to the main activity increase. In particular, in some parts of the country tourism is a major industry which has led to a number of tourist enterprises on farms. Where these remain a subsidiary activity to the core farming activity they can be included as farming profits. These activities range from the provision of holiday accommodation, livery stables, shooting and fishing fees to the use of land and water for sports activities. Rental income is discussed later in this Chapter. The selling of turf and the receipt of grazing rents (**6.4**) can both be treated as farming receipts. There has been a substantial increase in contract farming or management agreements over the past few years which has resulted in many clients receiving substantial amounts of contracting income. Strictly, this income is not considered to be derived from farming but the business of supplying contracting services (**5.4.1**).

5.2.1 Farming as one trade

All farming carried out by the same person or persons in partnership or a company, within the UK, is treated as one trade for tax purposes and chargeable to tax under Case 1 Schedule D or corporation tax. Therefore, where several farms in different parts of the country are operated by the same person or persons they will be treated as one business for tax purposes. This does not apply to any farming activities outside the UK where the profits are taxed under Schedule D case V. Market gardening is also separately defined as a trade in s53(1) ICTA 1988 but is not subject to the one-trade provision.

5.2.2 One estate election

This allows the transfer of surplus expenditure from one property to another, including the owner occupier's house (TA 1988 s26). It is available only for estates managed as one unit and where an election has been in force since 5 April 1963. It is to be abolished as from 2001/2002 for income tax and as from 1 April 2001 for companies (FA 1998).

It may be worth considering accelerating the timing of repair work in some instances.

5.2.3 Moving farm – time limits

A person or partnership moving from one farm to another, giving up, or taking on a farm or some land, will be treated as a continuing trade. However, where there is an interval between moving from one farm to another, the Revenue may not allow the trade to continue. This may be important where there are losses brought forward. Short periods of up to 12 months where there is no other income in the meantime can sometimes be justified as a continuation of the trade.

5.2.4 Interest and bonuses

Many farming businesses receive trade bonuses from co-operatives and deposit interest and these sums, unless they are significant, can be included in the farming profits. In practice small amounts of rental income are normally included. Rental income is discussed in paragraph **5.5**.

5.2.5 Farmhouses

Historically one-third of farmhouse expenses have been included as allowable expenses, however, the Revenue changed their attitude to this in 1993 (Press release, 18 February amending ESC B5) when they stated that each case will be judged on its merits and all allowed expenditure justified. In practice, the one third rule is still being adopted in many cases and accountants should be aware that the Revenue may question these in the future. Where there is more than one dwelling on the farm occupied by partners in the business the same principles apply. It is not advisable to identify one specific area of the farmhouse exclusively for business use because of the effect on principal place of residence relief from CGT.

The same comments apply to Agricultural Building allowances on farmhouses (CAA s124(1)).

5.2.6 Farmhouse rents

Farmhouse rents may pose problems in agreeing a private use adjustment because the rent for a farm is not usually apportioned between the land and the house. Historically two thirds of the gross rateable value was used. A comparison with open market rents will give a high figure and the difference between the rental value of the farm with and without a farmhouse may give a low figure. The Revenue will seek a figure somewhere between the two. In practice, many recent rent reviews for agricultural holdings will differentiate between the rent payable for the land and the farmhouse in the background calculations and, therefore, may be available if requested from the landlord's agent. Some landlords are specifically dividing the land and house and giving separate figures on the rent demand.

5.2.7 Recreational activities

Many farming businesses have recreational activities, the most common being horses and shooting. The expenditure and income from these as recreational activities are excluded. The control of vermin and the costs of keeping horses for tending stock or observing crops for disease etc., may be allowable expenses.

5.2.8 Woodland

Commercial woodland is outside the scope of tax (**6.10**), but costs of shelterbelts and small areas of woodland are allowable as general maintenance of the land and for stock shelter. In this situation the sale of the timber should be included as farm income. Receipts from the sales of Christmas trees and short rotation coppice should be included as part of the farm receipts.

5.2.9 Other allowable expenditure

Other allowable expenditure which is peculiar to a farming business will include working dogs, expenses of agricultural shows and societies, subscriptions and overseas business travel. College and training fees of farm staff are normally allowable. The allowability of agricultural course fees for the farmer's own children working on the farm will depend upon the circumstances in each particular case but could well be open to a challenge from the Inland Revenue.

5.3 Trading losses – hobby farming

5.3.1 Hobby farming rules

The general rules relating to the treatment of trading losses apply to farming and market gardening and therefore, in principle, are available to set off against other income as set out in s380 ICTA 1988. Because living on a farm is an attractive occupation, the Revenue experienced problems with taxpayers farming for recreational purposes and not commercial reasons, setting off losses against other income. Special legislation was introduced to restrict these losses:

- Section 397 ICTA 1988, which restricts the use of losses in a farming or market gardening trade where they have been incurred in each of the five previous years. These provisions are commonly referred to as the 'hobby farming rules'. For this purpose, the loss is calculated under Case 1 of Schedule D. The loss calculated is before the deduction of capital allowances and this also applies post self-assessment; after 1996/97. In new businesses the year of commencement is not counted, therefore the loss in the seventh year is relevant.
- Section 384 ICTA 1988, which restricts the use of losses for any business where the trade is not run on a commercial basis and with a view to the realisation of profits. A similar provision for the restriction of corporation tax relief is included in s393A(3).

If it is possible to prove that because of the particular type of farming activity carried out, it needs a longer time than the five years before profitability could normally be expected, it may be possible to extend the five year rule. The Revenue will normally allow up to 11 years' losses for certain horse-breeding businesses provided it can be shown that it is potentially profit making.

There are anti-avoidance provisions which prevent a change of partnership or the formation of a company breaking the five year rule if the same individuals are in control. In this context husband and wife are treated as the same person but a widow is not. Therefore when a trade passes to a widow on the death of her husband, a new run of five years' losses are available.

Where loss relief is precluded and the farmer is an owner-occupier, Extra Statutory Concession (ESC) B5 allows normal landlord's expenses such as the maintenance, repairs and insurance of the property to be set against other income, subject to the usual restriction for the private use of the farmhouse. This is not available to market gardening. ESC B5 is to be withdrawn with effect from 1 April 2001 for companies and 6 April 2001 for unincorporated businesses.

5.3.2 Losses and capital gains

The Finance Act 1991 allows losses from a farming trade to be set against capital gains by the same individuals from 1991/92.

5.3.3 Incorporation relief

The carry forward of trading losses by an individual, or a number of individuals trading as a partnership, may still be available if the business (not merely the trade) is transferred to a company. This is also known as carry-over relief or shareholder relief. The relief is available against the first subsequent income the individual receives from the company.

5.4 Averaging

Farming profits can be subject to considerable fluctuation outside the control of the farmer such as the weather and market prices. In particular there has been considerable reduction in farm profitability during 1997 and 1998 as a result of a reduction in market prices. In recognition of this, s96 ICTA 1988 allows the taxable profits of two consecutive years to be added together and averaged. This is available to sole traders and partnerships in the trade of farming and market gardening, but not to limited or unlimited companies. Farms or market gardens outside the UK are not included. A claim may be beneficial if by averaging the two years, the highest profit will no longer incur tax at the 40 per cent rate.

It is available if the profits of one of the years does not exceed 70 per cent of the other. A partial or marginal relief is available if the profit of one year does not exceed 75 per cent of the other. An averaging claim cannot be made for:

- the year of assessment in which the trade commenced or is ceased; or
- the year of assessment which precedes a year which has already been included in an averaging claim.

A trading loss is treated as a nil profit for averaging purposes. Therefore an averaging claim will not affect any loss relief that may be claimed.

An election to average must be made within 12 months after 31 January following the second year of assessment and the resultant averaged profit can be used in a subsequent averaging election. Once made, the averaging claim is irrevocable, therefore it is important not to make the election too early. Before making the claim, the effect on the net tax payable for the two years based on the total income, and not only Case 1 profits, should be considered. The impact on relief for pension payments should be considered.

Some farming partnerships include a company as a partner, and in these cases the total partnership profits excluding those attributable to any corporate partner, where the profit share is subject to corporation tax, will be the assessable profit to be used in an averaging claim. Other non-corporate partners including trustees, executors and sleeping partners are included for averaging purposes.

5.4.1 Other income and averaging

Averaging is available to the trades of farming and market gardening and, by ESC A29, to the trades of the intensive rearing of livestock or fish on a commercial basis for the production of food for human consumption. Strictly, averaging is only available on the normal farming income and not available where the trade is agricultural contracting or includes substantial non-farming income such as a tourist enterprise or haulage. In practice, it will depend upon the relative amount of other income in the farm accounts.

There has been a considerable increase in contract farming arrangements over recent years and most contractors in contract farming arrangements are also farmers and therefore will have a balance of both types of income.

Contract farming income, where the client is the contractor, is in principle excluded because the Inland Revenue consider the contractor not to be farming and chargeable under Case 1 Schedule D on profits as a contractor. It could be argued that as a large proportion of the divisible surplus (**2.15**) forms the remuneration to the contractor, the contractor is therefore directly affected by the adverse effects of fluctuating profits.

5.4.2 Self-assessment and averaging

The profit to be averaged prior to self-assessment was that adjusted for Case 1, Schedule D, before the deduction or addition of capital allowances and balancing charges.

Averaging is now available with the following changes:

(a) The profit that can be averaged will be the net Case 1 profits after the deduction or addition of capital allowances including agricultural buildings allowances and balancing charges.

(b) The profits to be averaged will be those of each individual partner rather than the total for the trade. It is not necessary for every partner in a trade to make an averaging claim.

(c) Averaging cannot apply to partners joining or leaving a partnership as in the pre self-assessment rules where averaging cannot apply to a partnership in the year of commencement or cessation.

Where one of the years to be averaged is the transitional year of 1996/97 the method will depend upon whether the other year is the preceding or following year.

(a) If the preceding year (1995/96) is averaged with 1996/97 the old rules will apply, i.e., profits before capital allowances and balancing charges and the claim will be for the whole partnership.

(b) If the following year is averaged with 1996/97 the new rules will apply, i.e., profits after capital allowances and the claims made by individuals.

The transitional period and the new rules under self-assessment open up some tax planning opportunities for individuals in partnerships and it will be worthwhile reviewing the profit share of individuals.

5.5 Rental income

An increasing number of farming businesses receive rental income from letting property and the Revenue practice, where the amounts received are not significant, and material to the normal trading income, is to treat them as part of the normal trading profits assessable to Schedule D Case 1. When the rental income exceeds what may be interpreted as significant, the Revenue may not allow this practice. It is advisable to warn all clients who receive rental income that this may happen and the resulting effect on their net tax position. Rental income from the letting of agricultural land used in a trade by another entity is taxable under the normal rules of Schedule A.

The tax regime for rental income from property received by individuals changed as from 6 April 1995, and after this date all income from property including furnished lettings are assessable under Schedule A as the profits of one activity according to the rules applicable to trading income. The old rules remained for companies until 31 March 1998. Furnished Holiday Lettings for individuals is treated as a trade (TA s 503) with the properties available for rollover and retirement relief and the income eligible as relevant earnings for pension contributions.

Rental income from accommodation temporarily surplus to normal business requirements is not usually separately treated in order to avoid apportioning expenses in the farming business. The Inland Revenue do, however, state conditions in circumstances where this treatment is accepted; they state that all of the following must apply:

(a) The rental income is relatively small in the farming business.
(b) The rents are for surplus business accommodation and not from land.
(c) A farming business is being carried on.
(d) The property is temporarily surplus to business requirements and has been used or intended to have been used in the business in the past.

(e)   The premises are partly used for business purposes and partly let, therefore making it difficult to apportion expenses.

5.5.1 The most common forms of rental, or similar income, from property in a farming business

These include:

(a)   Rents from farm cottages temporarily not required for housing farm employees, which are normally included as trading profits.
(b)   Rents from surplus farm buildings used for storage or light industry. These would normally require planning permission for change of use from agricultural use.
(c)   The rental income from a correctly constructed short-term grazing agreement where the landlord has some involvement in maintaining the grass, which is trading income (**6.4**).
(d)   Income from correctly constructed contract farming and share farming agreements (**2.15**) as discussed later in this Chapter is not rental income but trading income.
(f)   Long term furnished and unfurnished lettings of cottages particularly on country estates will normally not be allowed to be included as trading income and therefore assessed as Schedule A. In practice the size and scale of the rental income is important as referred to earlier in this Chapter.
(g)   Furnished holiday lettings which comply with the letting requirements on time limits (s503 & 504 ICTA 1988), are subject to special rules equivalent to Schedule D Case 1.

5.6 Grants and subsidies

The taxation of grants and subsidies adopts the same principles as standard commercial accountancy practice. The main difficulties encountered are:

- the distinction between capital and revenue; and
- the time at which the income should be recognised.

The general principles relating to the accounting treatment of grants and subsidies are set out in other Chapters (**2.7**, **2.8**, **2.10**) and the Revenue will generally not challenge the method of accounting as long as the grant or subsidy is fully accounted for at some stage, the method of accounting is consistent and where there is no substantial deferment of tax. (References are Tax Bulletin, issue 10, February 1994, p108 and issue 14, December 1994, p182).

Grants and subsidies which may cause difficulties are:

5.6.1 Annual management grants

In practice, some of the annual management grants (**2.10**) are paid as lump sums with the payment possibly relating to more than one year. Although these may seem capital in nature they relate to compensation for a reduction in production as a result of a restriction of commercial husbandry and management, therefore they are trading income.

5.6.2 Combination of compensation for loss of income and capital

Many grant schemes provide a mixture of capital and annual compensation payments, therefore it is important to differentiate between the two. Capital grants will relate to specific capital expenditure and the documentation accompanying the payment should be examined. The compensation for loss of profits will be trading income.

5.6.3 Farm woodlands

Farm Woodland Premium Scheme annual payments (**6.10**) are to compensate farmers for loss of agricultural profits when land is planted with trees and therefore are a taxable farming income. The remainder of grants available under the Woodland Grant Scheme are outside the scope of tax.

5.6.4 Milk quota

Both wholesale and direct sales milk quota have been reduced from the amount originally allocated, and compensation payments paid to milk producers. The compensation can be either a trading receipt or a capital receipt.

- The compensation for temporary cuts in milk quota are trading receipts.
- The compensation for a permanent reduction in milk quota is treated as compensation for a reduction in a capital asset and is therefore a capital receipt.

The compensation payments for permanent cuts have been paid in instalments over the past years along with single payments for temporary cuts, therefore making it difficult to identify the status of each payment.

Table 5.1 *Milk compensation payments and dates*		
1987/88	3.927 ppl per annum for 7 years	Capital
1988/89	3.927 ppl per annum for 7 years	Capital
1988/89	6.860 ppl as single payment	Trading
1989/90	7.054 ppl as single payment	Trading
1990/91	6.212 ppl as single payment	Trading
1991/92	5.465 ppl as single payment	Trading
1991/92	8.19 ppl per annum for 5 years	Capital

In addition, milk producers have received shares and interests in the following bodies following the demise of the Milk Marketing Board:

(a) *Milk Marque*
Certificates of entitlement issued in November 1994 not subject to tax. Interest on certificates of entitlement is income.
(b) *Dairy Crest*
Free shares issued in August 1996 are capital and pooled with rolling fund offer shares. Nil base cost.
Rolling fund cash offer and dividend are income.
(c) *Residual Milk Marketing Board*
Supplementary payment and B reserve fund distribution in June 1996 and March 1997 are income.
(d) *Genus*
Issue of Genus shares in December 1994 are capital with nil base cost.
(e) *National Milk Records*
Shares issued April 1997. Capital with base cost at 45 pence.

5.6.5 SLOM compensation

This compensation relates to milk producers who had entered into a temporary non-marketing of milk scheme which restricted them from producing milk for a period of five years. This five year period coincided with the introduction of milk quotas, therefore the producers did not produce milk in the reference period and were not allocated a quota.

Milk producers in Holland and Germany took court action which resulted in compensation being paid. The allocation of the compensation in the UK is covered by the Dairy Quotas (Amendments) Regulations 1990. There have been three compensation schemes:

- SLOM I was allocated in June 1989;
- SLOM II was allocated in December 1991;
- SLOM III was allocated in 1994 and was compensation for land

purchased which was subject to a milk production restriction and therefore not allocated a quota.

The compensation is treated as income and not capital, should be included as one sum in the year of entitlement and cannot be spread over the years to which it relates.

5.7 Capital allowances

The normal rules for capital allowances on plant and machinery apply to farm businesses. The distinction between capital allowances and depreciation of plant and machinery as shown in the annual accounts is generally not understood by farmers, many being under the impression that depreciation and any amount shown as a profit or loss on disposal of plant and machinery are taxable amounts.

5.7.1 Higher capital allowances for small businesses

Capital allowances were increased to 50 per cent in the first year only for the period 2 July 1997 to 1 July 1998 (F(No 2)A 1997 s42). This was extended for a further 12 month period to 1 July 1999 at 40 per cent (FA 1998 s94). Most farming businesses fall within the small business criteria where they have to satisfy two of the following; turnover less than £11.2 million, assets less than £5.6 million and employees less than 250.

5.7.2 Definition of plant

One of the most common problems faced by the accountant is the actual definition of plant, allowable up to 25 per cent, as opposed to expenditure allowable for agricultural buildings allowance at 4 per cent (**5.8**). Machinery and plant does not have a statutory definition, therefore their ordinary meanings apply. In general, for a piece of equipment to be eligible as plant and machinery it must perform a function in the business as opposed to functions being performed within or around it. In addition, its suitability for an alternative use can be considered. Where its use is specific to one function this supports the argument that it is plant.

The taxation treatment is dependent on the facts of each individual case and the following, where the construction contains integral and interdependent machinery, may be considered to be plant:

- milking parlours;
- silage clamps;

- glasshouses which form part of an overall environmentally controlled system;
- slurry pits containing integral equipment;
- fish tanks and ponds;
- grain silos; and
- specialist pig buildings.

5.7.3 Mixture of plant and building

In practice many projects on farms will consist of expenditure on both plant and buildings and care should be taken to allocate the correct amounts to plant. The Revenue will normally resist a claim that services on or in a building and being an integral part of the building are plant. However, it is important to consider each item because of the difference in allowances.

5.7.4 Capital losses

Capital losses on farm machinery is an area that is generally overlooked. Indexation allowance was available on disposals prior to 29 November 1993 and in some instances a capital loss may be claimed. The time limit for claiming capital losses is six years.

5.7.5 Balancing charges

If the proceeds of sales of machinery and plant exceed the pool figure plus additions during the period, a balancing charge occurs. This can occur in businesses where:

- most assets have been leased; and
- assets have not been substantially purchased since the higher rates of first year allowances were available.

In these situations the pool balance may be relatively low and careful consideration must be given as to the timing and method of funding of replacement machinery and plant (**2.16**).

5.7.6 Short-life machinery

The normal rules apply. An election may be made within two years of the accounting year, in which an asset is acquired to deal with short-life machinery separately from the pool. This may be relevant to computer systems and some items of farm machinery. Section 38 of CAA 1990 gives a list of eligible assets.

5.7.7 Motor cars

Most cars in a farming business have a dual private and business use and are often the subject of discussion with capital allowances scaled down for any private use. Four-wheel drive vehicles that have windows and seats in the rear are very common on farms and are regarded as cars by the Revenue. Motor cars costing more than £12,000 acquired after 10 March 1992 are maintained in a separate pool and the writing down allowance is restricted to a maximum of £3,000 per annum. This allowance is normally scaled down for any private use. The allowances on cars acquired under finance and operating leases are discussed later in this chapter.

5.7.8 Hire purchase and credit agreements

Many of the larger items of plant and machinery are subject to instalment finance agreements (**2.16**). These have become more diverse and complex over the past few years. The date on which the expenditure is incurred is the relevant date for capital allowances and this is the date the obligation to pay becomes unconditional and legal title passes. This rule is modified when an extended period of credit is given as discussed below. The distinction must be made between:

(a) *Hire purchase agreement:*
Capital allowances are available on the full capital cost of the asset, the balance being interest and therefore a trading expense. Strictly, capital allowances are restricted to the amount of capital payable under the hire purchase agreement until the asset is actually brought into use in the trade. The balance of unclaimed allowances is carried forward until further capital is paid or the asset is brought into use. Up to 25 per cent per annum of the allowances, including the unclaimed allowances brought forward, will be carried forward to subsequent years. In practice this is not usually a problem, however, it may be relevant to items such as combine harvesters that are mainly purchased during the winter months because of favourable credit terms and may not be delivered until the following spring. The definition of 'used in the trade' is not defined and is therefore open to interpretation.

(b) *Credit period under normal terms of trade:*
When an extended period of credit under normal terms of trade, which is not subject to an instalment finance agreement, is greater than four months, capital allowances are not available until the due date for payment. This is irrespective of when the asset is brought into use or when the payment (even if earlier than the due date) is actually made.

(c) *Finance lease (SSAP 21)*
Capital allowances not available to the lessee (**5.9**).
(d) *Operating lease (SSAP 21)*
Capital allowances not available to the hirer unless the hirer
purchases the asset during or after the hire period. (**5.9**).

It is recommended that the original documents are always requested
from the client and inspected (**2.3.1**). Should there be doubt regarding
the construction of the agreement it is suggested, with the permission of
the client, to discuss the agreement with the finance company.

Some finance companies offer Conditional Sale agreements (**2.16.4**)
which are not subject to the rules of hire purchase agreements regarding
the title of the asset. Conditional sale agreements are essentially loans
and were used extensively for funding machinery when grants were
available on their purchase. MAFF would not provide grants on machinery subject to hire purchase agreements. These agreements should be
considered in situations where there is an element of risk of the Inland
Revenue not allowing capital allowances where assets are not brought
into use in the trade for a period of time after purchase.

5.8 Agricultural buildings allowance (ABA)

The allowances for agricultural buildings was restricted to four per cent
per annum in FA 1985 and 1986 from an effective 100 per cent tax relief
over a ten year period. As a result of the difference between the four per
cent ABA and the 25 per cent available on plant and machinery and
repairs and replacements which are wholly allowable as a business
expense, it is important to differentiate between them.

5.8.1 Eligible expenditure

Capital expenditure on farmhouses, farm and market garden cottages
and buildings, fences, roads, walls, drains including land drainage, ponds
and reservoirs and reclamation of agricultural land are disallowable as
revenue expenditure but subject to ABA. Farmhouses are subject to
private use restriction with up to one third allowable depending upon
the nature and size of the house relative to the size and nature of the
farm. There has been considerable case law relating to the eligibility of
farmhouses and cottages.

5.8.2 Eligible claimants

The allowances may be claimed by the owner occupier, tenant or landlord of a let farm who has incurred the expenditure.

5.8.3 ABA versus repairs

Replacements of old drainage systems would constitute a repair or replacement and it should be remembered that most farmland apart from hill areas has been drained in the past. Replacements of parts of buildings without improvement will normally qualify as being wholly allowable.

5.8.4 Sale, purchase and transfers of farms and land

A new owner of the land, whether by purchase or transfer, acquires the unused portion of the ABA's calculated on a time apportioned basis for the year of change. Unused allowances from an outgoing tenant revert to the landlord unless the incoming tenant pays the outgoing tenant for the assets.

5.9 Finance and operating leases

The capital value of leased assets cannot qualify for capital allowances as at no time do they belong to the lessee. However, the revenue accept that the 'properly computed commercial depreciation' of the asset applied under *SSAP 21* is allowed as a tax deduction. A tax adjustment will thus normally be necessary if the whole depreciation charge for the year has been added back in the computations. The interest element of payments to the lessor normally qualifies as a business expense.

The situation for leased assets set out above applies for tax purposes to leases entered into after 11 April 1991. Prior to that date the whole of the rental instalments were tax deductible when they became due. The revenue changed this practice because of the perceived abuse of the system in the case of front-loaded leases that gave accelerated tax relief to the lessee. The new practice was introduced in the Revenue Statement of Practice SP 3/91.

Depending upon the finance company involved, the lease agreement will specify the amount of any sale proceeds that may be received by the lessee. This will range from 100 per cent down to around 90 per cent. In practice the asset will normally be traded in as a part exchange for a new one and the proceeds used as a deposit. The remittance advice issued by the finance company will detail any deductions due such as a settlement figure and a retention which, as stated, is normally expressed as a percentage of the proceeds. The sale proceeds of leased assets are termed 'rebate of rentals' and are wholly taxable.

Secondary period rentals are wholly allowable against tax as they fall due.

5.9.1 Expensive cars on finance leases

Where a car, for which the retail price when new exceeds £12,000, is leased for business purposes, the accounting charge (annual depreciation) is treated as reduced for tax purposes in the hands of the lessee. The restriction is half the excess of the car's cost over £12,000 divided by the price.

	£
Example 5.1 *Expensive car on a finance lease*	
Retail price	20,000
Limit for 'expensive cars'	12,000
Excess price	8,000
Half of excess	4,000
Half of excess divided by price (4,000/20,000)	1/5
Full accounts depreciation charge	5,000
Less restriction (5,000 × 1/5)	1,000
Lease depreciation allowable for tax purposes	4,000

The restriction on the tax relief for the car rental does not apply to any agreed maintenance element. The Inland Revenue has agreed that if the contract includes a specified amount for any running costs as opposed to capital costs then that part of the rental may be excluded from the formula for calculating the disallowance. The finance company should be able to provide the details if the client cannot.

5.9.2 Operating leases

Tax relief is given when the rentals fall due and therefore if there is any 'front loading' to the payments the lessee will receive an accelerated tax advantage. No capital allowances are available. At the end of the agreement the machine is sold to a third party with no rebate of rentals as occurs in a finance lease agreement. The rules that apply to 'expensive cars' regarding disallowable expenses and maintenance elements under finance leases, also apply to operating leases.

5.10 Herd basis

5.10.1 Introduction

The rules relating to the herd basis are contained in ICTA 1988 Sch 5 and are available in the Inland Revenue booklet IR9. The normal treatment of farm animals is as trading stock, however, some animals are kept for the whole of their lives for their products or progeny such as milk, eggs, pigs, calves and lambs. The herd basis, therefore, allows these classes of mature animals to be treated as assets and excluded from the trading stock valuation. The main benefits of the herd basis is that the ongoing movement in value of the production animals does not distort taxable profit, and if they are eventually sold without replacement, the proceeds are tax free. The herd basis is not available for companies.

The decision as to whether to elect or not depends upon the long-term plans of the individuals in the business and the forecast movement in stock values over the long term. One of the problems of electing is that there will be no tax relief on any reduction in value of the animals.

5.10.2 Election for herd basis – time limits

An election for the herd basis must be seriously considered as it is irrevocable. It can be made when a farmer starts a production herd of a certain class of animal and that class of animal has not been kept by the same individual or group of individuals in the previous five years. It must be made in writing and specify the class of animal. A special form is not available. There are specific time limits to make an election:

(a) *Pre-self-assessment – 1995–96 or earlier*
For sole traders, partnerships or companies, within two years after the end of the first accounting period when that class of production herd is kept or, in a commencement, within two years after the end of the first accounting period.

(b) *Post self assessment – 1996-97 or later*
Within 12 months after the fixed filing date for the year of assessment in which the production herd is first kept.

Where a herd that is not on the herd basis has been compulsorily slaughtered, the opportunity exists to make an election or alternatively elect for the compensation to be spread over the three years following the year in which the compensation is received (**6.2**).

5.10.3 Class of animal

An election will be required for each different class of mature animals. For example, a dairy herd for milk production and a suckler cow herd producing beef calves will be the subject of two elections. Different breeds within each class are ignored. Only mature animals can be subject to herd basis and animals are deemed mature when they give birth for the first time. Immature animals can be included in acclimatised hill sheep flocks where the replacements are bred on the farm.

5.10.4 'Flying' herds or flocks

Herds of cows and flocks of sheep are sometimes kept with individual animals sold at the end of their production cycles, such as dairy cows sold at the end of their lactation, and new cows purchased to replace them. These are termed 'flying' herds or flocks and are not eligible for herd basis.

5.10.5 Change in a partnership

Any change in a partnership, for example, by the introduction of a wife or son, will require a new election for the herd basis. (Tax Bulletin May 1992, p20 and Tax Bulletin June 1997, p42). The Inland Revenue treat the partnership as the farmer and not the individuals within the partnership (ICTA 1988, Sch 5, paras 2(3) and 5). Therefore a farmer (partnership) carrying on a trade before a change is not the same as a farmer (partnership) after the change. If a claim is not made within the time limits the opportunity will be lost and the production animals will be valued as trading stock.

5.10.6 Share farming or shares in individual animals

In November 1990 ESC B37 allowed the herd basis to apply to shares in animals which is common in share farming arrangements (**2.15, 5.11.2**) or shares in such animals as pedigree bulls.

5.10.7 Operation of the herd basis

The initial costs of the animals forming the herd is not an allowable deduction and is excluded from the trading stock valuation, it is dealt with as a herd capital account. (ICTA 1988, Sch 5, para 3).

Unless sufficiently detailed records of production costs are maintained, animals giving birth for the first time are transferred into the herd capital account at their deemed value (**2.17**). If an animal in the herd is replaced by an animal of similar quality, the herd capital account is not altered. The sale proceeds of the animal replaced and the cost of the replacement (if home reared, at deemed value) are dealt with through the trading account.

If the number of animals in the herd is increased, the cost of the additional animals is added to the herd capital account.

If a herd animal is sold and not replaced, the herd capital account is reduced by transferring the cost of the animal to the trading account and the sale proceeds are credited to the trading account.

5.10.8 Sale of the whole or a substantial part of the herd

If more than 20 per cent of the herd is sold in a 12 month period without replacement, the profit or loss arising from the difference between the sale proceeds and the base cost in the herd capital account is not liable to tax as trading profits or as a capital gain.

5.10.9 Replacement of herd

If any animals of the same class are replaced within the following five years they are treated as replacements. Therefore, the sale proceeds of the animals sold in the previous five years are credited to profit when the replacement animals are purchased.

When the whole herd is replaced, any difference in costs or receipts as a result of an increase or decrease in numbers are taken into account in the Schedule D tax computation. If the decrease is 20 per cent or more the profit is not taxable.

5.10.10 Special provisions

Special provisions apply in the following circumstances:

- when the herd is subject to compulsory slaughter (**6.2**);
- when animals of inferior quality are purchased after compulsory slaughter;
- the transfer of a herd between connected parties below commercial value. Anti-avoidance provisions apply as set out in paragraph 5, Schedule 5 ICTA, 1988;
- a change in the purpose of a class of animal on the herd basis; and
- share farming where the herd was previously on herd basis or one of the parties is not eligible.

5.11 Contract and share farming

5.11.1 Introduction

These structures are described in Chapter **2** and the comparison between farm business tenancies and contract farming or contract management agreements are described in Chapter **6**. In practice there are a multitude of agreements operating in the farming industry, many of them with inadequate or no written documentation. Unless the written agreements, and of greater importance, their operation in practice, are very similar to the structures described in Chapter **2**, the client must be warned that the trading as a farming business status may be questioned by the Revenue.

All clients should be encouraged to have all agreements reviewed by a solicitor who has experience in this field.

Correctly constructed agreements which are also followed in practice should achieve the following:

- both parties treated as separate businesses for VAT and tax;
- income assessed under Case 1 of Schedule D for both parties;
- capital gains tax rollover relief;
- capital gains tax retirement relief; and
- agricultural property relief, assuming vacant possession available within the time limits.

5.11.2 Share farming agreements

In practice the amount of income assessable will be similar under Schedule D and Schedule A, but it is the reliefs from capital gains tax and inheritance tax that are important. Care must be taken, as the Revenue may agree that each party is trading separately but their agreement may be restricted to income tax only. They may reserve judgement regarding the capital tax status until after a detailed examination of the agreement, which may not be looked into until an event involving a capital tax occurs and a computation submitted.

Share farming has now become generally acceptable by the Revenue to be trading as a farmer. However, in the past there have been occasions when the whole principle has been questioned.

One of the dangers of an incorrectly constructed agreement, particularly to the landlord, is that a partnership may be formed. In this event the commercial implications are more important than the tax implications.

Agreements that account for all of the income and costs of a farming business could be construed as a partnership, whereas, if only restricted items of costs are included, the agreement may be more related to share farming. It is recommended that all share farming agreements follow the model agreement from the Country Landowners' Association which has had Revenue approval.

5.11.3 Contract farming

A correctly constructed agreement is more straightforward than share farming with one party supplying contracting services to a landowner (**2.15**).

Most contractors involved in these agreements also farm in their own right, therefore their contracting income is in addition to their income from the trade of farming which, depending upon the relative amounts, will be accepted as farming income (**5.2**). Contractors that do not farm land and derive all of their income from contract farming arrangements will be treated by the Revenue as contractors and not farmers. This will still be taxed as Case 1, Schedule D but averaging provisions (**5.4**) will not be available. Clients with substantial contract farming income should be warned that a proportion of their income may not be treated as the trade of farming, and the contracting income may have to be excluded in any averaging calculations.

There may be VAT implications for clients with substantial contracting income, this is discussed in **5.17**.

5.12 Employees

5.12.1 Introduction

The minimum wages of agricultural workers are set out in *The Agricultural Wages Order* which is published at least annually and usually operative from the first of June each year. Two wages orders were published in 1999; Number 1 effective from 1 April 1999 dealing with the National Minimum Wage and Number 2 proposed from 1 June 1999. Although the minimum rates of wages are below £8,500 per annum for some age and grade categories, most full-time agricultural workers earn more than £8,500 including taxable benefits per annum. The value of benefits are applicable to PAYE and NIC.

5.12.2 Housing

It has been customary for employers to provide free housing for agricultural workers, however, as more farmers are aware of the value of commercial rental income of cottages an increasing number of farm employees are now encouraged to purchase or rent houses independently.

Most agricultural workers irrespective of the level of their remuneration, other than company directors, are exempt from tax on the value of living accommodation as long as they satisfy that they have to live in that particular property for the better performance of their duties (TA s145(4)(a)). The employee is therefore the representative occupier for the employer. This exemption also extends to council tax but did not extend to community charge. It may be difficult to claim that a worker who lives in a property away from the farm is living there for the better performance of duties.

Company directors who own more than 5 per cent of the shares or are not full-time working directors will be assessed on the rental value of any accommodation provided by the company.

5.12.3 Board and lodging

There is provision for the value of free board and lodging, for employees who earn less than £8,500, provided either by the farmer or somebody else, not to be treated as part of the pay for PAYE purposes (ESC A60). To be eligible, the worker must only receive the net cash wage and the farmer either retains the amount for board and lodging or pays it direct to a third party. The Revenue will accept the employee's mother as a third party but not a spouse. The national minimum wage regulations are now incorporated in the 1999 (Number 1) Wages Order. Only £19.95 is allowed to be deducted for lodging alone, compared with the previous £62.28 board and lodging deduction.

Employees who earn more than £8,500 will be taxed on the value of free board and lodging and included on the form P11D. It is still advisable to pay the employee the net cash wage and include the value of board and lodging on form P11D as the value will then not be subject to NIC.

The value or cost of board and lodging is an allowable expense of the farming business.

5.12.4 Other benefits

There are a number of other benefits that can be provided for the personal use of employees and their families earning less than £8,500 per annum without incurring any tax. These include farm produce such as vegetables and milk, and fuel and grazing such as free grazing for family ponies.

Employees earning more than £8,500 are taxed on the value of all benefits apart from free or subsidised housing referred to in paragraph **5.12.2** above.

5.13 Casual workers

The Agricultural Wages Board in the Agricultural Wages Order define a casual worker as a worker who is employed on a temporary basis by the hour or day to undertake specific tasks and who has not been continuously employed for more than 20 weeks excluding any holiday entitlement. The order sets out the minimum rate of pay per hour according to the age of the worker.

With the general reduction in full-time workers employed in agriculture there is an increasing number of part-time or casual employees including the sharing of employees between two or more businesses. Farmers take on additional staff during peak work periods such as harvesting or lambing. Farms that grow vegetables and fruit in particular sometimes employ large numbers of casual workers. Tax evasion has been a problem in these situations and the Revenue have liaised with the DSS, NFU and other interested parties to attempt to produce guidelines which can be operated in practice. In principle PAYE has to be applied to all workers with some agreed exceptions:

- payments made to gang masters who supply large numbers of casual workers;
- students who complete the declaration on form P38(S);
- workers who complete form P46 where they earn less than the PAYE threshold;
- daily casual workers who are employed for one day and paid at the end of the day; and
- self-employed workers. There is a difficult distinction between employed and self-employed workers in some situations and the employer should verify with the tax office that they accept the self-employed status of the worker.

In all situations where PAYE has not been deducted the farmer should maintain records of names, addresses and amounts paid so that a return can be made to the Revenue. The National Farmers' Union has been liaising with the NI Contributions Agency in 1998 regarding the practical difficulties facing farmers. As a result local contributions agency inspectors have been issued with guidelines informing them to take account of the practical difficulties farmers have with identifying harvest casual workers.

5.14 Quotas

5.14.1 Introduction

A quota system exists for various commodities and functions in several ways. In all cases the quota are treated by the Revenue as capital assets and are subject to capital gains tax and inheritance tax and the standard qualifications for reliefs. The current quotas are:

- suckler cow quota allowing a producer to claim headage payments on suckler cows;
- sheep quota allowing a producer to claim headage payments on ewes and ewe lambs;
- milk quota, which allows dairy farmers to produce a certain amount of milk per annum without having to pay a levy termed 'superlevy';
- potato quota. All restrictions relating to potato quota have been abolished as from 1996 resulting in the quota having no value; and
- sugar beat quota which does not trade.

All quota apart from sugar beat quota can be leased or sold between different farmers subject to specific trading periods. For tax purposes there are two types of transaction: temporary transfers and permanent transfers. 'Back to back' transactions are increasingly used whereby 'used' (sometimes termed 'dirty') quota is sold and 'unused' (sometimes termed 'clean') quota purchased on the same day.

5.14.2 Temporary transfer of quota

Temporary transfer is when the quota reverts back to the original owner at the end of the agreement period. This is normally for a 12 month period, however, there are some milk quota temporary transfers for periods up to three years. In these instances the receipts and payments are not capital. The expenditure for leasing in quota is an allowable deduction. How the receipt for leasing out quota is treated depends upon the individual circumstances. If the quota is leased out because it is only temporarily surplus to the business it will normally be treated as Schedule D Case 1. If, however, the enterprise to which the quota relates has ceased and the quota not been sold, for example, the sale of a suckler herd or a dairy herd, the income for leasing out the quota will probably be treated under Schedule D Case VI.

5.14.3 Permanent transfer of quota

These are sales and purchases of capital assets and in the case of milk quota can be subject to very complex rules with a substantial amount of case law (**6.5**). The same principles apply as set out in **5.14.2**; if the enterprise ceases and the quota is leased to another producer, the asset is no longer used in the business of farming and is therefore not eligible for retirement relief and agricultural property relief. Roll-over relief may be restricted to the proportional time the asset was used in the business (**6.5**).

5.14.4 Back-to-back transactions

In order to obtain additional milk quota in a production year to meet actual milk production it is possible for a milk producer to purchase unused quota and sell used quota for a lower price on the same day. In commercial terms the difference in price can be compared with the cost of leasing additional quota; both methods achieving the same result of acquiring additional quota for incresed milk production.

These are capital transactions and governed by the pooling rules for securities (TCGA 1992, s104) for quota acquired prior to 6 April 1998 (**6.5.9**). The changes to the pooling rules (FA 1998) ceased the pooling of milk quota for quota purchased on or after 6 April 1998. Therefore 'back-to-back' transactions of quota since 6 April 1998 will not be pooled and subject to a last in/first out basis.

5.14.5 Potato quota

Potato quota now has nil value, therefore a claim for the capital loss should be considered under Section 24(2), Taxation of Chargeable Gains Act 1982. The loss is calculated with reference to either the purchase price or the value at 31 March 1982. In order to fully utilise annual exemptions available to individuals, this should only be considered in a year when there are chargeable gains above the annual exemption or no gains. It may be advisable for companies to claim a loss as soon as possible. The quota must be in existence and of negligible value when the claim is made, therefore once the Potato Marketing Scheme ceases to exist, the quota will no longer exist and a claim may not be accepted.

5.15 Capital gains tax

5.15.1 Introduction

There has been a considerable increase in the value of agricultural land and property over the past few years which has resulted in a substantial increase in tax liabilities on the disposal of assets. The downturn in the profitability of agriculture has had a dampening effect on the price of land in some geographic areas, however, there is still a reasonably strong demand from neighbouring farmers and properties with residential value.

There are a number of reliefs available from capital gains tax and their application to farming assets are discussed below. As in all capital tax planning, farming clients should be encouraged to discuss their plans and wishes with their accountant at the earliest opportunity and preferably a few years before any transactions and disposals occur.

Capital gains tax planning in relation to agricultural assets has become complex, in particular in relation to milk quota and when land has been, or is, subject to tenancies. In these instances unless the accountancy practice has the relevant experience and expertise it is advisable to seek assistance from a suitable individual or firm, either another accountant or a solicitor. In some instances a suitably qualified land agent may also be required.

The interaction of capital gains tax and inheritance tax should not be overlooked in planning the handing down of assets within a farming family. With 100 per cent agricultural property relief available on farming assets, including tenanted land since 1 September 1995, consideration should be given to passing down the assets on death rather than a lifetime transfer, therefore benefiting from the tax-free base uplift for future capital gains purposes.

There is no capital gains tax on any disposals between husband and wife.

5.15.2 Roll-over relief

The standard rules apply to agricultural assets (TCGA 1992 s152). Care must be taken to ensure that the asset disposed is eligible. For example, assets not used in the trade would be quota leased out (**6.5.10**), and in some circumstances properties let outside agriculture.

The use of this relief and also Hold over relief (**5.15.8**) is very important in tax planning in agriculture and is often used. There is no limit to the number of times a gain can be rolled over, therefore assets sometimes have a complicated cost history. Therefore it is important to investigate the full cost history of assets prior to sale, paying particular attention to:

- March 1982 values;
- previous gains rolled over;

- previous gains held over;
- probate values;
- tenancies including the value of a tenancy to a tenant.

Taper relief (FA 1998) (**5.15.6**) is not available on the base cost of assets rolled over or held over.

Land subject to a tenancy including family tenancies is normally not eligible however. Statement of Practice D11 (SPD11) allows relief to the owners of assets let to a trading partnership of which they are a member. Business taper relief would also apply in these circumstances. The asset must be used for the purpose of the trade and satisfy all other conditions.

Qualifying agricultural assets for reinvestment include:

- land and buildings;
- fixed plant (relief for ten years or until sold without replacement);
- milk quota;
- ewe and suckler cow premium quota;
- fishing licences; and
- furnished holiday letting.

Care must be taken, particularly with the self-assessment rules, when roll-over relief is claimed on the purchase of complete farm units. Full relief is often claimed successfully on the total purchase price, however, some of the purchased assets may be fixed plant and subject to the ten year rule.

It is common for agricultural land to be jointly owned by members of a family. Extra Statutory Concession D26 allows relief for the joint interests in land (including tenanted land) and milk quota to be partitioned to individuals.

Roll-over relief is not available in respect of a gain arising on the disposal of part of an asset within 12 months of its purchase as a single asset (*Watton* v *Tippett*, 1996). The remaining asset cannot be treated as a new asset. Consideration should be given to separating assets prior to acquisition when there is a possibility of sales taking place within a 12 month period resulting in a gain.

Therefore it is important to plan ahead before any intending sale, gift or restructuring of assets and in many cases a second opinion may be advisable to ensure the most efficient use of reliefs.

5.15.3 Retirement relief

This relief is particularly useful for individuals involved in farming businesses as the business usually consists of a number of enterprises and the land can be used for several sources of income. It is important to distinguish between:

- a disposal of part of the business – relief is available;
- a disposal of business assets – relief is not available.

The important point is whether or not a disposal involves sufficient 'interference' with the whole business to constitute a disposal of part of the business.

Therefore it is possible for a farmer to dispose of a substantial part of the business excluding the land and carry on the trade of farming (*McGregor* v *Adcock*, 1977). In particular, this applies to a dairy farmer retiring and selling the dairy herd and milk quota, and using the land for another enterprise. Each case will be considered on its own merits and particular care must be taken with the timing of the disposal of assets in this situation as relief can be denied. (*Wase* v *Bourke*, 22 November 1995) (**6.5.3**).

Relief is also due where shares in a family company are disposed of or where an asset is sold which was used rent-free in a family business.

In some instances it is important to consider the interaction of retirement relief and hold over relief. Retirement relief, being an exemption, has priority and it may not always be desirable to use the retirement relief. This may be overcome by transferring the asset to a spouse not eligible for retirement relief before gifting.

Retirement relief is being phased out over the period 1999 to 2003 at 20 per cent per annum being replaced with taper relief (**5.15.6**). Taper relief will not have full effect until the tax year 2007/08 while retirement relief will be abolished from 2003/4. Therefore planning for retirement in the ten year phasing period (1998/9 to 2007/8) needs careful consideration. In general terms, taxable gains peak in 2003/4 but depend upon the extent of the gain. Over the ten year period gains below £500,000 result in a higher taxable amount whilst gains above £500,000 result in a lower taxable amount. However, each case will need to be individually considered as there are ownership and indexation issues that need to be taken into consideration.

5.15.4 Reinvestment relief

Capital gains tax can be deferred on the sale of assets, providing that proceeds equal to the capital gain are reinvested in ordinary shares in unquoted trading companies. Prior to 29 November 1994, shares in farming companies did not qualify and the value of the company's interests in land had to be less than half the total asset value of the company. These restrictions were abolished as from 20 November 1994 which opened up tax planning opportunities and it was possible to roll over from any disposal into a qualifying company which included farming, property development and commercial shooting as eligible trades. Individuals or trustees who sold assets subject to substantial capital gains were able to issue shares in a newly formed company equal to the capital gain and purchase farmland with the resultant cash in the company. This offered scope for tax planning within family businesses and possibly contributed to the increase in land values in some areas.

With effect from 6 April 1998 (FA 1998 s12(1)) farming, market gardening, forestry and other property based activities are excluded trades.

5.15.5 Indexation

For the period from 30 November 1993 to 5 April 1995, capital losses arising from indexation allowance were restricted to a maximum of £10,000. From 6 April 1995 indexation allowance is not available to create or increase a capital loss. Therefore the scope for using indexation to create capital losses by transferring assets with potential gain including their associated losses into trust has been lost. Indexation from 31 March 1982 to 5 April 1998 is in the region of 100 per cent, therefore it is important to ensure that indexation is fully utilised in all asset sales as shown in Example 5.2.

With the introduction of taper relief, indexation relief has been frozen for individuals and trustees as from 6 April 1998, but will continue to apply to gains subject to corporation tax.

5.15.6 Taper relief

Introduced in FA 1998 replacing indexation and retirement relief. Relief is available at different rates for business and non-business assets. The new taper relief may be advantageous to assets that have a nil or very low base cost such as land previously subject to a tenancy and milk quota with a nil base value. As discussed in **5.15.2**, roll over and hold over are very common reliefs used in agriculture. Taper relief starts at zero with the change of ownership, apart from transfers between spouses (FA 1998

217

sch 20 (15). Therefore care needs to be taken in planning reorganisations and replacement of assets.

5.15.7 Part disposals

Relief for part disposals of land may be available provided that proceeds are less than:

- 20 per cent of the current market value of holding before disposal; and
- proceeds are less than £20,000.

A part disposal formula can be used to allocate a base cost to a part of a single asset where previous disposals, if any, have not been treated as separate assets. This method works particularly well with the sale of relatively high value assets, such as cottages or small blocks of land with planning permission. The calculated base cost should be deducted from the cost or value in March 1982 of the remaining asset. The Revenue must be satisfied that the asset is a single asset.

(Sale proceeds) divided by (sale proceeds added to the value retained) multiplied by (total 1982 value)

or

$$\frac{A}{A + B} \times \text{Total 1982 value}$$

Where A is the sale proceeds and B is the value retained.

Example 5.2 *Part disposal calculation*

This example disregards the possible availability of retirement relief, taper relief and rollover relief.

A farmer wishes to sell two cottages which were purchased or acquired together with 200 acres of agricultural land as one unit prior to 1982.

The 1982 values are

200 acres at £2,000 per acre	400,000
2 cottages at £10,000 each	20,000

Current values are

200 acres at £2,500 per acre	500,000
2 cottages at £60,000 each	120,000
The cottages are sold at £60,000 each	120,000

It can be seen that the sale of the cottages as a single asset will give rise to a capital gain of £80,000 being £120,000 less the indexed base value at 100 per cent of £40,000.

The part disposal calculation

$$\frac{120,000}{120,000 + 500,000} \times 420,000 \qquad\qquad 81,290$$

Indexation at say 100%	81,290
Indexed base value	162,580
Proceeds	120,000
Notional loss on cottages	42,580
Capital gains tax	NIL

5.15.8 Hold over relief

Capital gains tax can be deferred on the gift of assets which are qualifying at the time of the gift between individuals, including the following:

- business assets including shares in unquoted trading companies;
- land and buildings qualifying for agricultural property relief for inheritance tax purposes;
- heritage properties and maintenance funds; and
- gifts with an immediate charge to inheritance tax.

It is important to explain to the recipients that any gain has been deferred until a subsequent disposal of the asset.

Taper relief is not available on held over gains therefore it may not be beneficial to claim hold over if the asset may be sold.

5.15.9 Agricultural tenancies

Statutory compensation is normally available when a tenant protected by the Agricultural Holdings Acts is given a valid notice to quit. The compensation is up to five or six times the annual rent of the farm and will not give rise to capital gains tax liability (*Davis* v *Powell*, 1977). A payment received by a tenant as compensation for a voluntary surrender of a tenancy may be chargeable to capital gains tax, therefore great care must be taken by tenants to fulfil all of the requirements for the statutory compensation procedures.

The key issue regarding capital gains tax is the value of the tenancy upon disposal and its base value as at 31 March 1982. There have been several cases on this subject and the valuation of a tenancy for tax purposes is still subject to considerable debate. In practice the grant of a tenancy for a full rent is not a disposal by the landlord. Therefore tenancies granted since March 1982 are likely to have a nil base value and any subsequent surrender may lead to a chargeable gain. This is a complex area and the appropriate professional assistance should be sought in all cases to avoid missing any opportunities.

5.15.10 Machinery

Plant and machinery are subject to capital gains and losses. Prior to 29 November 1993, indexation could be taken into account in calculating capital losses and restricted to a maximum of £10,000 to 5 April 1995. On large items of machinery it may be worthwhile claiming any calculated losses.

5.15.11 Trading losses

Trading losses in a farming business can be used to offset a capital gain incurred by the same individual. Losses from the same year or preceding year to the gain can be used (s72 FA 1991). It should be noted that losses must be used initially against income and any remaining losses set against a capital gain. Trading losses take priority over the annual exemption, therefore, depending upon the amounts, care must be taken to fully utilise the exemption. Farming companies, in general, have greater flexibility in their use of trading losses against capital gains.

5.16 Inheritance tax

5.16.1 Introduction

Inheritance tax is charged on both death and lifetime transfers (IHT Act 1984). However, there are several reliefs available which in most cases and with prudent planning, will minimise the impact of this tax on farming families.

5.16.2 Agricultural property relief (APR)

This is available by reducing the agricultural value (IHTA 1984 s115(3)) of eligible agricultural property, subject to qualifying conditions, by:

- 100 per cent relief for land with vacant possession or subject to a tenancy taken out after 1 September 1995;
- 50 per cent relief for all other land.

The relief is only available on the agricultural value of property, therefore any enhanced value such as hope or amenity value is not subject to the relief. In this instance business property relief may apply.

5.16.3 Agricultural property eligible for APR (IHTA 1984 s115(2))

This includes:

- undeveloped agricultural land;
- farmhouses, including land occupied with the house that is of a character appropriate to the property;
- cottages and farm buildings including buildings used with intensive livestock and fish farming, again of a character appropriate to the property;
- woodland ancillary to the agricultural land;
- sporting rights but not fishing rights;
- property used for the grazing and breeding of horses on stud farms;
- shares to the extent where they reflect the value of the property within the company;
- milk quota included in the value of agricultural land may be eligible; and
- short rotation coppice from 6 April 1995 (FA 1995, s154(2),(3),(5)).

The Revenue's current internal guidelines (CTO Manual L.231) on the elegibility of farmhouses state that the case should be referred internally where there is a farming business but the following apply:

221

- the amount of land occupied either as owner or tenant is small (less than 20 acres);
- the farmhouse is valuable (over £250,000) and the land farmed is less than 100 acres.

5.16.4 Occupation of agricultural property to be eligible for APR

The relief is only available subject to occupancy conditions. The agricultural property must have been occupied for the purposes of agriculture as follows:

(a)   owner occupiers who have occupied the property for the purposes of agriculture in the previous two years prior to transfer. This occupation can be with other partners or by a company where the owner has control of the company (IHTA 1984 s117(a)); or

(b)   the property must have been owned in the seven year period ending with the transfer (IHTA 1984 s117 (b)).

These periods of occupation can be transferred between spouses on death.

5.16.5 Vacant possession

Agricultural Property Relief is available at 100 per cent on agricultural property subject to vacant possession or the right to it within 12 months (IHTA 1984 s116(2)(a)). The 12-month period is extended to 24 months by ESC F17 for transfers after 13 February 1995. Where vacant possession is not available within these time limits the relief is available at 50 per cent. This is particularly important in family partnerships where the relief may be lost when assets are handed down to the younger generation and the occupancy tests are not satisfied. Land that is share farmed or contract farmed under a correctly constructed agreement will normally qualify as being occupied (**2.15**).

5.16.6 Tenancies

Land subject to a tenancy commenced after 1 September 1995 is nearly always eligible for 100 per cent APR subject to the ownership and occupancy conditions being satisfied. Where an agricultural tenancy is surrendered it is generally considered that a transfer of value is being made. This is a very complex area covered by s10 IHTA 1984. There are also capital gains tax implications on the surrender of tenancies. The grant of a tenancy for full commercial consideration is not normally a transfer of value for inheritance tax purposes.

The Revenue have argued for many years that a value attaches to agricultural tenancies. The Revenue base their arguments around a hypothetical sale of an assignable tenancy in an open market situation. The value of a tenancy has been generally considered to be 50 per cent of the difference between the vacant possession value and the tenanted value of the land. Land let on an agricultural tenancy prior to 1 September 1995 is generally considered to have a value in the region of 50 per cent of the full vacant possession value. Therefore, based on these assumptions, it can be argued that the value of the tenancy is 25 per cent of the vacant possession value. This method of valuation has recently been challenged in the courts (*Walton* v *CIR*, 1996) (**6.11**).

5.16.7 Potentially Exempt Transfers (PET)

Lifetime transfers are normally treated as Potentially Exempt Transfers with the tax only becoming payable when the transferor dies within seven years of making the gift. The availability of APR at 100 per cent, whilst it continues at that rate, makes a PET of less importance.

5.16.8 Business Property Relief (BPR)

Agricultural property relief takes precedent over BPR. BPR will be applicable to the assets in the farming business other than those eligible for APR, subject to the normal qualifying conditions. It should be noted that APR is only available on the agricultural value of property.

5.16.9 Reservation of benefit

This is of particular importance in farming family partnerships. Where the donee continues to benefit from the asset after making the gift, the gift is not considered to be a transfer of an asset for inheritance tax purposes. There are several methods of overcoming this; however, it is of less importance with 100 per cent APR as an owner can retain assets until death and obtain the full relief at that stage.

5.16.10 Double discount relief

This is also sometimes referred to as transitional relief and applies to tenanted land that qualified for full-time working farmer relief prior to 10 March 1981. Subject to the tenancy remaining in force since 10 March 1981 to the date of transfer, and the right to vacant possession not being available, 100 per cent relief is available against the tenanted value on the first transfer. Many of these exist within the industry and in most circumstances they should be maintained. There are several issues that are relevant in tax planning relating to this relief. Initially every effort should be made to preserve the tenancies, the relief is subject to

the previous working farmer relief restrictions of a maximum of
£250,000 or 1,000 acres and care must be taken not to utilise the relief
on inter-spouse lifetime transfers.

5.16.11 Assets charged as security on borrowings

Consideration should be given to charging assets that are not eligible for
APR or BPR as borrowings secured against specific assets will effectively
reduce their value for IHT purposes (IHT Act 1984 s162(4)). By con-
structing borrowings in this way and whilst 100 per cent APR and BPR
relief is available the total liability to IHT may be reduced. This could be
put in place by the lender including a clause in a loan agreement stating
that a loan is charged firstly against a specific asset or property (not
subject to APR/BPR), secondly against a possible further asset or property (not subject to APR/BPR), and in so far that the proceeds of these
assets are insufficient to discharge the loan then against other assets of
the business. Therefore, the lender is prioritising the charges on the
assets that would normally be subject to IHT.

5.17 Value added tax (VAT)

5.17.1 Introduction

Farming is a taxable business activity which must be registered for VAT
where taxable supplies exceed the VAT threshold. Many of the sales
from farming businesses are zero-rated whilst the costs are standard
rated, therefore most farming businesses will be net reclaimers of VAT.

All farm owners derive the vast majority of their income from the land
they own or lease. Where this land is farmed in hand, the VAT consequences are relatively straightforward.

Where the land is farmed by someone else, where farmland is being
bought or sold, or where agricultural land and buildings are being put to
a non-farming use, the VAT consequences are more complicated.

Most farmers account for VAT on a monthly or quarterly basis. Many
operate an accounting system based on cash as opposed to a double
entry system (**4.3.7**). Customs and Excise normally accept this practice
as most farmers are net reclaimers of VAT and the net VAT is reclaimed
at a later date than it would normally be. However, they will expect VAT
to be paid on standard-rated sales when goods or services are sold, not
when payment is received, for example, contracting services.

5.17.2 Registration

VAT registration is obligatory where the value of taxable (i.e., standard rated plus zero-rated) supplies is above a certain limit (the VAT Registration Limit).

Currently the VAT Registration Limit is £50,000. Farmers with annual taxable income above this limit are obliged to be registered.

Farmers with annual taxable income below this limit can voluntarily register for the tax.

The main benefit of being VAT registered is the ability to reclaim VAT incurred on purchase.

Farmers with taxable supplies above the registration limit making mainly zero-rated supplies who do not wish to be VAT registered can apply for exemption from registration.

Farmers who choose exemption from registration give up their ability to reclaim VAT on purchases. However, they avoid the administrative burden of keeping VAT records or submitting VAT returns.

Alternatively, farmers who wish to avoid the administrative burden of VAT registration can opt to join the flat rate scheme (**5.17.15**).

5.17.3 VAT on sales

VAT is a tax on supplies made in the UK for a consideration where the person engaged in making those supplies does so by way of business. The amount of tax due on such supplies depends upon the VAT liability of the supplies being made.

Currently the VAT liability of supplies made by farmers will be either:

- taxable at   standard rate – currently 17.5 per cent
  zero rate   – currently 0 per cent
- exempt   no VAT to charge

All supplies made by farmers will be subject to VAT at the standard rate unless specifically zero-rated or exempted.

Broadly speaking, farmers can zero-rate:

- food of a kind used for human consumption. At present Customs accept that industrial crops grown on set-aside land are zero-rated, provided the produce is of a type normally grown for food etc., (for example industrial oil seed rape);

- animal feeding stuffs (but not pet food). Includes grass keep agreement other than that seen twice daily (**6.4**);
- seeds used to propagate food for humans or animals, but does not include pre-germinated grass seed; and
- live animals which are used to produce food for human consumption.

5.17.4 VAT on land transactions

The sale of, granting a right over, or licence to occupy agricultural land or buildings would normally be exempt from VAT.

Broadly speaking exemption applies to:

- sales of freehold;
- agricultural tenancies;
- farm business tenancies;
- mineral rights; and
- cottage rents but not holiday cottages.

5.17.5 Exclusions to exemptions

Specifically excluded from exemption and, therefore, automatically subject to VAT at the standard rate are, amongst others:

- sale of farm buildings less than three years old;
- the right, licence, etc., to take fish or game;
- holiday or bed and breakfast accommodation;
- seasonal caravan pitches;
- camping facilities;
- parking facilities; and
- the right to fell and remove standing timber.

'Land' includes anything attaching to the land. Therefore, the sale of land with standing crops is, potentially, exempt from VAT.

5.17.6 Opting to tax

Since 1 August 1989 it has been possible to change the liability of exempt land transactions. This involves 'opting to tax'. Transactions involving 'opted' land are normally subject to VAT at the standard rate. Extreme care needs to be applied when opting to tax, particularly as there is extremely complicated anti-avoidance legislation in this area.

Opting to tax has the benefit of allowing the farmer to recover any VAT incurred on expenses relating to the land transactions (**5.17.4**).

The option to tax should, therefore, be considered where significant costs are likely to be incurred; for example, converting buildings from agricultural to non-agricultural use, selling development land for which planning permission has been acquired, etc.

5.17.7 Other income

All other income received by a VAT registered farmer is, potentially, liable to VAT at the standard rate. For example:

- grass keep agreements where stock is looked after and seen twice a day or more (**6.4**);
- contracting work;
- supply of staff;
- sale of fertilisers and manure;
- sale of farm equipment;
- sale of sheep dogs;
- sale of horses;
- full livery for horses (DIY livery will be either exempt, zero rated or a mixture of the two);
- shooting rights;
- fishing rights;
- bed and breakfast;
- holiday accommodation;
- sale of quotas without land (**5.17.10**);
- sale of firewood; and
- sale of straw is zero rated unless the straw is specifically held out for sale as only suitable for bedding or not suitable for feeding animals.

5.17.8 VAT on purchases

VAT can be reclaimed on purchases made by a farmer provided:

- the farmer receives the benefit of the goods or services purchased; and
- the purchase is made for business, as opposed to private, purposes;
- the goods or services purchased are used to make taxable (as opposed to exempt or outside the scope) supplies; and
- the farmer holds a VAT invoice from the supplier.

VAT cannot be reclaimed on the following items, even though the conditions above may have been satisfied:

- the purchase of a motor car, other than those used exclusively for business, e.g., pool cars (n.b., 'cars' include most range rovers and many models of land rovers, jeeps, twin cab pickups etc.);
- 50 per cent of the VAT incurred on the lease hire of a motor car;
- business entertaining;
- domestic accommodation (including farmhouses) provided to company directors and their immediate family (but see also **5.17.13** below); and
- business gifts.

5.17.9 Hire purchase, leasing and contract hire

There are differences between the VAT treatment of hire purchase and lease payments. In essence the purchaser under a hire purchase agreement contract can, subject to the normal requirements, claim input VAT on the capital cost of the equipment purchased at the time of supply. Conversely, the lessee under a finance or operating lease agreement can claim only the input VAT on the instalments as and when they fall due, again subject to the normal rules.

There are restrictions on claims for input VAT where there is a non-business use of the assets. It is important to ensure that clients have a system that both distinguishes between hire purchase, finance and operating lease agreements in their accounting records and copes with the different VAT treatments.

The rules for VAT recovery on cars were significantly altered with effect from 1 August 1995. Prior to that date, apart from certain limited circumstances, VAT incurred on the purchase of a new car could not be recovered. Farming businesses could, however, recover the business portion of VAT charged on lease rentals. The new rules in summary are:

(a) businesses which purchase cars wholly for business use will be able to reclaim all of the VAT on the purchase price. This will apply mainly to leasing companies and businesses with pool cars;
(b) if there is any non-business use, then all of the VAT on a car purchase is irrecoverable.

5.17.10 Milk quota

The treatment of VAT on milk quota transactions was defined on 1 April 1994 (Dairy Produce Quotas Regulations 1994).

The following transactions are standard rated:

- sale of quota without land;
- sale of quota with a grazing agreement;
- leasing of quota without land; and
- sale of quota with land where the landowner has elected to register for VAT on land transactions as discussed in **5.14.3** above.

The following transactions are exempt or outside the scope of VAT:

- sale of quota with land;
- sale of quota with a short term tenancy;
- payment by landlord to a tenant as compensation following a notice to quit or following a voluntary surrender; and
- compensation for temporary and permanent quota cuts and SLOM.

5.17.11 Grants

In the UK, agricultural grants are currently treated as being outside the scope of VAT.

This treatment is consistent with rulings given by the European Court of Justice in two recent cases involving German farmers being paid to cease or reduce production. In both cases the decision was that because there was no consumption (i.e., reducing or ceasing production was for the general benefit of the community as a whole) there was no supply liable to VAT.

However, as with recent cases in the UK regarding grant payments made under the Home Energy Efficiency Scheme, the implication is that if the payment of the grant results in a supply to a specific consumer the payments are subject to normal VAT rules.

At the time of writing, and as a result of the cases brought by the German VAT authorities, a review of the VAT treatment of agricultural grants is being undertaken.

It is expected that the conclusions of this review will be the same as those reached by the ECJ.

Provided the recipient of a grant continues to pursue a business activity subject to VAT, VAT incurred on expenses should be reclaimable, subject to the normal rules.

5.17.12 Partial exemption

Farmers who receive exempt income (**5.17.4**, **5.17.5**) are 'partly exempt'.

Partly exempt businesses cannot, normally, reclaim all of the VAT they incur on purchases.

Farmers making exempt supplies may, therefore, be unable to reclaim all of the VAT incurred on their business expenses.

However, where VAT on such expenses is relatively small, full recovery may be possible.

Currently full recovery is allowed where VAT on purchases used to make exempt supplies is *both:*

- less than £625 per month on average; the average being established over a period of 12 months, therefore totalling £7,500; and
- less than 50 per cent of all VAT incurred on purchases.

5.17.13 Common problem areas with purchases

Particular problems arise over the recovery of VAT on purchases by farmers and landowners in the following areas:

(a) repair and maintenance of farmhouses. Customs now accept claims of up to 70 per cent of the VAT incurred by sole proprietors and partnerships. Limited companies are likely to be restricted to a far lesser proportion, and may be unable to reclaim any at all (see **5.17.8** above);
(b) telephone expenses, an apportionment for private use is required;
(c) heating and lighting expenses (an apportionment for private use is required);
(d) landlord's contributions to capital projects;
(e) capital goods (**5.17.14**);
(f) business assets put to a private use.

5.17.14 Capital goods scheme

Buildings, extensions to buildings and building refurbishments costing more than £250,000 are subject to the capital goods scheme.

Under this scheme the recovery of any VAT incurred on the purchase or construction of the building is reviewed over a ten-year period. Buildings which are extended or substantially reconstructed may also be subject to the capital goods scheme.

Any change in the use of the building during that ten-year period may result in a claw back of some of the VAT originally reclaimed on the purchase or construction of the building.

This claw back of VAT may apply even if the building was constructed by the previous tenant or landowner.

Care is, therefore, needed when, for example, selling agricultural buildings or converting them to non-agricultural uses.

5.17.15 Agricultural flat rate scheme

Any business involved in crop production, stock farming, forestry, fisheries or supplying agricultural services can apply to join the flat rate scheme.

Those who qualify for the scheme have their VAT registration cancelled and are allowed to add a 'flat rate addition' of four per cent to all sales made to VAT registered customers.

This flat rate addition is retained by the farmer but reclaimed from Customs by the customer.

The retention of the flat rate by a flat rate farmer is designed to recompense them for being unable to reclaim any VAT incurred on expenses.

As net reclaimers of VAT, not many farmers have chosen to join the scheme. However, significant benefits may be available to farmers whose produce is subject to VAT at the standard rate and which is sold direct to the public, e.g., nurseries, horse breeders, maggot farmers, etc.

5.17.16 Common problem areas with VAT

(a) Farmers need to consider carefully the VAT consequences of part exchange deals and barter deals.
(b) Farmers should ensure that they account for VAT at the right time on standard rated supplies. Except where trading income is below £350,000 per year, Customs will expect VAT to be accounted for at the time of sale not the date payment is received.
(c) Where equipment is being purchased on credit finance the farmer needs to know whether the agreement is HP, lease purchase or lease

hire. Generally, VAT on HP and lease purchase deals can be reclaimed at the start of the agreement. VAT on equipment purchased on lease hire can only be reclaimed each time an instalment payment is made.

(d) Contract and share farming agreements often involve transactions between the landowner and the contractor or share farmer. Some of these transactions involve seeds, fertilisers and sprays, in addition to contracting services, and the VAT must be accounted for where appropriate.

(e) Approved alterations made to listed buildings used as houses, flats, etc., should not attract VAT. Landowners or farmers who own or occupy listed houses or cottages should ensure that they do not pay VAT unnecessarily on the cost of any alterations.

(f) It should also be possible to avoid VAT on the costs of converting agricultural buildings, e.g., barns, into houses, flats, etc. However, professional advice is recommended to ensure that the necessary transactions are properly structured.

(g) Where income subject to VAT at the standard rate is below the VAT Registration Limit, consideration should be given to running a separate business for those activities, e.g., the farmer's wife running a separate bed and breakfast business. However, care must be taken to ensure that the two businesses are financially and administratively separate. Failure to do so could result in Customs treating the two businesses as one for VAT purposes and demanding VAT on the standard-rated income (**5.17.17**).

(h) Special rules apply to racehorse owners, with different treatment accorded to breeders and trainers. Farmers and landowners who own, breed or train racehorses, therefore need to ensure that they meet the terms of these rules before reclaiming any VAT incurred on their racing, breeding or training activities.

5.17.17 Artificial separation of business activities

HM Customs and Excise issued Notice 700/61 in June 1997 on the artificial separation of business activities to remain below registration thresholds (FA 1997 s31). The new measures focus on the affect rather than the reason for the separation and a direction can only be made when:

- the separation results in the avoidance of VAT;
- the separation is artificial;
- the parties involved have close financial and economic links.

The following are advisable when running a separate business alongside

the main farming business and a certain amount of discipline is required
to maintain them:

- separate bank account;
- separate books maintained and separate accounts prepared;
- there should be no cross subsidisation.

Customs and Excise will be looking for the following links between the
main farm business and the other activity such as bed and breakfast:

(a) Financial links such as one business relying on the profit from the
    other. One business would not be financially viable without the other.
(b) Economic links where the activities of one business benefit the other
    and they both have the same economic objective.
(c) Organisational links where the two businessses have shared manage-
    ment, employees, equipment and premises.

5.17.18 Shooting syndicates

Since Lord Fisher's case (*C & E Commissioners* v *Lord Fisher* (1981) STC
238) it has been possible to run a shooting syndicate on a farm outside
the scope of VAT. However, a more recent case reversed this decision
(*J O Williams* v *C & E Commissioners* LON/95/2173A).

In simple terms a syndicate who share the costs of a shoot would
normally be regarded as not making taxable supplies. Following Lord
Fisher, Customs & Excise provided guidelines on 7 April 1981 indicating
the requirements for a shoot not to be treated as a business activity:

- only relatives and close friends are allowed to shoot;
- the shoot must not be advertised;
- the landowner makes a contribution, or is responsible for the loss at
  least equal to the average contribution from other syndicate
  members;
- the landowner's contribution must be personal and not come from
  the estate or farm business.

Williams was found to be running a business based on a number of
important differences from Lord Fisher, in particular:

- syndicate members had to pay a specific amount in advance;
- the shoot was let commercially on a number of occasions compared
  with once; and
- VAT had been reclaimed on all costs without distinguishing between
  the commercial lets and the in-hand days.

The correct organisation of a shoot is therefore extremely important.

5.18 Landfill tax

With effect from 1 October 1996, anyone carrying on an activity requiring a waste management license is, potentially, a 'landfill site operator' and, therefore, obliged to register for, and pay, landfill tax.

It is the licence holder and not the waste producer or disposer who is the person liable to register and pay the tax.

Landfill tax is payable on all licensed operations, including those which take place wholly within the curtilege of a farm and which simply involve the disposal of waste created by the farmer or landowner's own operations.

Since 1 April 1999, landfill tax was increased from £7 per tonne to £10 per tonne on active waste taken to a licensed landfill site. £2 per tonne is currently payable for inert waste. As from 1 October 1999, inert waste used in the restoration of landfill sites and quarries will become exempt from landfill tax.

All farmers and land owners currently undertaking an operation for which a waste management license is required, and all those currently in the process of applying for such a licence, should investigate their obligations to be registered for landfill tax.

5.19 Stamp duty

The rate of stamp duty was increased in the FA 1998 s149 to:

- £60,000 to £250,000   1%
- £250,001 to £500,000   2%
- £500,001 plus   3%

The increase in the value of land and property over the years, coupled with the increased rate of stamp duty, has made it an important additional cost. Therefore it is worth planning for minimising the liability to stamp duty. In simple terms, savings can sometimes be made in the following instances:

(a) By avoiding the re-selling of property to other members of the family after initial purchase.
(b) The identification of chattels included within sales marginally above the thresholds.

(c)   The appropriate treatment of partnership interests upon retirement from a partnership by a partner. The withdrawal by a partner of the capital from a partnership may not constitute a sale and may therefore not be subject to stamp duty. On the other hand, the sale of an interest in a partnership by an outgoing partner to the remaining members will attract stamp duty.

(d)   The introduction of a new partner. In these circumstances, an incoming partner introducing capital to the partnership will not normally attract stamp duty whereas if the incoming partner is purchasing a share in the business it will be subject to stamp duty.

Therefore bearing in mind that stamp duty is payable on documents and not property it is important to ensure that the correct documentation is prepared by the solicitors. It will be beneficial for the accountant to discuss any partnership changes well in advance with the solicitor with regard to stamp duty planning in addition to capital tax planning.

Chapter 6 – Problem areas and planning opportunities: commercial application of accounting and taxation

6.1 Introduction

This Chapter contains some of the more common questions and situations encountered by accountants from their farming clients, based on the experience of the author. It is structured as a series of independent topics that concentrate on the application and interpretation of accounting and taxation, referred to in earlier Chapters, to specific circumstances.

6.2 Accounting and taxation implications of BSE

6.2.1 Introduction

The link between BSE and human health risks was announced on 20 March 1996 and has had a dramatic effect on the beef industry. There have been several compensation schemes in force since that date and the following paragraphs deal with some of the accounting and taxation implications.

6.2.2 Year end valuations

Many farming businesses have financial year ends on 31 March or 30 April and the public concern over BSE has resulted in the market for some classes of livestock being non-existent at these times. For tax purposes the year end valuations are taken as the lower of cost of production or the net realisable value of the stock (**2.13.8**). It is common to value home bred or substantially home bred animals at the year end for tax purposes at 60 per cent of their market value as an estimate of their cost of production. Because the market value was not available, the Inland Revenue on 29 April 1996 set out the procedures and accepted the following as the market values of stock during the period between 20 March 1996 to 31 May 1996, both dates inclusive :

(a) the compensation that was paid on the slaughter of the animal, being 1 ECU or 85.66 pence per kilogram liveweight plus the relevant top up payment, set initially at 25 pence per kilogram.

An adjustment was necessary for the change in weight of the animal between the balance sheet date and the date of slaughter.

(b) the compensation rate per kilogram times the estimated liveweight of the animal at the balance sheet date.

(c) the latest normal market value prior to the announcement by the government on 20 March 1996, less :
  20 per cent for beef cattle
  30 per cent for cull cows
  40 per cent for bull calves born to dairy cows.

Deemed cost was then calculated as 60 per cent of the calculated market value. The full details are contained in Inland Revenue Press Release 78/96 of 29 April 1996. Since these dates normal valuation procedures apply.

6.2.3 Self-assessment transitional period

Many farming business with accounting year ends prior to 6 April 1996 were half way through their two year transitional period, therefore the value of stock at this point was irrelevant for tax purposes. The Inland Revenue have stated that they will welcome the preparation of a two year account for the whole of the transitional period. However, one of the advantages of preparing accounts with year ends prior to 6 April is that if a tax loss is created, the whole of the loss may be immediately available against total income. There is also the potential for using any excess relief against capital gains and in some circumstances consideration should be given to crystallising capital gains to take advantage of excess losses.

Businesses with financial year ends after 5 April 1996 will have completed their two year period and the valuation will be important. A low valuation will reduce the profit but only 50 per cent of this reduction will get tax relief, again unless a tax loss is made. Should the market recover, the whole amount will be subject to tax in the following year and the farming business will have lost out on up to 50 per cent of the reduced value in calculating taxable profits.

If the BSE crisis has a major effect on the profitability of a farming business, consideration should be given to tax planning using averaging or cessation rules.

6.2.4 Compensation payments

There are four main compensation schemes in addition to the extra premium payments under the beef special premium scheme and the suckler cow premium schemes (**1.6**, **1.7**):

- over 30 month slaughter scheme;
- calf processing aid scheme;
- selective cull – voluntary slaughter for cattle born between 1 July 1989 and 14 October 1990; and
- selective cull – compulsory slaughter for cattle born after 15 October 1990.

The tax treatment of the compensation payments will depend upon the scheme, the percentage of the herd slaughtered and whether a herd basis election is in force (**5.10**). Extra Statutory Concession (ESC B11) allows compensation for compulsory slaughter to be treated as trading income for tax purposes and to be spread over a three year period following the year of slaughter and deducted in computing the trading profit or loss for the year of slaughter.

Compensation payments for the compulsory slaughter of trading stock (i.e., those not on the herd basis) which are replaced by inferior and cheaper animals are subject to special provisions. This may occur because a farmer may not be able to purchase similar quality animals in the required time to maintain production. The compensation money will be restricted to the cost of the new, inferior and cheaper replacement, the balance being tax free.

(a) Over 30 month and calf processing schemes

The Inland Revenue have indicated that ESC B11 does not apply to the Over 30 Month Slaughter Scheme nor the Calf Processing Scheme as the compensation is not compulsory and does not relate to whole herds. The logic behind this decision is that the animals will be slaughtered in their normal trading period and the compensation received per animal will fall in the same accounting period as if the animal was normally sold. If more than 20 per cent of a herd on the herd basis are slaughtered including the over 30 Month Scheme then herd basis provisions may apply.

(b) Voluntary selective cull

The compensation is treated as a normal commercial sale unless in total, more than 20 per cent of the herd is sold when the herd basis provisions, if an election is in force, will apply.

(c) Compulsory selective cull

If a herd basis election is in force and more than 20 per cent are slaughtered and not replaced within five years then the proceeds are tax free. If the herd basis provisions do not apply then the compensation may be subject to ESC B11 and the special provisions of replacement by inferior animals. .

6.2.5 Herd basis

In the case of compulsory slaughter most farming businesses will be on the herd basis and the normal rules will apply. For those farmers not on the herd basis, if a substantial part (normally 20 per cent or more) of the herd is subject to compulsory slaughter an opportunity is given to elect for the herd basis in respect of that class of animal. The effect of the election is to ensure that any profit arising because the compensation payment exceeds the opening stock valuation will be tax free, unless the herd is replaced within five years. Correspondingly no relief would be available if a loss arose, therefore the opening stock valuation will be necessary to assess whether an election is beneficial. If opening valuations are relatively high an election may not be worthwhile.

Where a herd is on the herd basis, then compensation payments will be treated as though they represent normal sale proceeds of the animals. Thus, if 20 per cent or more are disposed of in a 12 month period, any profit over the original herd cost will be tax free, unless the herd is replaced within five years. Where the whole or a substantial part of the herd is compulsorily slaughtered, most farmers will probably replace within five years and in that circumstance they would obtain a tax deduction for the net cost of replacing their production animals.

6.2.6 Commercial considerations

Farming businesses that have weak balance sheets and in particular tenant farmers, may suffer from a low valuation of their trading stock recorded in their balance sheets. In some circumstances tax planning may not be the primary consideration when valuing the stock, particularly if their market value increases over time after the balance sheet date.

6.3 Comparison of farm business tenancies and contract farming businesses

6.3.1 Agreements

Farm Business Tenancies (FBT) were introduced on 1 September 1995 (Agricultural Tenancies Act 1995) and any land let for agricultural purposes after this date will be subject to an FBT. In simple terms the FBT will replace the following arrangements, but it is important to note that it is not retrospective and will not interfere with existing arrangements:

- Pre-Agricultural Holdings Act 1986 tenancies which contained the rights to two successions;
- Land let under the Agricultural Holdings Act 1986 which provided lifetime rights;
- *Gladstone* v *Bower* arrangements (usually 23 months);
- Ministry Licences (usually 5 years); and
- Seasonal cropping agreements.

The Agricultural Tenancies Act 1995 does not replace the following arrangements:

- Grass keep arrangements (**6.4**)
- Share farming (**2.15**)
- Contract management agreements (**2.15**).

6.3.2 Taxation considerations

Capital gains tax
When land is let under a Farm Business Tenancy, the landowner is no longer trading and will probably not be eligible for retirement relief should the land be sold. Roll-over relief on any capital gain that may arise will usually be restricted on a time apportioned basis. Under a correctly structured contract management agreement the landowner is still trading and using the services of a contracting farmer to provide labour, machinery and management. Roll-over relief is available to the owners of land let to a trading partnership of which they are members (SP D11, IR 131, 1996).

Inheritance tax
One hundred per cent Agricultural Property Relief is available for land let under a Farm Business Tenancy, but under existing rules the land to be eligible must have been either owned for seven years or have been

240

farmed in hand for at least two years ending in the transfer. Therefore new owners of agricultural land should ideally contract farm the land for the first seven years before letting it on a farm business tenancy to secure Agricultural Property Relief at the earliest opportunity. In this situation the relief will not be available for the first two years.

Income

Rental income under a Farm Business Tenancy is treated as Schedule A for tax purposes, whereas trading income under a contract management agreement is Schedule D. The expenses that are allowable against Schedule A income are restricted to the costs directly attributable to land ownership, therefore many costs will not be eligible for tax relief, such as telephone and electricity costs.

6.3.3 Pension provision

Pension premiums can only be made when there is taxable Schedule D income. Therefore, when land is let premiums cannot be made.

6.3.4 VAT

As with the restriction on trading expenses VAT is equally restricted.

6.3.5 Trading losses

When all the land in a business is let and it was previously farmed in hand, the trade of farming will be discontinued and any trading losses within the business from past trading will be lost. Normally losses can be carried forward and used against future taxable profits.

6.3.6 Commercial considerations

Working capital

Most contract management arrangements involve cropping enterprises although they have been successfully used in dairy, beef and sheep enterprises.

The working capital required to fund the variable costs on typical arable combinable crop enterprises will be in the region of £100 per acre (seeds, fertilisers and chemicals). In a contract management agreement the landlord usually funds the working capital with the contractor providing labour, machinery and management (**2.15**). Should the contractor wish or be offered the land under an FBT he will have to have access to additional working capital (**4.5.4**).

Risk

The landowner involved in a contract management agreement will inevitably be exposed to an element of risk as a result of fluctuating production and prices. In essence a landowner will continue the trade of farming and the degree of risk will depend upon the structure of the actual agreement. The landowner's risk is minimised under an FBT when an agreed rental income is received.

In many contract management agreements the contractor is not paid the fixed fee and profit share (**2.15.5**) until after all crop proceeds have been received by the landowner. At this stage the contractor is exposed to substantial risk, particularly if the variable costs have also been funded by the contractor.

To minimise the risk to the contractor it is preferable to include within the agreement a clause giving the contractor the option to purchase the grain at the prevailing market price. The grain can then be immediately sold by the contractor for the same prevailing market price. In practice, most agreements state that the contractor has full responsibility for marketing the grain as agent on behalf of the landowner. As long as the contractor can show that he/she purchased the grain for the current market price he/she does not contravene the agreement. The contractor will have acted professionally and will be able to contra any amount owing from the landlord for work done from the payment for the grain.

Security

Contract management agreements are usually for a fixed period of up to three years, although many have been in existence for a number of years on an ongoing annual basis. This does not provide security for the contractor who will not be able to plan machinery purchases and obtain bank funding efficiently. Many FBTs are for short periods of up to three years and again do not provide sufficient security.

6.3.7 Accounting and bookkeeping

Accounting and bookkeeping is much simpler in an FBT where only the rent has to be recorded.

	FBT	*Contract agreement*
landowner:	receives rent	retains part of gross margin
tenant/contractor:	pays rent, retains gross margin	receives contracting income

6.4 Short-term grazing agreements

6.4.1 Introduction

Grazing agreements are also called grass keep arrangements and are very common in dairy farming areas such as the west country, although they are found in most parts of the country. Essentially a landowner allows another farmer to graze animals on the land for a set period, usually from the first week in April until October. Many agents hold auctions of such parcels of land.

6.4.2 Options for letting

There are several options available for letting land for grazing :

(a) a grazing tenancy giving exclusive possession of the land for agricultural business purposes under the Agricultural Tenancies Act 1995 (**6.3.1**);
(b) a grazing tenancy giving exclusive possession of the land for private purposes;
(c) a grazing tenancy for a non-agricultural business such as a riding establishment will fall under the Landlord and Tenant Act 1954; or
(d) short-term seasonal grazing agreements.

6.4.3 Taxation

The construction of the agreement and the responsibilities of the landlord and the grazier or tenant can have far-reaching taxation consequences. The first three agreements allow exclusive possession of the land to the tenant and therefore the landlord receives rental income taxed as unearned income under Schedule A income tax. In addition, there may be loss of entitlement to capital gains tax roll-over and retirement reliefs, and Agricultural Property Relief on inheritance tax may be lost (**6.3.2**).

In order to retain the taxation reliefs and for the landlord to be treated as a farmer for tax purposes, a correctly constructed grazing agreement must be used. In this instance it is essential that the landowner is responsible for growing the grass and looking after the land, such as re-seeding, fertilising, ditching, draining and fencing.

6.4.4 Period of agreement

Where the land is let for more than a grazing season, or more than 365 days, the Revenue may treat the income as Schedule D.

6.4.5 Accounting

It is advisable to account for a short-term grazing agreement in the form of a gross margin, showing the rental income as the output and costs such as seeds, fertilisers and sprays as deductions to arrive at a margin.

6.4.6 Commercial considerations

Therefore as in a contract management agreement it is possible for:

(a) A landowning farmer to retire from active farming, realise the working capital in the business and retain a farmer status for tax purposes. For example, a livestock farmer may sell his livestock and let another farmer graze the land under a short-term grazing agreement and be treated as continuing in the same trade.

(b) An investor in agricultural land, through the use of management agreements and grazing licences, will be able to enjoy the tax status of a farmer and, subject to other qualifications, be able to obtain roll-over and retirement reliefs on capital gains and agricultural property relief from inheritance tax on the land and farmhouse.

6.5 Cashing in on milk quota values – the taxation implications

6.5.1 Introduction

The Agenda 2000 CAP reform measures provisionally agreed on 11 March 1999 state that milk quota will remain until at least 2006 with a reduction in intervention prices in the future. The general reduction in profitability in the dairy sector has reduced quota prices during 1998 and the early part of 1999. As a result of the reduced profitability, many dairy farmers are considering taking the opportunity of selling their quota and dairy herd and retiring from active dairy farming.

What appears to be a relatively straightforward business decision could prove to be a very expensive and complex situation. There is considerable case law relating to the ownership and taxation of milk quota. The notes below are very brief and simplistic relative to the complexity of the subject and aim to provide indications of some of the main factors to be taken into consideration when the sale of quota is under consideration.

Milk quota is treated by the Inland Revenue as a separate and distinct asset for capital gains tax (CGT) purposes, (*Cottle* v *Coldicott*, July 1995). Producers who acquired allocated quota on 2 April 1984 at no cost can potentially face a pure capital gain if the quota is sold without retiring or reinvesting the proceeds. This is because there is no cost to set against the proceeds as it cannot be valued as at March 1982 and, having no base cost, indexation allowance is not available. The disposal of milk quota cannot be treated as a part-disposal of the land (IR Tax Bulletin No 6 February 1993).

6.5.2 Quota ownership

One of the first things to establish is the actual ownership of the quota; it may be apportioned based on several factors. Milk quota is attached to land and registered with the producer farming the land. It will be apportioned across the land used for milk production even though the land may be in different ownership.

When there is a formal tenancy (other than a seasonal grazing agreement or *Gladstone* v *Bower* tenancy) allocated quota will be owned by the landlord with compensation due to the tenant upon termination of the tenancy (Schedule 1, Agriculture Act 1986). However, the Inland Revenue consider that upon the termination of a tenancy milk quota 'reverts to the landlord' (para 77942 CGT manual). In practice, the value of the quota will be apportioned between the landlord and the tenant as 'landlord's fraction' and 'tenant's fraction'. The tenant's fraction is calculated based on a formula involving the standard amount of quota per hectare and the rental value of the tenant's dairy improvements. Quota purchased by a tenant will be owned by the tenant.

Farming partnerships often farm land owned outside the partnership by one or more of the individuals. For example, the parents may own land in their own names and the land farmed under a tenancy by a family partnership which includes the parents. In this situation, the quota ownership is likely to be with the landlord, with compensation available to the tenants.

Many farming partnerships do not have written partnership agreements, or have agreements that are silent regarding the proceeds from any quota or compensation In these situations it can be argued that as quota is attached to land, the quota, or the compensation to the tenant, will follow the land ownership or tenancy rather than being a separate and distinct asset of the partnership. This is important in situations where a partner dies and a partnership is dissolved upon the death, (*Faulks* v *Faulks* 1982). The Revenue have disregarded the decision in *Faulks* v *Faulks* in relation to capital gains tax.

When there is a limited company involved, the company may own some or all of the quota or, if it is a tenant, receive compensation. In this case a sale will result in cash being realised and possibly taxed within the company. There may be an additional tax liability in order for the individual shareholders/directors to be able to obtain the cash from the company.

Once the ownership has been established, the reliefs available on any capital gain can be considered.

The quota sale may also involve the sale of the herd and possibly land. In simple terms, cows on the herd basis will not be subject to income tax when 20 per cent or more of the herd is sold in a 12 month period and numbers are not built up again within five years (**5.10**). Any land sold will usually have a base value as at March 1982, subject to a rebasing election, or acquisition cost if later, plus indexation to April 1998 for individuals and trusts. Because the land and the quota are treated as separate assets by the Inland Revenue, when land and quota are sold, any calculated loss on the land, as a result of indexation, will be restricted to a nil gain and cannot be used against any gain on the quota.

6.5.3 **Retirement relief** (see **5.15.3**)

The main relief that should be considered is retirement relief from CGT, although it is being phased out from 6 April 1999 over the subsequent four years and replaced by taper relief. It will still be important over this period because most quota will have a nil or negligible base value. Retirement relief is available for individuals over 50, or earlier on grounds of ill health, where the whole or part of a business is sold. In 1999/2000 retirement relief allows full relief on gains to a maximum of £200,000 and 50 per cent relief on gains between £200,000 and £800,000. Gains potentially qualify in full if the individual, partner or shareholder has been in business for ten years. The asset itself does not have to be owned for ten years. Below ten years a proportion of the relief is available rising from ten per cent (the minimum) after 1 year to 100 per cent after ten years. In order to qualify the individual must dispose of the whole of the business or a part that constitutes a material disposal and not merely an asset that has been used in the business. This has been termed the 'interference test' (*McGregor* v *Adcock*, 1977). Whether the disposal of a dairy enterprise alone is sufficient is currently open to question. The Inland Revenue has recently lost an appeal case on this point (*Jarmin* v *Rawlings*, 1994).

The timing of the disposal of transactions is vital, in particular where quota is sold some time after the sale of the herd, retirement relief may not be available (*Wase* v *Bourke*, 1996). When there is a complete retirement from all farming activities, assets can be disposed of up to 12 months after cessation (s163(2)(b) TCGA) which allows some flexibility in the marketing of the quota.

In a family partnership where the landlord is also a partner in the business, retirement relief may be available in full or in part on the landlord's portion of quota when it can be argued that a tenancy was granted prior to milk quota existing and the rent charged to the partnership does not reflect the value of the milk quota apportioned to the landlord. It can therefore be argued that the landlord has allowed the tenant to use the quota for no interest or rent (associated disposals, Sch 6 TCGA).

Retirement relief is available to each individual in a farming partnership but is not available to limited companies. Therefore any milk quota and any other assets that are owned by a limited company and sold for a gain will not be eligible for retirement relief and will be subject to corporation tax, currently at 20 per cent for most farming businesses. If the limited company is subsequently disposed of, retirement relief may be available on the share values.

6.5.4 Taper relief

The introduction of taper relief from 6 April 1998 and the associated phased withdrawal of retirement relief will be important in the planning of retirement from dairy farmimg. Concepts introduced in taper relief include the business and non business relief, time apportionment and the holding period an asset is held.

6.5.5 Crystallising gains

In some circumstances where the individuals wish to continue farming but may retire in the near future, consideration should be given to crystallising a gain on milk quota without disposing to a third party. This can be achieved in several ways such as the use of retirement relief trusts (s70 TCGA), transferring a business, including assets, from a partnership to a company. Ideally the gains should be completely covered by retirement relief, however, holdover relief may be available. Great care must be taken to ensure that any future use of taper relief is not jeopardized by any such transactions and that the cost of any stamp duty is taken into consideration.

6.5.6 Roll-over (see 5.15.2)

Sale of quota that gives rise to a chargeable gain can be rolled over into qualifying business assets acquired during a period of one year prior to the sale and ending three years after the sale. The new asset must be brought into use immediately but it need not be used in the same trade. It should be remembered that to obtain full relief the whole gross proceeds will have to be invested, not merely the gain.

In family partnerships it may be possible for individuals, particularly younger generation partners, to roll over their gains into land owned by the older generation. This has the effect of transferring assets to the next generation and maintaining the cash within the family. There are inheritance tax implications of this course of action that should be fully considered.

6.5.7 Reinvestment relief (5.15.4)

It was possible up to 6 April 1998 to roll over the gain provided that proceeds equal to the capital gain were reinvested in eligible shares in unquoted trading companies including the trade of farming, and many of these companies now exist. A similar relief is still available under the Enterprise Investment Scheme, however farming is an excluded trade.

6.5.8 Holdover relief (see 5.15.7)

Capital gains tax can be deferred on the gift of qualifying business assets including land and buildings qualifying for agricultural property relief. Quota gifted with land is eligible for holdover relief.

6.5.9 Pooling of quota for sale

The rules relating to pooling were amended as from 5 April 1998 except for companies. Milk quota acquired or allocated prior to this date is normally pooled (s52(4) TCGA). For example, in a situation where a partner in a farming business owns a proportion of the allocated quota and quota purchased by the partnership, the purchased quota will have a base cost and indexation applied to the date of the sale. It is impossible for the individual to elect to sell only the purchased quota and fully use its base cost as the Inland Revenue will apportion the base cost and indexation across the total amount including the allocated quota, thus reducing the base cost and increasing the gain. A gain could arise even if the quota is sold for less than the purchase price. As from 5 April 1998, milk quota held prior to this date will be held in a seperetely identifiable pool brought forward. Subsequently purchased quota is separately identified.

Milk quota disposals after 5 April 1998 will fall within the new identification rules and will be matched against the following in order:

- same day acquisitions;
- acquisitions within the following 30 days;

- previous acquisitions after 5 April 1998, latest acquisitions first;
- milk quota held in the pool brought forward at 5 April 1998.

In a situation where a tenant receives compensation as a result of the sale of quota, it can be argued that the compensation is a different asset to any other quota owned by the individual and, if successful, pooling may not occur.

6.5.10 Leasing out quota

Great care must be taken if cows are sold and the quota leased out prior to final retirement. Leased quota may not be treated as a business asset by the Inland Revenue. The capital gain on the eventual sale may no longer be eligible for retirement relief and roll-over relief will be restricted to the number of years the asset was used in the business, however, the new, non-business taper relief will normally apply. It is advisable to have a period of use for milk production of at least 12 months within the business before disposal to be eligible as a business asset.

There are many farming businesses in this situation at present and the leasing income net of tax has to be compared with the capital gains tax payable on its sale net of any non-business taper relief. A potential fall in the capital value of the quota also needs to be taken into account. In situations where quota has been leased out, the option of using the quota for milk production within the business for a 12 month period may need to be considered. This could be achieved by hiring in cows under a contract arrangement. A commercial decision will have to be made in these circumstances and a large sum of money could be at stake. If the leasing income is substantial relative to the total farm income it may not be treated as farming profits.

Inheritance tax reliefs may also be lost if the quota is no longer considered to be used in the business.

6.5.11 Conclusion

Therefore seeking professional advice, planning ahead and making full use of the available tax reliefs could mean the difference between retiring from dairy farming successfully and facing an unwelcome tax bill that could make such a move impractical. The timing of transactions is crucial and considerable planning opportunities arise in this complex area.

6.6 The economic price of arable farmland

6.6.1 Introduction

The demand for additional land continues to be strong with many farmers looking to expand their existing units. There are various methods of acquiring additional land: purchase, rent or contract farm.

6.6.2 Land purchase

Before considering a land purchase, a marginal costing exercise needs to be carried out to calculate the break-even price based on the potential of the land.

Example 6.1 *Land purchase*

A 700 acre farmer is considering the purchase of 100 acres of arable land adjoining the existing farm. The land is eligible for arable area payments and an average gross margin including set-aside of £230 per acre is expected. This gives a total arable gross margin of £23,000 for the additional land.

The purchase of the land would not require the purchase of any additional machinery. However, it is estimated that expenditure on fuel and machinery repairs would be £20 per acre, making a total of £2,000. The average working capital per acre is projected at £66 per acre or £6,600. The interest charges on the fixed costs and working capital at eight per cent total £648 per year.

This results in a total net margin for the 100 acres before tax of £20,352. If the farmer is in the 40 per cent tax bracket this additional gross margin is taxed accordingly. The net gross margin after tax is £12,211 per year. This is the annual net cash inflow for the additional land before finance charges on the land purchase. From this we can calculate the break-even purchase price as shown below:

Annual net cash flow before finance & after tax
Projected ongoing cost of money after tax relief

Capital repayments as well as interest charges should be included in the ongoing cost of money to ensure viability of the proposed purchase. A 20 year loan at 8 per cent per annum has a total cost including capital repayments of 10.2 per cent per year or 8.0 per cent after 40 per cent tax relief on the average interest portion. Therefore, if this annual cash flow continues in perpetuity, the break-even purchase price is:

$$\frac{£12,211}{8.0\%} = \qquad £1,526 \text{per acre}$$

If the farmer is in the 23 per cent tax bracket, the annual net cash inflow before finance and after tax is higher at £15,671. The total cost of money is now 8.7 per cent after 23 per cent tax relief on the average interest portion of the loan. If this annual cash flow continues in perpetuity the break-even purchase price is:

$$\frac{£15,671}{8.7\%} = \qquad £1,801 \text{ per acre}$$

These figures are based on borrowing all of the money for the purchase. However, if a farmer has surplus cash available to fund all or part of the purchase, the cost of money will be the opportunity cost, and therefore the break-even price will be higher.

If there is to be a cash surplus from the additional land, the farmer needs to pay less than these figures. If he pays more, then the cash deficit made on the 100 acres needs to be funded from the existing 700 acre unit until the loan is repaid and then the additional land will begin to contribute to the overall business.

It is important to realise that the business may be able to afford to pay more than the break-even price and accept an annual cash deficit for the period of the loan. Land is often purchased for higher than the break-even price in order to secure the purchase for the next generation and for the long-term expansion of the business, especially if the additional land neighbours the existing unit.

The irony is that even though more profits overall are made, at 40 per cent tax the break-even purchase price on a marginal costing basis for the additional land is lower than for a 23 per cent tax payer. This is because all the additional income is taxable but there is no tax relief on any capital element of land purchase.

If the purchase of additional land is being considered, the process described above should be carried out. It is important that no relevant factors are missed in the calculation. It should be noted that the above example is very simple and there are often other factors when buying land which complicate the calculations.

6.6.3 Rent and contract management agreements

Currently short-term rents have reduced to £100 to £120 per acre for good arable land and land owners can expect similar returns under contract farming agreements. How should you calculate what you can afford to bid for short-term rents or contract farming land?

The first step is to work out the lowest amount you as the tenant/contractor can afford to receive from carrying out all the operations and this should be based on standard contractor rates. This must include grain handling in and out of store and possibly cleaning. For a mainly combinable crop farm the total figure may be in the region of £90 to £100 per acre to carry out all operations. It should be noted that this includes a profit element.

In addition, you then need to add on a figure for the management of the crops, arranging the purchase of inputs and sale of crops and generally overseeing all operations. This may range from about £10 to £40 per acre depending upon the value you put on your own time and responsibility.

Therefore the minimum amount the tenant or contractor may require is £100 to £140 per acre. The land currently has a potential gross margin of say £230 per acre and therefore the maximum return to the land-owner is £90 to £130 per acre.

The high rent figures of up to £160 per acre that have been paid in recent years are largely because of the prosperity in the arable sector. The net return to the contractor or tenant in these agreements has dropped substantially and will be subject to renegotiation at the end of the initial agreement period. Many of these agreements may continue for several years and the initial, relatively high rent therefore needs to be considered as a premium for securing the additional land. When entering into a short-term rental agreement or contract farming agreement it is important to ensure that provision is made for flexibility in the future if arable incomes decline. This can be achieved by structuring contract farming agreements appropriately.

When taking on additional land, whether purchased, rented or contract farmed, it is important to consider the effect on the whole business. Expansion should not be at any cost!

The above examples are based on arable enterprises, however, the same principles apply to livestock enterprises. If livestock enterprises are to be expanded as a result of taking on additional land, a considerable amount of additional capital may be required to fund quota and animals. The interest on this additional capital should be taken into account in the calculations.

6.7 Pension schemes and farming businesses

6.7.1 Introduction

Historically it was possible to obtain 100 per cent tax relief on the capital cost of machinery and equipment used in the business, however, nowadays, subject to certain limitations, pension premiums are the only method of obtaining 100 per cent relief.

For a 40 per cent taxpayer, even though 100 per cent tax relief is available, there will still be a net cash cost of £600 for every £1,000 invested. Many farmers see this cash locked away and unavailable until retirement, whereas there are probably a multitude of uses for the cash within the business. It is possible to overcome this problem by setting up a pension scheme. There are two types:

- Small Self Administered Scheme (SSAS) for limited companies.
- Self Invested Personal Pension (SIPP) for sole traders and partnerships.

These schemes allow the members the opportunity to invest the funds within a defined range of investments including quoted stocks and shares, and commercial property, including agricultural land. Residential property is not allowed.

Many individual farmers have their own pension schemes with a traditional Insurance Company or Life Office, making regular contributions. There will be a fund building up, which at retirement will be used to provide a tax-free lump sum and to purchase an annuity (an income for life). It is possible to transfer the fund at any stage before retirement to another pension fund and this includes a SSAS or SIPP. This has the effect of obtaining the liquid cash from an existing pension which has traditionally been thought of as being unavailable, and using it to purchase agricultural land or other assets. A transfer value can be obtained for any existing pension policy which will provide the amount in the fund available for transfer. The transfer value will normally be less than the actual fund.

Both types of schemes are very similar, however, an important distinction is that a SSAS can purchase land currently owned by the company and therefore, in effect, a sale and leaseback arrangement can be made. A

SSAS can also purchase shares in a farming company and provide a loan for a commercial purpose.

A SIPP is only allowed to purchase farmland from an unconnected party, therefore it will have to be additional land to the business.

All income and capital growth within the funds are free of tax.

The ideal situation for setting up a fund is where there is a family farming business, therefore two generations can be contributing at the same time which can allow greater flexibility when parents retire. It must be remembered that the purpose of a fund is to provide a cash sum sufficient to purchase a pension for a retiring member. If insufficient cash is available, any farmland owned by the fund will have to be sold to an unconnected party which obviously defeats the object.

Premiums attract tax relief at the marginal rate of tax paid by the individual or the company.

The maximum pension contribution for an individual will vary, depending upon age and range, from 17.5 per cent of net relevant earnings at 35 or under up to 40 per cent over 60. The maximum net relevant earnings from 6 April 1999 is £90,600. For individuals who have not contributed into a pension scheme, the contribution limits can be used from the previous seven years against current taxable income. This will be particularly useful for owners of potato and onion enterprises where taxable profits have been high in some recent years.

The maximum contribution to a company scheme will vary depending upon length of service and age of the directors.

The schemes cannot be set up for the benefit of the existing farming business but are strictly controlled and all transactions have to be on a commercial basis. Therefore a commercial rent will have to be paid to the fund for land. Likewise the interest on loans from company schemes will have to be on a commercial rate. Tax relief through the business is available on the rent paid, and in effect is very similar to actual pension contributions, as the rental income remains within the fund until used to provide a pension upon retirement.

Example 6.2 *Self-invested personal pension scheme to purchase land*

	£	£
Existing pension scheme funds:		
premiums	80,000	
interest earned	20,000	
Transfer value	100,000	
Set up a SIPPS:		
transfer existing fund to SIPPS	100,000	
single premium into SIPPS	20,000	
borrow into SIPPS	30,000	
Total fund to purchase land 60 acres at £2,500	150,000	150,000
Tax relief on single premium £20,000 at 40%	8,000	
Tax relief on previous premiums £80,000 at 40%	32,000	
Total tax relief	40,000	(40,000)
Effective cost of land		110,000
Effective cost of land per acre		1,833
Ongoing income into SIPPS:		
pension premium partner 1		2,500
partner 2		2,500
rent 60 acres at £50		3,000
Total per annum		8,000
Net cost per annum after tax relief on £8,000 at 40 per cent		4,800

6.8 Farming partnerships

6.8.1 Introduction

Most farming businesses trade as a family partnership. There is no law which requires a partnership agreement to be in writing and as long as there is an oral agreement which is reflected in the annual accounts and in the actions of the partners, a written deed is not essential. In the absence of any agreement the Partnership Act 1890 will dictate the partnership.

A partnership agreement may need to change with time. Personal circumstances change and tax legislation is amended. Agreements should be regularly reviewed to ensure that they meet both the needs of the partners, and also safeguard the tax position.

It is recommended that a partnership deed be drawn up for every farming client with the accountant drafting up the heads of agreement for the solicitor to draw up the legal document.

It is assumed that the reader is familiar with the basic structure of partnerships; the following paragraphs comment on specific points that often arise when dealing with family farming partnerships.

6.8.2 Partnership structure

As a minimum, a partnership agreement should cover the following:

(a) Nature, place and name of the business.
(b) Date of commencement and duration of the business.
(c) How and in what proportion the capital of the partnership is provided and ownership of the underlying assets is arranged, particularly land and property.
(d) Calculation of profit and its division between the partners.
(e) Management of the business and the time to be devoted by each partner to it.
(f) The keeping of records and the preparation of annual accounts.
(g) Death or retirement of a partner.

When sons or daughters are introduced into a partnership consisting of husband and wife (the parents), clauses relating to the following may also be included in the partnership agreement:

(a) The signing of cheques to be by two partners of which the father or mother shall be one signatory.
(b) Capital provided by the parents shall be with reference to the last balance sheet. Freehold and leasehold land may be excluded including any mortgages on the land.
(c) Capital provided by the son or daughter shall be a fixed amount. For example, the current annual gift exemption from inheritance tax of £3,000, being a transfer from the capital accounts of the parents.
(d) The son or daughter to have a fixed salary and a small profit share such as ten per cent.
(e) The son or daughter to devote whole time to partnership business and not engage in any other business or occupation.
(f) The son or daughter not to enter into any transaction greater than say £1,000 without the consent of the parents.

(g) Partnership meetings to be held at defined periodic times.

(h) Structure of voting powers to be defined and chairman of meetings stated. For example, when a father brings two sons into partnership it will be important to define the voting rights of each individual. In this instance it will be important for the father to have two votes and the sons one each, with the father having a casting vote.

(i) During the first two or three years of the partnership the father and mother will have the right, by notice in writing, to expel the son or daughter from the partnership if any serious breaches of the partnership agreement are committed.

(j) Sons or daughters brought into partnership, who may later wish to leave, must not be allowed to upset the viability of the family business. Hence there must be no dissolution, or revaluation of assets. The departing junior partner must only be allowed to take out the capital that has been gifted and built up. Such capital to be withdrawn by instalments, say six half yearly. Interest must be allowed on the outstanding balance at a commercial rate.

6.8.3 Diversification and VAT

Many diversification activities supply services to the public such as bed and breakfast and furnished holiday lettings. These will normally be subject to VAT when the activity is carried out through the main trading partnership. It may be possible to run a separate business for these activities; the most common method being the farmer's wife as a sole trader. The separate business should not comprise the same individuals as the main partnership and must be financially and administratively separate (**5.17.17**).

6.8.4 Introducing new partners

Care should be taken when introducing individuals into a partnership purely for tax reasons. The Revenue may look at the introduction of new partners to ensure that they are genuine and take an active and effective part in the management and running of the partnership business affairs. In particular this applies to farmers' wives and younger members of the family.

6.8.5 Self-assessment

Prior to self-assessment the partnership is treated as a distinct entity and assessed to income tax. This is apportioned to the partners based on their relative profit shares and the individual partners are held jointly and severally liable for income tax.

After the transitional period a partnership, for taxation purposes, will not be treated as a separate and distinct entity. Each partner will be assessed as an individual trader on that individual's share of the partnership trading income. Partnership changes will not be treated as a cessation as the commencement and cessation rules will apply to the individuals joining or leaving the partnership.

6.8.6 Capital gains tax

Changes in the partnership, or profit shares, can have capital gains tax implications, being disposals and acquisitions of chargeable assets. The most common situation when a capital gains disposal is made is when a new partner is introduced and assets transferred.

6.8.7 Inheritance tax

Land and other assets can either be held by individuals or by the partnership on behalf of the individuals. Where the partnership holds assets a frequently used clause is where there is a binding contract for sale on the death of a partner of his or her interest to the surviving partners. This can mean that agricultural and business property relief are not available under existing legislation. These 'accruer' clauses are common in older partnership agreements and should be amended or removed.

6.8.8 Tenancies and succession

It may be desirable to bring a successor to a tenancy into partnership with the tenant to improve the chances of being eligible and suitable under the succession regulations.

In situations where some land is owned in addition to tenanted the potential successor must prove that the main source of income was derived from the tenanted holding. Therefore bringing a son into a partnership encompassing the total land farmed may not be advantageous. In this instance consideration should be given to farming the tenanted land as a separate partnership to include the tenant and potential successor, with the latter having the majority profit share. The owned land should trade as a separate partnership or sole trader and the potential successor to the tenancy should ideally not be involved.

6.8.9 Commercial considerations

A partnership is a very flexible vehicle to enable members of the younger generation in a family partnership to gradually enter the business. Initially the new partner may only receive a profit share without any transfer of assets and at a later stage assets may be transferred and possibly a share in future capital profits may be introduced. Profit shares need not be shared in the same proportion as capital profits. Shares in losses need not be the same as shares in profits.

It is a convenient method of transferring assets between individuals through their capital accounts in the balance sheet; in particular capital tax exempt annual gifts to the younger generation.

A certain amount of tax planning can be undertaken by varying the profit shares of individuals. This will be of increasing importance under self-assessment where each individual will be able to claim losses and make averaging claims (**5.4.2**).

Profit shares can be in the form of a prior charge on profits or a salary plus a share in the balance after the salary. This enables certain partners who may provide the majority of manual labour or junior partners with a fixed amount plus a profit share. Interest on capital can also be incorporated in profit shares.

Partners are able to draw anticipated profits out of the business without incurring income tax.

It is relatively easy to set up different partnerships or sole traders within the family to cater for individual circumstances, for example, succession to tenancies (**6.8.8**).

The liability for the debts that other partners may incur in the business is unlimited apart from limited partnerships.

The balance sheets of farming partnerships frequently contain partnership assets at less than their true current market value. For example, land and property at original cost, production herds and flocks on the herd basis and acquired milk quota. These balance sheets are frequently referred to in retirement clauses in partnership agreements where the remaining partners have the option to purchase the share of the retiring partner at a sum equal to the amount standing to the credit of the retiring partner in the last annual accounts. It can be argued that this method is unjust, however, it does ensure that the partnership will be able to continue trading and avoid paying out large sums of capital to retiring partners or the estates of deceased partners.

6.9 Limited companies

6.9.1 Introduction

Many farm businesses trade as companies, having an identity separate from that of the individual shareholders. This can have a number of advantages and disadvantages compared with a partnership structure.

Some of the main taxation and commercial considerations are discussed below.

The main reasons for the formation of companies in the past was for taxation and limiting the liability of the shareholders. There are an increasing number of farming businesses that trade as unlimited companies (**6.9.8**).

Some of the larger farming businesses trade as companies and partnerships, with the company being one of the partners. This structure can provide a degree of flexibility in the allocation of profit but in some cases can lead to a complex and bureaucratic structure which may outweigh the benefits.

6.9.2 Limited liability

Shareholders are not normally responsible for the debts of a company with their liability restricted to their fully paid up shares.

It may be difficult to obtain credit facilities from a bank because of the limited liability status; a lender may request the directors of a farming company to give personal guarantees in addition to requiring security over the assets of the farm. This can effectively negate the protection gained by trading through a limited company.

6.9.3 Wrongful trading

Directors are also at personal risk under the 'wrongful trading' provisions of the Insolvency Act 1986. If the directors allow trading to continue when it was, or should have been, clear that insolvent liquidation was inevitable, then the liquidator may apply to the court for an order requiring the directors to contribute personally.

6.9.4 Transfer of ownership and control

Family farming companies are useful vehicles to transfer shares to younger members of the family and in some situations to farm managers and other key employees as minority shareholders, providing them with an interest in the business. It normally would not be appropriate to bring managers and other employees in as partners. It is important to retain more than 50 per cent of the shares and voting rights with the core family members to ensure that the control of the business is maintained.

6.9.5 Pension schemes

A self-administered pension scheme can provide a great deal of flexibility in managing the assets of the family as well as providing the directors with a pension. They offer more flexibility than the self-invested scheme which can be set up by a partnership (**6.7**). In addition, directors have the option of a personal pension arrangement or an occupational pension scheme.

6.9.6 Company tenancies

A limited company that holds a tenancy over agricultural land prior to September 1995 has a value, as the tenancy will continue indefinitely. In normal circumstances it is not advisable to disturb these arrangements.

6.9.7 Accounting requirements and privacy

Limited companies have to be audited and have administrative requirements which are a cost. The statutory financial statements have to be filed with the Companies Registration Office and are available for the general public to obtain copies. Smaller and medium-sized companies do not require statutory audits and have exemptions regarding the form of the accounts that are needed for the Companies Registration Office (**3.2**).

6.9.8 Unlimited companies

It is possible to trade as an unlimited company. This has several advantages, such as the privacy of not having to file financial statements, while enjoying the advantages of a company. This may be advantageous for tenants who wish to trade as a company; the landlord will not be able to identify the profitability of the farm.

6.9.9 Corporation tax considerations

The highest rate of tax for sole traders and partners is currently higher than corporation tax. A limited company offers the flexibility of retaining profits within the company which will be taxed at corporation tax rate, as opposed to individuals where the top band of income could be taxed at 40 per cent, whether or not the profit is retained in the business. Advanced corporation tax was abolished with effect from 6 April 1999.

Company trading losses are not available to set against other income of the shareholders, whereas the losses in a partnership could be used against other income of the partners.

Averaging of profits is not available to farming companies. Self-assessment will be introduced for companies for accounting periods ending on or after 1 July 1999.

When most of the profits of a company are paid out to directors as remuneration and assessed under Schedule E, tax will be paid earlier than if the directors were trading as sole traders or a partnership.

6.9.10 Capital tax considerations

Taper relief introduced in FA 1998 s121 does not apply to companies where indexation continues to apply (**5.15.6**). In normal circumstances it is not advisable for land to be owned by a company because of the double tax charge on capital gains which can arise on the sale of the land and the winding up of the company.

Retirement relief is not available on assets sold by companies but, subject to conditions being satisfied, will be available on the sale of the shares.

Individuals have annual exemptions from capital gains tax but a company does not and will pay corporation tax on a chargeable gain.

6.9.11 Farm houses

Principle private residence relief is not available on houses owned by companies and lived in by a director of the company. This would be available in a partnership.

Tenant farmers who, according to their tenancy agreement, have to reside in the tenanted farmhouse are able to obtain principle private residence relief on a second home and also let it out on a commercial basis until required for retirement. This is not available if the tenant farmer trades as a company.

6.9.12 Disincorporation

It can be said that recent legislation has made farming companies more attractive than in the past. However, there may be instances where a company may no longer be required. A company structure can be difficult to unravel.

The following are some of the most common pitfalls of disincorporation:

(a) Losses in the company cannot be carried forward outside the company.

(b) Capital gains may arise on taking assets out of the business which may not be possible to mitigate.

(c) Capital gains may arise on the individual shareholders. This is often the case when small shareholdings have been acquired by gift or inheritance with low base costs.

(d) Company law requirements with regard to the distribution of the company's reserves have to be met.

6.10 Farm woodlands

6.10.1 Introduction

There has been an increasing interest in planting trees on farms and estates over the past few years, with many farmers planting small blocks on the most unproductive land and in field corners. Generally this has been in the context of a relatively prosperous period in agriculture but the current downturn in profitability is likely to have an impact on the amount planted. On the one hand, many farming businesses will not contemplate woodlands as they strive to retain profitability, and on the other hand, land prices may fall to a level that will make investments in land for planting a viable proposition.

The current grant scheme, the Woodland Grant Scheme (WGS), came into force on 19 September 1994 and in April 1997 incorporated the Farm Woodland Premium Scheme. The several amendments over the years have resulted in many landowners being confused with the grants available and professional assistance is usually required to complete all of the paperwork and supply, plant and sometimes manage the trees. The aims of the current grants available include recreational, environmental and general socio-economic benefits in addition to the production of timber.

6.10.2 Taxation of farm woodlands

Income tax and corporation tax
The occupation of woodlands in the UK managed on a commercial basis with a view to profit was taxed under Schedule B; sale of timber was tax free and the expenditure was not allowable against any taxable profits. Owners, however, had the option to elect for Schedule D to apply. Profits were then treated as profits or gain from a trade but without bringing in the value of the trees into stock. Elections were therefore made for Schedule D when land was planted and continued in the early years of the crop when costs always exceeded income. Losses arising could be set against other income at the marginal tax rate and repayments of tax obtained. It was not possible for the same owner to

revert back to Schedule B. When the timber matured, a change could usually be effected by changing the occupier (often involving creating a lease within the family). Thus tax relief could be obtained on all the costs, but the ultimate proceeds were not taxed.

After much publicity involving high profile public figures and planting in sensitive areas, the Government considered that the tax advantages had been abused and abolished them on 15 March 1988 subject to transitional provisions which came to an end on 5 April 1993. In addition, the rights of tax relief on interest on loans taken out to acquire an interest in commercial woodlands was also abolished. The objective of the FA 1988 was to take woodlands out of the income tax system. The growing of timber on a commercial basis is now exempt from income tax and corporation tax and likewise the costs associated with the income is not tax deductible.

It is possible to obtain losses from commercial woodlands and forestry abroad set against trading income in the UK but this is a complex area of taxation.

On many farms and estates there are woods which are not managed on a 'commercial' basis but nevertheless maintenance expenditure is incurred. In these circumstances it is often possible to obtain tax relief on this expenditure as part of general farm and estate maintenance expenditure. There are no strict rules or guidelines on this.

Correspondingly the sale of timber from 'non commercial' woodlands would be subject to income tax.

6.10.3 Capital gains tax (CGT)

Profit from the sale of trees is exempt from CGT but any profit from the sale of the land is liable to CGT subject to reliefs of:

- indexation;
- enhancement expenditure; and
- rebasing of asset values at their 31 March 1982 valuation.

Roll-over relief is available on land for timber production where the standard qualifying conditions are met. It is also possible to roll over UK capital gains into the value of the land and trees in the USA.

Hold-over relief is available on gifts.

Retirement relief is not available.

6.10.4 Inheritance Tax (IHT)

Commercial woodlands (trees and land) qualify for Business Property Relief, which is 100 per cent providing it has been owned for a minimum of two years.

When planning for IHT, decisions have to be made as to whether to make a lifetime gift, being a potentially exempt transfer, or leave a woodland by will. Gifting a woodland during lifetime may incur capital gains tax whereas leaving a woodland by will result in the uplift on the land on death to be free of CGT. Should the donor die within the seven year period after the date of the gift care must be taken to ensure the donee remains eligible for Business Property Relief during the seven year period. If the donee sells the woodlands during this period and does not replace them then they would become subject to IHT at the value at the date of the gift.

6.10.5 VAT

The sale of land and standing timber is exempt from VAT unless the landowner has elected to charge VAT at the standard rate.

Sales of felled timber is normally standard rated and the grant of a right to fell and remove timber is also standard-rated.

Timber held out for sale as domestic fuel is currently subject to VAT at five per cent, whereas firewood supplied to a business acting as a wholesaler will be standard rated.

In practice, woodland owners may make no taxable supplies for long periods of time whilst timber matures. Nevertheless they will incur input tax on expenditure. This VAT can be reclaimed as being attributable to future taxable supplies. If not already registered it is possible to obtain VAT registration as an 'intending trader' providing woodland is managed on a commercial basis with a continuing intention to make taxable supplies in the future.

If the woodland is sold before a vatable supply takes place, or the intention to make a taxable supply in the future changes, the appropriate professional advice should be sought.

6.10.6 Christmas trees and tax

Christmas trees are taxed as a trade (*Jaggers* v *Ellis*, 1996) and, together with short rotation coppice planted on farm land, should be included as part of the farm receipts.

6.10.7 Woodland Grant Scheme

Administered by the Forestry Authority for the purpose of establishment, restocking and maintenance of woodland.

Grants for new woodland

(a) Planting Grants

These are paid in two instalments: 70 per cent after planting, 30 per cent in year five although the trees must be managed for a further five years to retain the grants.

	£ Per Ha
Conifers	700
Broadleaves less than 10 Ha	1,350
Broadleaves 10 Ha or more	1,050

The density of planting must be a minimum of 2,250 trees per Ha. 1,100 trees per Ha is acceptable by agreement for amenity woodland, new native woodland, poplar plantations or agroforestry.

Up to 20 per cent of the area planted can be left as open ground and remain eligible for the grant.

(b) Restocking and Natural Regeneration Grant

This is paid 100 per cent after planting new trees or paid when natural regeneration has been established. There are minimum densities of 2,250 for conifers and 1,100 for broadleaves. There are two elements, the first an agreed discretionary payment for preparatory work and a payment per hectare.

	£ Per Ha
Conifers	325
Broadleaves	525

(c) Challenge Funds and National Forest Tender Schemes

Various funds are available in specific geographic areas.

(d) Supplemental payments

Several other grants are available in addition to the planting grants.

(i)   *Better Land Supplement*
      Paid 100 per cent after planting for new woodland on improved grassland or existing arable land. Paid in addition to planting grant but not available for short rotation coppice.

266

(ii)   *Community Woodland Supplement*
       A £950 per Ha premium is payable after planting new woodland
       within five miles of a village or town that can be used for informal
       recreation.

(iii) *Locational Supplement*
       £600 per Ha available in specific geographic areas to encourage
       planting.

(iv)   *Farm Woodland Premium Scheme*
       This comprises annual payments for 15 years where more than 50
       per cent of the area is broadleaves and/or scots pine. The payments
       are reduced to ten years if 50 per cent or more of the area is
       conifers. Trees must not be felled for 20 years. The rates of payment
       depend upon the land type:

Arable land eligible for AAP	£ Per Ha
Outside less favoured areas	300
Disadvantaged areas	230
Severely disadvantaged areas	160
Cropped and improved grassland	
Outside less favoured areas	260
Disadvantaged areas	200
Severely disadvantaged areas	140
Unimproved land	
All less favoured areas	60

Land in receipt of the Farm Woodland Premium Scheme and
eligible for arable area payments can be used towards set-aside
obligations. Set-aside payments will not be received.

(e) Short rotation coppice

£600 per Ha grant for planting on non set-aside land and £400 per Ha
on eligible set-aside land available for planting willow and poplar where
an end use is confirmed. Payable 100 per cent after planting. Supplements are not available, however, set-aside payments are available on
eligible land.

Grants for existing woodland

(a) Annual Management Grant

£35 per Ha per annum available for any age of woodlands to maintain
and improve woodlands where there are environmental benefits and/or
public access.

(b) Woodland Improvement Grant

A discretionary capital payment of 50 per cent of costs for work on existing woodland for environmental benefits and/or public recreation.

(c) Livestock Exclusion Annual Premium

£80 per Ha per annum payable for up to ten years in less favoured area or environmentally sensitive areas to exclude livestock from woodland of environmental importance.

6.10.8 Woodlands and set-aside

Woodlands planted on eligible set-aside land can count towards the obligation to set-aside land under the Arable Area Payments Scheme (AAPS). The normal woodland grants are available instead of the set-aside payment. Short rotation coppice on set-aside land will receive set-aside payments instead of Farm Woodland Premium Scheme.

6.10.9 Christmas trees and grants

Christmas trees do not attract grants, however it is possible, by agreement, to grow christmas trees for sale in areas of woodland receiving grant.

6.10.10 Taxation of grants

Annual payments under the Farm Woodland Premium Scheme and Livestock Exclusion Payments are subject to tax as they are compensation for lost revenue. Other grants are outside the scope of tax. The costs and revenue from christmas trees are subject to tax.

6.10.11 Economics of farm woodlands

With this background of taxation and grants we can now consider the economic viability of establishing and managing woodlands on lowland commercial farms and estates.

The key issues that are considered by the average farmer are:

(a) Grants have been and are difficult to understand because of the many options available and the frequency with which they have changed.
(b) The long term nature and lack of flexibility compared with normal enterprises. There is no room for errors.
(c) The drop in value of the land planted. Land eligible for the Woodland Premium Scheme would hold a value of between £1,500 to

£2,500 per acre at present, whereas land growing trees could be valued at around £500 per acre.
(d)   There is a general lack of understanding of the commercial woodland industry by the average landowner.
(e)   Existing woodlands are seen to be a financial liability and are neglected.

Against this are some positive considerations:

(a)   There is an increasing awareness of the environment and pressure on farmers to farm environmentally.
(b)   A small percentage of woodland on a farm will help maintain if not increase the asset value.
(c)   Woodlands enhance the sporting value on farms.

6.10.12 The current economic situation

Most enterprises are facing a downturn in margins at present with gross margins on cropped land down to £200 per acre. The gross income from set-aside land which currently is 10 per cent of cropped area is in the region of £100 per acre. Therefore, farmers may not need to consider other, non-traditional enterprises for economic reasons.

The establishment of woodlands on commercial farms is usually considered on the difficult and poor areas. However, with the advent of non-rotational set-aside these areas have been taken out of production and can produce a gross income of £100 per acre without any fencing or other capital costs and with the flexibility of bringing them back into production in the future, if required.

6.10.13 Woodlands v commercial farming

The comparison of a woodland enterprise with arable or livestock production needs to be carried out as a marginal costing exercise. Therefore the gross margins per acre need to be compared. As only a small area of land relative to the total farm is usually considered for planting, there will be minimal if no effect on the overheads of the business such as labour and machinery.

Assuming only a small area of most commercial farms is considered for planting, the drop in value of the land planted on an acre for acre basis needs to be ignored in the comparison.

Comparisons can be made based on annual cashflows over the productive life of an area of woodland from initial fencing and planting to clear felling, net of the tax on the Woodland Premium Scheme, and discounted to a net present value.

This net present value can then be compared with the net present value of an annual income stream over the same period, net of tax, to represent the annual gross margin from an agricultural enterprise.

The main components of viability that need to be considered in the comparison are:

- profitability – in this instance gross margin per Ha; and
- feasibility – annual and cumulative cashflow.

There are many variables involved in the costings of establishing woodlands and it can be assumed that farm staff are available to carry out most of the ground preparation, fencing if required, planting and some of the maintenance.

In particular, the cost of fencing has a major effect on the profitability and cash flow. The requirement for fencing will depend upon the species of tree and the number of rabbits and deer in the area. Poplar can be grown without fencing.

In economic terms the main variables are:

- requirement for fencing;
- length of time until harvest;
- yield class of the trees; and
- final quality of the timber such as veneer planking.

6.10.14 Conclusion

In theory the grants available provide significant incentives for farmers to respond to the Government's encouragement to reduce the 90 per cent gap in our timber needs currently filled by imports.

The current financial incentives are aimed at either:

- planting new woodlands; or
- associated with amenity and conservation.

In practice, at present farmers will be reluctant to respond in a significant way because there is no long-term replacement of their farming profits. In addition, once planted, there is no going back. Flexibility is lost. In an uncertain time, with the advent of the full impact of the GATT agreement, many farmers will want to keep their options open.

There is a great deal of work currently being carried out in the genetic improvement of trees: in the increasing of growth rates and therefore in the time to maturity and harvest, as has been carried out over the years with arable crops. This coupled with:

- planting being permitted on set-aside;
- greater understanding of the industry by farmers;
- professional management being used;
- the possibility of joint ventures in the industry; and
- the continuation of grants;

will lead to an increase in the amount of trees that will be planted on agricultural land in the future.

6.11 The value of agricultural tenancies created before 1 September 1995

6.11.1 Introduction

There has been considerable discussion, debate and case law regarding the valuation of agricultural tenancies depending upon the individual circumstances and whether it is beneficial to argue for a high or a low valuation. At the time of writing the position is still evolving and extremely unclear with interested parties currently discussing the way forward. The following notes are very simplistic compared with the complexity of the subject and merely provide some background.

Accountants who encounter situations where a tenancy is involved, either at present or at March 1982, without the necessary expertise should consult the appropriate assistance. A current common example is a tenant farmer purchasing the freehold of his property and selling a portion at vacant possession to fund the purchase. In this situation, the base value will be the purchase price at say 50 per cent of vacant possession value, plus the value of the tenancy at March 1982 with indexation to April 1998.

It is a fact that there is a difference between land values with vacant possession and land subject to tenancies. Land let before 1 September 1995 under the Agricultural Holdings Act 1986 is generally considered to have a value in the region of 50 per cent of its vacant possession value (**5.15.5**).

6.11.2 Vacant possession premium

Land subject to an agricultural tenancy under normal farming circumstances cannot be disturbed unless there is mutual agreement between both the landlord and the tenant that they wish to end the agreement and to release the land from the restriction of the tenancy. Based on the mutual agreement argument it follows that both the landlord and tenant share the difference between the tenanted value and the vacant possession value of the land. Therefore the value of the tenancy to the tenant under normal circumstances will be 25 per cent of vacant possession value.

6.11.3 Inland Revenue valuation

The Revenue have strongly argued this point for many years. However, because there is no commercial market in tenancies to arrive at this basis of valuation they have had to assume:

- a hypothetical sale;
- an assignable tenancy; and
- an open market situation.

This argument is theoretically consistent with the situation when both landlord and tenant realise the vacant possession premium by mutual consent, as the values will normally be based on negotiations by both parties to arrive at a commercial outcome.

The logic of this method of valuation is challenged in some situations where two parties do not come together by mutual agreement to lift the tenancy restriction and realise the increased land value. An example of this is a tenancy within a family partnership arrangement where a determination of the tenancy is as a result of family reorganisation and the land continues to be farmed. The subsequent uplift in its value will not be realised in cash by the landowner or the tenant.

The results of *Walton's Executors* v *IRC* upheld this view and the agreed value of a tenancy was reduced from 50 per cent of the vacant possession premium of £100,000, argued by the Revenue, to £12,645 based on a capitalised rental formula.

The results of this case mean that the Revenue cannot use their blanket approach in the valuation of tenancies in the future and each case must be considered on its own merits. It must, however, be noted that the Lands Tribunal made comment that when the vacant possession premium is realised by mutual agreement, the 50 per cent share of the premium as a method of valuation may be appropriate. It can be assumed, therefore, that the Revenue will continue to argue the vacant possession premium method of valuing tenancies in situations where the individuals seek to improve their positions.

6.12 Employees and labour

6.12.1 Introduction

The benefits to employees and the use of casual workers are discussed in **5.12** and **5.13**. The notes below relate to other aspects of employing labour in farming businesses.

6.12.2 Terms and conditions of employment

All employees whose contract of employment normally involves working more than eight hours per week, and who are not independent contractors, are entitled to written terms and conditions. A model form can be obtained from the National Farmers' Union or the Country Landowners Association. Some staff such as estate and domestic workers may not be covered by the Agricultural Wages Act 1948 and a different agreement will be required for these employees.

6.12.3 Service cottages

It is customary to supply service accommodation to agricultural employees. These can be protected by a number of alternative acts depending upon the start date of employment, whether a rent is charged and the terms and conditions of employment. It is recommended that an employer considers all of the alternatives when taking on an employee:

- Rent (Agriculture) Act 1976.
- Rent Act 1977.
- Assured shorthold tenancy under the Housing Act 1988.
- Assured agricultural occupancy under the Housing Act 1988.

There is provision in the Rent (agriculture) Act 1976 and an assured agricultural occupancy under the Housing Act 1988 for retired workers to remain in occupation of the service accommodation after retirement. In addition, a widow or widower or any member of the family living with the retired employee has succession rights after the death of the retired employee.

6.12.4 Salaries

There is an increasing tendency to employ staff on a salary basis and include an amount for housing when service accommodation is not provided. Staff on a salary may find it easier to obtain mortgages to purchase their own houses, lenders being reluctant to provide mortgages based on a considerable amount of overtime.

A salary may not be appropriate for all levels of staff as a certain amount of self-discipline will be required by the employee regarding hours worked.

6.12.5 Agricultural workers' sick pay scheme

A specific scheme for agricultural workers is operational, the details are contained in the Agricultural Wages Order. Employees must be full-time workers or regular part-time workers, including flexible hours, and must have been employed for more than 52 weeks.

6.12.6 Transfer of undertakings

These regulations protect the interests of employees when a business or part of a business is transferred to a new owner by preserving the contracts of employment they enjoyed immediately prior to the transfer. These regulations are important in farming businesses because they apply when a farm is sold, a new tenancy is granted or a farm taken in hand.

It is also considered likely that the regulations apply when a farmer decides to run his business under a contract management arrangement where the incoming contracting farmer will take on the existing contracts of the workforce.

It may be possible for the vendor or the previous farmer to make the existing staff redundant based on economic, technical or organisational reasons prior to a new farmer taking over the farm, or prior to a contracting farmer managing the land.

6.12.7 Self-employed contractors or employees

There are a large number of independent contractors that provide services to farming businesses. The line between self-employed and an employee is not very clear and is a question often asked by farmers. Often the answer must be based on a balance of the relevant factors.

Some of the main relevant factors are:

(a) If a worker supplies his own equipment and is not required to work regular hours, but is merely carrying out a specific operation and is able to delegate, then that person will normally be self employed.

(b) If a worker supplies a personal service to an employer without the ability to delegate to a substitute than that person will normally be an employee.

(c) The amount of control and direction that the employer gives to the worker is relevant.

An employer is at risk if a worker is wrongly treated as a self-employed person. The employer can be liable for the tax and the National Insurance Contributions.

6.13 Capital gains tax planning

6.13.1 Introduction

The current farming recession has resulted in many farming businesses reviewing their assets and identifying the ones that may be surplus to the efficient running of the business and therefore with the potential for sale to raise capital.

In many situations the capital is required to repay borrowings and a calculation needs to be carried out to compare the income lost and the benefit gained (**4.7.12**). It is unfortunate in many instances that capital gains tax needs to be paid out of the capital raised. Therefore the comparison is the income potential from the asset versus the after tax proceeds which in some cases may be not much more than 60 per cent of the capital raised given a 40 per cent tax rate.

The following uses Example 5.2 (**5.15.6**) to indicate the planning opportunities available to minimise capital gains tax on the disposal of assets. Most land used for commercial agricultural purposes has an inherent indexed capital loss compared with its base value. It is important to utilise this loss effectively when other assets with inherent capital gains are sold. The assets must have been treated as a single asset and any previous disposals must not have been treated as separate assets (**5.15.6**).

Example 6.3 *Disposal of assets using part disposal rules and the effective use of indexation.*

This example disregards the possible availability of retirement relief, taper relief and roll-over relief.

A farmer wishes to sell 200 acres of land and two cottages to raise capital to repay borrowings. They were purchased or acquired as one unit prior to 1982. It is assumed that the land is not subject to a tenancy. The example goes through the various options available.

1. *Sale as a whole treated as a single asset*

	£	£
200 acres at £2,500 per acre		500,000
2 cottages at £50,000 each		100,000
Total proceeds		600,000
1982 value		
200 acres at £2,000 per acre	400,000	
2 cottages at £10,000 each	20,000	
Indexation 1982 to 1998 say 100%	420,000	
Indexed base value		840,000
Notional loss		240,000
Capital gains tax		NIL

It should be noted that since 30 November 1993 indexation allowance cannot be used to create or augment a loss (**5.15.5**). Therefore the land has an indexed loss of £300,000 and the cottages have a gain of £60,000 resulting in a net notional loss of £240,000.

2. *Sale in lots treated as separate assets*

When considering the marketing of the land and cottages it may be prudent to market them separately to raise more capital. In the following example, the land is sold at the same price and the cottages sold for £60,000 each; an additional £20,000 is raised before tax. The contracts for sale are exchanged on the land before they are exchanged on the cottages.

200 acres at £2,500 per acre		500,000
1982 value		
200 acres at £2,000 per acre	400,000	
Indexation 1982 to 1998 say 100%	400,000	
Indexed base value at 100%		800,000
Notional loss not allowable		300,000

The cottages are subsequently sold

2 cottages at £60,000 each		120,000
1982 value		
2 cottages at £10,000 each	20,000	
Indexation 1982 to 1998 say 100%	20,000	
Indexed base value		40,000
Capital gain		80,000
Tax at 40%		32,000

Therefore the net proceeds are £620,000 less £32,000, being £588,000 compared with the sale in one lot £600,000.

3. *Sale using part disposal method*

It is now assumed that the land and cottages are still sold in two lots but the contracts for sale are exchanged on the cottages first. The part disposal formula (**5.15.6**) is then used and deducts the calculated base cost of the cottages from the base cost of the land.

Sell two cottages at £60,000 each

$$\frac{120,000}{120,000 + 500,000} \times 420,000 \qquad 81,290$$

Indexation at 100%	81,290
Indexed base value at 100%	162,580
Proceeds	120,000
Notional loss on cottages	42,580
Capital gains tax	NIL

The land is subsequently sold	
200 acres at £2,500	500,000
Base cost 200 acres and cottages	420,000
Less cost of cottages sold	81,290
Adjusted base cost	338,710
Indexation at 100%	338,710
Adjusted indexed base cost	677,420
Notional loss on land	177,420
Capital gains tax	NIL

Therefore it is important that clients are encouraged to discuss any potential sales of assets with their accountant in advance and the accountant and agent should liaise at an early stage.

6.13.2 Assets subject to a tenancy

Should the land and cottages be subject to a tenancy in favour of a farming partnership or company, the tenancy must be surrendered in order for the asset to be sold freehold. The surrender of the tenancy will be a disposal of an interest in land which may give rise to a capital gain. In many instances the parties involved are members of a family and therefore connected parties, the arrangements may be loose with regard to the rent being paid and the preparation of written agreements.

The key considerations for the adviser in these circumstances are:

(a) Does a tenancy exist ?
    (i)   is there a written tenancy
    (ii) is rent being paid
    (iii) is rent being recorded in the annual accounts
    (iv) the rent may be shown in the accounts in the form of interest paid on borrowings secured on the land which is held outside the business by the owner.
(b) Are the tenant and landowner connected parties?
(c) Did the tenancy exist at 31 March 1982? If so it may have a base value and indexation may be available.
(d) Is the tenancy which is being surrendered part of a tenancy over a larger single asset enabling a part disposal calculation to be made?
(e) If the tenancy is in favour of a partnership the members of the partnership may each have a share in the value in proportion to

their share in the partnership and each partner may have a disposal of an interest in land upon the surrender.

(f) When the parties are members of a family it is usual for the surrender to be for nil consideration and in these circumstances it may be possible for a holdover claim to be made on the imputed value.

(g) If a landlord rents land to a company and that individual is also a shareholder in the company, a surrender of the tenancy for nil consideration may be treated as a distribution.

(h) The breach of a tenancy agreement, for example, by subletting a property may make it possible for a valid notice to quit to be served therefore circumventing the need for a surrender of the tenancy. This may be particularly useful for houses or cottages where a part disposal calculation is not possible.

6.14 Borrowing in euros (2.18)

6.14.1 Introduction

Whilst the UK remains outside European Monetary Union, borrowing in euros will be exactly the same as borrowing in any foreign currency with the same exchange rate risks. It has always been possible to borrow in foreign currencies and the general rule is that there should be an income stream in the same currency to repay interest and capital.

There is a possibility that subsidy payments and grain receipts may be available to farmers in euros even if the UK remains outside EMU which would provide an opportunity for farming businesses to:

- take out a euro loan at a relatively lower interest rate to repay sterling borrowings or to purchase additional assets;
- to purchase inputs or machinery in euros;
- to arrange a hire purchase agreement for an asset, with repayments in euros.

On an average combinable crop farm in the region of a third of the income may be in subsidy payments. If the option to receive these in euros is taken, they must be matched to expenditure in euros otherwise there may be a surplus or shortfall which will be subject to exchange rate risks.

16.14.2 Euro loans

The calculations and key issues that need to be considered are:

(a) There is currently a lower interest rate in euros in the region of 2.5 per cent to 3 per cent compared with sterling.

(b) It is likely that the differential between sterling and euro interest rates will reduce over the next few years, therefore the advantage is short to medium term.

(c) If sterling interest rates reduce relative to euro interest rates it is logical that sterling may weaken relative to the euro. However, there are many other factors that could influence the value of sterling.

(d) The relative timing of receipts in euros and repayments on euro loans will be crucial otherwise sterling may have to be converted at a spot rate to pay euro instalments. The converse of this will be a surplus of euros on deposit for part of the year which could result in an increased overdraft in the business.

(e) A euro loan will normally be taken out over several years, therefore consideration will need to be given to the income stream in euros continuing over the full period of the loan.

(f) Should it no longer be beneficial to continue with a euro loan the conversion back to sterling may not be advantageous.

(g) Whilst sterling remains relatively strong against foreign currencies, current sterling loans when converted to the foreign currency will result in a relatively higher level of borrowing in a foreign currency.

(h) It is likely that there will be costs such as arrangement fees on new loans and redemption fees on existing sterling loans which will need to be taken into account when comparing interest rate savings.

Example: *£100,000 existing sterling loan converted to euro loan*

At £0.7 to a euro the amount of euros that need to be borrowed to repay the £100,000 are   142,857 euros

But consider if sterling dropped to £0.8 to euro as interest rates reduced in the UK during 1999 and 2000. (14.28 per cent reduction in value of sterling).

The 142,857 euros owed assuming no capital repayments had been made at £0.8 to the euro is now the equivalent of   £114,286

Therefore the sterling equivalent of the euro loan in the balance sheet of the business will be greater than the original sterling loan of £100,000 as   £114,286

Therefore an additional £14,286 has been borrowed by taking the euro loan out whilst the £ was relatively high in value and subsequently weakened.

In the above example, if an income stream in euros continues to be available throughout the term of the euro loan, the relative sterling values are not important as they will have no effect on the business in cash terms. Whilst the euro remains as a foreign currency the sterling equivalent of the outstanding loan will be included in the balance sheet and in some situations may be higher than the original sterling loan in the early years.

6.14.3 Purchasing commodities in euros

The most likely commodities that may be purchased are fertilizer, chemicals and machinery. Some of the more important considerations are:

(a) Products manufactured outside Europe will not provide potential benefits.
(b) Many chemical products require approval and re-labelling prior to importation.
(c) Membership of buying groups may be beneficial.
(d) Machinery purchases are most likely to be funded by credit agreements such as hire purchase, therefore borrowings will have to be arranged with finance companies in order for payment to be made in euros.
(e) The operating of a business in two currencies will require an increase in the level of management and relatively sophisticated office and control systems.

At the present time it is likely that many farming businesses will not benefit from receiving a proportion of their income in euros to fund loan repayments and purchase commodities as the additional management and risk will normally outweigh the potential benefits.

6.15 Business reorganisation and quota

6.15.1 Introduction

Accountants are often involved in the restructuring of a farming businesses, for example:

• the introduction of the next generation into a business;
• the introduction of a spouse into the business;
• the death of a partner or shareholder;
• the retirement of the elder generation;
• reorganisation as part of an estate planning exercise; and
• amending the shares in a partnership or company.

Most of these changes occur at the financial year end of the business and if this happens to fall within some of the time limits or retention periods of the quota rules and regulations, great care is required. This is particularly relevant to sheep quota.

The following details are a brief synopsis of the relevant issues and full details are available in the Explanatory Guides available from MAFF Regional Service Centres (Appendix **4**).

6.15.2 Sheep quota

Sheep quota can be in the name of an individual, a company or a producer group. A partnership is a producer group. The most important factor is that all individuals within a producer group must hold quota in their own names as individuals in the same proportion as their relative shares in the sheep flock which is usually based on their shares in the partnership. Each member must individually comply with all of the time limits and retention periods. If this is not the case MAFF may withold payments.

Therefore after changes in a partnership, quota may have to be transferred or leased. Apportionment changes which affect less than ten per cent of the group's flock cannot be accepted by MAFF, therefore apportionment changes of less than ten per cent should not be made. Normally transfers of quota (not leases) are subject to a 15 per cent siphon to a national reserve with certain exemptions:

(a) Transfers between a producer group on the undertaking that both the transferor and transferee remain members of the group and eligible for premium for a period of three years after the transfer year.
(b) Transfers followed by retirement from the group including the transfer of the share in the business.
(c) Transfers including the transfer of the whole farm.
(d) In the event of the death of a producer, the quota automatically transfers into the hands of the executors of the estate.

Sheep quota is designated within five ring fences in Great Britain and cannot be moved between ring fences. Therefore care must be taken when land is purchased, sold or rented (including short term lettings and licences) in a different ring fence as this could change the designation of the ring fence area and possibly make the quota ineligible. In these circumstances the sheep quota will have to be sold and replaced with the appropriate quota.

6.15.3 Suckler cow premium

Suckler cow quota can be held in the name of an individual, partnership or a company and if held by a partnership, is not subject to the producer group rules as in sheep quota. The same rules apply if the quota is held in individual names as opposed to the partnership name. Any changes should be notified to the appropriate Regional Service Centre (Appendix **4**).

The ring fence and siphon rules apply as in sheep quota.

6.16 Farm staff and working time regulations

6.16.1 Introduction

As farmers continue to utilise bigger and better machines, the number of workers on farms has declined. Those that remain need high skill levels to cope with the varied tasks that they have to perform. Consequently, farm business managers invest large amounts of time and money on training their employees.

Not only has the size of the workforce declined, but the make-up has also altered. More managers are taking on a share of the outdoor workload; strategic use of part-time labour is rising; and more employees are salaried rather than being paid a weekly wage with overtime.

This is against a backdrop of diminishing returns in the industry. As commodity prices fall, margins get tighter and there is increasing pressure to cut fixed costs. Consequently, employees are responsible for increasing numbers of livestock or acres and their total workload is rising. There is a temptation, both on the part of the employer and the employee, to work the extra hours involved. However, this practice is to be curtailed under the latest government regulations.

6.16.2 The working-time regulations

For the first time in UK law, rules exist covering the number of hours worked in a week, the length and timing of rest breaks and rest periods, night work and entitlement to annual leave. They were introduced under the title 'The Working Time Regulations' and came into force on 1 October 1998. They are applicable in all cases, except where the 'Agricultural Wages Order 1988 (Number 2)' is more beneficial to the employee (for example rest periods during the working day) in which case the AWO will apply.

The regulations are designed to protect all workers, and especially adolescents, from the detrimental effects of working long hours without suitable periods for recovery. Apart from the genuinely self-employed person, they cover all workers including casual and freelance workers.

The main points in the two pieces of legislation are:

(a) the working week will be restricted to 48 hours, including overtime;
(b) employees will be entitled to an unpaid 30 minute rest period if their working day exceeds 5 hrs 30 mins;
(c) they will also be allowed 11 hours continuous rest every 24 hours;
(d) rest periods of 24 hours must be given every seven days (although these may be averaged over a two week period for non-adolescents);
(e) there is an entitlement to annual leave after 13 weeks continuous employment (this includes casual labour);
(f) paid annual leave shall be a minimum of three weeks (rising to four weeks after 23 November 1999); and
(g) genuinely self-employed people are exempt from the rules.

Applying these as they stand to many farm businesses, be it livestock or arable, immediately highlights potential problems, for example, the labour requirements during the peak workload occurring in late summer/autumn during harvest and autumn cultivations. Hours worked are likely to exceed the 48 hour maximum working week. There are practical measures that can be taken to either make the regulations fit the business or to fit the business to the regulations.

6.16.3 Practical measures

Changing the system
There may be scope to spread the workload more evenly throughout the year by incorporating more spring crops into the rotation. The peak workload may also be reduced by employing more minimal cultivation and direct drilling techniques. This has the potential to reduce labour requirements, but may also improve timeliness of crop drilling, leading to agronomic and other benefits. It is important that the impact on all areas of the business is assessed before changes to the system are implemented.

6.16.4 Flexibilities within the legislation

48 hour maximum working week
There are some inbuilt flexibilities in the regulations to compensate for peculiarities of a particular industry. For example, employees can enter into individual agreements to work more than 48 hours per week. The

agreement must be in writing and should specify the period of notice (up to three months) for terminating the agreement – the default period is seven days.

If a worker decides he does not want to opt out of the 48 hour maximum working week, as he is perfectly entitled to do, then employers can use the averaging procedure to determine average hours worked over a particular reference period. This reference period is normally 17 weeks but can be extended to 26 weeks under certain circumstances.

It may be advisable to agree beforehand that the reference periods will run consecutively. If there is no agreement the reference period will become a 'rolling' period. On the average arable unit it would mean that the employee could only work very few hours in the weeks immediately before harvest, to ensure the weekly rolling average never exceeded 48 hours.

Rest periods

The rest periods specified also allow some flexibility. For example, the entitlement to daily and weekly rest does not apply to a worker where:

> '....on account of the specific characteristics of the activity in which he is engaged, the duration of his working time cannot be measured or predetermined or can be determined by the worker himself.../'

Essentially this applies to workers who have complete control over the hours they work and whose time is not monitored or determined by their employer. Deciding whether this applies to individual businesses depends upon official interpretation of the above rule, and how applicable it is in each situation. An indicator may be if the worker has discretion over whether to work or not on a given day without having to consult their employer, although official interpretation will emerge from industrial tribunals. Examples of personnel to whom this exemption may apply include farm and estate managers who have total responsibility for the day-to-day running of the farm.

There are other situations where rest periods may not apply, including where there is a need for continuity of production or where there is a foreseeable surge in activity, for example, during harvest periods or whilst calving or lambing livestock.

However, if rest periods are withdrawn for any reason, employers must provide their workers with compensatory rest, equivalent to the rest period they missed. This must be provided in reasonable time – the guidelines at present suggest about two weeks for daily rest and around two months for weekly rest.

The need to provide rest periods is likely to cause many problems within the agriculture sector, as there is no opportunity to opt out of it.

Annual leave
Eligibility for annual leave applies to all of the workforce. Employers should be aware that casual workers employed for more than thirteen weeks immediately become entitled to paid annual leave.

6.16.5 Self-employed

The regulations state that self-employed people are exempt from the rules. However, this only applies to the genuinely self-employed, a term which probably excludes people who do work for a single business but pay their own national insurance and so are technically self-employed (**6.12.7**). This is an area where it may be advisable to err on the side of caution.

6.16.6 Summary

The regulations stipulate a maximum average working week of 48 hours. Therefore, if the nature of the business indicates that this limit may be exceeded, it is important for employers to take the necessary action.

(a) Firstly, allow employees to opt out of the 48 hour week if they want to.
(b) If they do not want to opt out, agree when the reference period for averaging number of hours worked begins.
(c) Ensure that weekly timesheets are completed and saved for future reference whether employees have opted out of the 48 hour week or not.
(d) If you do not yet have one, complete a Statement of Terms of Employment for each employee.

It is important for all owners of businesses to study the regulations and to abide by them. They cover many more areas than those above, and contain extra protection for adolescents and school age employees. There is an inbuilt complaints procedure for any worker who is dismissed or subject to a detriment simply for asserting a right under the working time regulations, enforced by the health and safety executive and local authorities. In all cases, the driving force behind the legislation is protection of workers and if an employer can be shown to be treating the health and safety of his workforce as of less than paramount importance, then he or she could be liable to prosecution.

Draft Statement of Terms of Employment, Draft Individual Agreement to Disapply the 48 hour Maximum Working Week and an example timesheet for employers can be obtained from the NFU.

6.16.7 Useful contacts

NFU Orderline   0891 338700
For existing members of the NFU to order documents
Draft Statement of Terms of Employment Ref 150
Working Time Regulations   Ref 162

Workright   0845 6000 925
A Guide to Working Time Regulations

MAFF   0645 556000
A Guide to Some Aspects of the Working Time
Regulations for Those Engaged in Agriculture

MAFF Regional Service Centres   Various
Agricultural Wages Board   0171 238 6540
Agricultural Wages Order

Appendix 1 – Specimen statement of accounts

Alpha Beta Estates

Mill Stream Farm statement of accounts: year ended 31 March 1998

Contents

[Page 1]

288

Profit and loss account
For the year ended 31 March 1998

	Note	1998 £	1998 £	1997 £	1997 £
Gross margins					
Livestock	1	**81,499**		106,693	
Arable	2	**264,178**		313,146	
Contracting		**22,447**		–	
Total gross margins		**368,124**		419,839	
Fixed costs					
Labour		**74,999**		70,510	
Power and machinery		**117,834**		96,605	
Property		**32,918**		40,736	
Administration		**13,429**		40,865	
Tillages		**(2,235)**		(1,670)	
			236,855		219,046
Profit before rent and finance			**131,269**		200,793
Other income	6		**10,750**		20,259
Profit on asset sales			**2,129**		2,508
			144,148		223,560
Rent		**55,000**		52,000	
Finance costs	4	**7,647**		6,244	
			62,647		58,244
Profit after rent and finance			**81,501**		165,316
Unrealised profit – stock	11		**2,212**		(1,904)
Deferred income	11		**(8,997)**		8,554
Financial profit for the year			**74,716**		171,966
Appropriation of profit					
Mr Andrew Grant		**37,358**		85,983	
Mr Christopher Thornton		**37,358**		85,983	
			74,716		171,966
			74,716		171,966

[Page 2]

289

Balance sheet at 31 March 1998

	Note	1998 £	1998 £	1997 £	1997 £
Fixed assets					
Property	8		**38,124**		39,000
Plant and machinery	9		**262,714**		228,554
			300,838		267,554
Long term assets					
A C T Ltd			**45**		45
			300,883		267,599
Current assets					
Valuation	10	**218,863**		219,010	
Debtors and prepayments		**69,142**		64,553	
Cash at bank and in hand		**108,245**		156,932	
		396,250		440,495	
Current liabilities					
Trade creditors		**38,179**		43,637	
Deferred income	11	**16,113**		7,116	
Leasing and hire purchase		**26,539**		12,459	
		80,831		63,212	
Net current assets			**315,419**		377,283
Net assets			**616,302**		644,882
Financed by					
Current accounts	12		**577,511**		602,186
Loans	13		**38,791**		42,696
Capital employed			**616,302**		644,882

[Page 3]

Notes to the accounts year ended 31 March 1996

1 Livestock

	1998		1997	
	£	£	£	£
Livestock summary				
Dairy		**81,306**		102,844
Followers		**4,285**		6,548
		85,591		109,392
Hay straw and silage				
Opening valuation	**795**		600	
Purchases	**3,677**		2,894	
	4,472		3,494	
Closing valuation	**380**		795	
		(4,092)		(2,699)
Livestock gross margin		**81,499**		106,693
Dairy				
Closing valuation	**39,925**		52,000	
Sales − culls	**9,610**		12,901	
		49,535		64,901
Transfers in	**8,510**		9,000	
Opening valuaiton	**52,000**		49,350	
		60,510		58,350
		(10,975)		6,551
Milk		**144,256**		151,812
Dairy gross output		**133,281**		158,363
Bought feed	**31,881**		35,126	
Own grown feed	**6,391**		5,358	
Veterinary fees and medicines	**3,698**		4,098	
Hire of bulls	**220**		200	
Haulage	**154**		166	
Spares and sundries	**3,103**		3,814	
Forage seeds	**−**		235	
Forage fertiliser	**6,132**		5,822	
Forage sprays	**396**		700	
		51,975		55,519
Dairy gross margin		**81,306**		102,844

[Page 4]

Appendix 1 – Specimen statement of accounts

	1998 £	1998 £	1997 £	1997 £
Followers				
Closing valuation	**16,930**		24,000	
Transfers out	**8,510**		9,000	
Sales	**17,360**		17,955	
Subsidies	**2,464**		1,940	
		45,264		52,895
Opening valuation	**24,000**		26,500	
		24,000		26,500
Followers gross output		**21,264**		26,395
Bought feed	**6,364**		5,741	
Own grown feed	**6,822**		10,716	
Veterinary fees and medicines	**611**		806	
Haulage	**242**		219	
Spares and sundries	**616**		561	
Forage seeds	**213**		119	
Forage fertiliser	**1,876**		1,092	
Forage sprays	**235**		593	
		16,979		19,847
Followers gross margin		**4,285**		6,548

[Page 5]

292

2 Arable

	1998		*1997*	
	£	£	£	£

Arable summary – 1997 harvest

Barley	**49,335**		65,291	
Wheat	**137,436**		155,484	
Oats	**–**		14,141	
Beans	**11,740**		13,541	
Oilseed rape	**62,510**		58,120	
Industrial oilseed rape	**9,846**		6,450	
Set aside	**–**		2,410	
		270,867		315,437
Unallocated variable costs				
Contract work	**4,267**		3,000	
Hire of machinery	**1,340**		841	
Baler twine	**–**		64	
Miscellaneous	**205**		149	
		5,812		4,054
Arable gross margin		**265,055**		311,383
(Deficit)/Surplus from 1996 harvest		**(877)**		1,763
Total arable gross margin		**264,178**		313,146

[Page 6]

	1998		1997	
	£	£	£	£

1997 harvest

Barley

Sales		**34,410**		53,932
Area payments		**22,069**		24,945
Own use feed		**13,213**		6,768
Barley gross output		**69,692**		85,645
Seeds	**4,240**		4,351	
Fertilisers	**6,148**		6,756	
Sprays	**9,480**		8,817	
Other variables	**47**		13	
Contract work	**88**		49	
Weighbridge and levies	**354**		368	
		20,357		20,354
Barley gross margin		**49,335**		65,291

Wheat

Closing valuation		**41,000**		20,377
Sales		**100,435**		130,405
Area payments		**55,589**		52,177
Wheat gross output		**197,024**		202,959
Seeds	**10,680**		8,622	
Fertilisers	**19,423**		15,568	
Sprays	**27,967**		22,274	
Other variables	**196**		17	
Contract work	**588**		93	
Weighbridge and levies	**7,343**		901	
		59,588		47,475
Wheat gross margin		**137,436**		155,484

[Page 7]

294

	1998		1997	
	£	£	£	£

1997 harvest – continued

Oats

Sales		–	3,294
Area payments		–	7,734
Own use feed		–	9,306

Oats gross output   –   20,334

Storage charges	–	814	
Seeds	–	1,349	
Fertilisers	–	1,802	
Sprays	–	1,882	
Contract work	=	346	
	–		6,193

Oats gross margin   –   14,141

Beans

Sales	**7,334**		7,910
Area payments	**7,970**		10,048

Beans gross output   **15,304**   17,958

Seeds	**1,617**	1,952	
Fertilisers	**318**	384	
Sprays	**1,629**	2,081	
	3,564		4,417

Beans gross margin   **11,740**   13,541

[Page 8]

	1998		1997	
	£	£	£	£
1997 harvest – continued				
Oilseed rape				
Sales		**47,073**		43,560
Area payments		**35,884**		29,045
Oilseed rape gross output		**82,957**		72,605
Seeds	**2,925**		2,355	
Fertilisers	**7,117**		5,417	
Sprays	**9,093**		6,202	
Contract work	**1,312**		511	
		20,447		14,485
Oilseed rape gross margin		**62,510**		58,120
Industrial oilseed rape				
Sales		**7,366**		4,560
Area payments		**8,043**		4,830
Industrial oilseed rape gross output		**15,409**		9,390
Seeds	**915**		525	
Fertilisers	**1,922**		1,137	
Sprays	**2,726**		1,278	
		5,563		2,940
Industrial oilseed rape gross margin		**9,846**		6,450
Set-aside				
Area payments		–		2,760
Set-aside gross output		–		2,760
Contract mowing		–	350	
		–		350
Set-aside gross margin		–		2,410

[Page 9]

| | *1998* | | *1997* | |
| | £ | £ | £ | £ |

1996 harvest

Barley

Sales	–		10,532	
Less opening valuation	–		8,433	
		–		2,099

Wheat

Sales	**19,500**		32,144	
Less opening valuation	**20,377**		32,480	
		(877)		(336)
(Deficit)/Surplus		**(877)**		1,763

3 Fixed costs

	1998		1997	
	£	£	£	£
Labour				
Regular	**52,984**		47,328	
Casual	**–**		428	
PAYE and NIC	**21,925**		22,754	
		74,909		70,510
Power and machinery				
Fuel	**28,385**		22,864	
Licences	**250**		210	
Insurances	**4,865**		4,320	
Machinery repairs	**20,639**		14,763	
Loose tools	**203**		141	
Leasing charges	**200**		200	
Hire of machinery	**1,687**		1,007	
Depreciation	**61,605**		53,100	
		117,834		96,605
Property				
General rates	**2,344**		2,171	
Water rates	**4,087**		3,875	
Sewerage	**612**		589	
Electricity	**5,123**		4,816	
Repairs – farm buildings	**4,658**		7,088	
Repairs – general	**3,289**		3,224	
Repairs - farmhouse	**1,093**		6,495	
Drainage	**3,500**		5,000	
Depreciation	**8,212**		7,478	
		32,918		40,736
Administration				
Telephone	**1,455**		1,390	
Office expenses	**899**		425	
Subscriptions	**674**		709	
Secretarial services	**1,444**		1,352	
Sundry expenses	**2,038**		4,334	
Bank charges	**1,667**		1,255	
Accountancy	**3,250**		2,500	
Professional fees	**1,078**		900	
Depreciation	**924**		–	
		13,429		12,865

[Page 11]

	1998		1997	
	£	£	£	£
Tillages				
Opening valuation	**35,870**		34,200	
Closing valuation	**(38,105)**		(35,870)	
		(2,235)		(1,670)
Total fixed costs		**236,855**		219,046

4 Finance costs	1998	1997
	£	£
Interest - finance leases	**7,647**	6,244
Total finance costs	**7,647**	6,244

5 Turnover	1998	1997
	£	£
Total livestock and crop sales	**510,366**	611,038

6 Other income	1998	1997
	£	£
Rents received	**6,654**	6,269
Hay and straw sales	**2,985**	7,144
Wayleaves	**93**	89
Contract work	**–**	3,302
Miscellaneous income	**1,018**	3,455
	10,750	20,259

[Page 12]

7 Depreciation

Depreciation is calculated to write off the cost or valuation of all assets over their expected normal useful lives.

The rates and method of depreciation are:

Category of asset	Rate	Method
Freehold improvements	10	Straight line
Plant and machinery	20	Reducing balance
Tractors	15	Reducing balance
Motor vehicles	25	Reducing balance
Office equipment	30	Reducing balance

8 Fixed assets: property

	Freehold improvements £	Total £
Cost		
At 1 April 1997	74,775	74,775
Additions	7,336	7,336
At 31 March 1998	82,111	82,111
Depreciation		
At 1 April 1997	35,775	35,775
Provided in the year	8,212	8,212
At 31 March 1998	43,987	43,987
Net book value		
At 31 March 1998	**38,124**	**38,124**
At 31 March 1997	39,000	39,000

[Page 13]

9   Fixed assets: **Plant and machinery etc.**

	Plant and machinery £	Tractors £	Motor vehicles £	Total £
Cost				
At 1 April 1997	330,302	130,192	32,456	492,950
Additions	97,860	–	–	97,860
	428,162	130,192	32,456	590,810
Disposals	5,722	–	–	5,722
At 31 March 1998	422,440	130,192	32,456	585,088
Depreciation				
At 1 April 1997	182,416	61,607	20,373	264,396
Provided in the year	49,221	10,288	3,020	62,529
	231,637	71,895	23,393	326,925
Disposals	4,551	–	–	4,551
At 31 March 1998	227,086	71,895	23,393	322,374
Net book value				
At 31 March 1998	**195,354**	**58,297**	**9,063**	**262,714**
At 31 March 1997	147,886	68,585	12,083	228,554

Plant and machinery includes where relevant:
Fixtures and fittings
Office equipment

[Page 14]

10 Valuation

The valuation was made professionally and is stated at the lower of cost and net realisable value.

	1998 **£**	*1997* *£*
Livestock	**56,855**	76,000
Produce	**42,835**	20,000
Feedstuffs	**1,741**	2,822
Seeds, fertilisers and sprays	**78,652**	82,793
Goods in store	**295**	730
Hay, straw and silage	**380**	795
Tillages	**38,105**	35,870
	218,863	219,010

11 Unrealised profits and deferred income – adjustment

	At cost *£*	*Estimated realisable values* *£*	*Unrealised profit* *£*	*Deferred income* *£*
Opening valuation				
Wheat	20,000	20,377	377	7,116
	20,000	30,377	377	7,116
Closing valuation				
Wheat	42,835	41,000	(1,835)	16,113
	42,835	**41,000**	**(1,835)**	**16,113**

Unrealised profit and deferred income **Decrease/(Increase)**	**2,212**	**(8,997)**

For management purposes, certain stocks, as above, are included at market values. The above note shows the difference between market values and cost of production, such unrealised profit having been adjusted to reflect the financial profit.

Deferred income represents the proportion of area payments relating to unsold stock of the 1997 harvest at the year end.

[Page 15]

302

12   Current accounts

Partners:
A.G. is Mr Andrew Grant
C.T. is Mr Christopher Thornton

	Partner *A.G.* £	*Partner* *C.T.* £	*Total* £
At 1 April 1997	306,749	295,437	602,186
Share of profit	37,358	37,358	74,716
	344,107	332,795	676,902
Drawings	31,760	25,296	57,056
Life assurances	1,061	824	1,885
Tax and Class 4 NIC paid	21,332	18,478	39,810
Class 2 NIC	320	320	640
	54,473	44,918	99,391
At 31 March 1998	**289,643**	**287,877**	**577,511**

12   Loans

	1998 £	*1997* £
Long term leasing	**38,791**	42,696
	38,791	42,696

[Page 16]

Alpha Beta Estates
Approval of accounts and accountants' report: year ended 31 March 1998

Approval of accounts to 31 March 1998

We approve the attached accounts and confirm that we have made available all relevant records and information for their preparation and give our authority for their submission to the Inland Revenue.

Signed . . . .

. . . .

Date . . . .

Accountants' report to Alpha Beta Estates

We have prepared without audit the accounts and notes for the year ended 31 March 1998 set out on pages 1 to 15 from the books and information supplied to us.

Date . . . .

[Page 17]

Alpha Beta Estates
Five year summary: year ended 31 March 1998

Year end	1998	1997	1996	1995	1994
(Harvest year)	(1997)	(1996)	(1995)	(1994)	(1993)
Livestock area (in acres)	178	178	178	178	178
Arable area (in acres)	1,055	1,055	1,055	1,055	1,055
Contracting area (in acres)	160	–	–	–	–
Total effective area (in acres)	1,393	1,233	1,233	1,233	1,233
	£	£	£	£	£
Livestock margin per acre	458	599	545	504	535
Arable margin per acre	250	297	313	250	229
Contracting margin per acre	140	–	–	–	–
Farm gross margin per acre	248	343	348	287	273
Fixed costs per acre					
Labour	54	57	55	53	52
Power and machinery					
Depreciation	44	43	47	35	48
Repairs and spares	15	12	11	15	14
Other	25	23	25	25	20
Property	24	33	24	23	25
Administration	10	10	11	12	11
Tillages	2	1	–	–	–
Total fixed costs per acre	170	177	173	163	170
Profit before rent and finance	78	166	175	124	103
Other income	8	16	17	16	15
Profit on asset sales	2	2	7	4	3
Rent – land	39	42	42	41	42
Finance costs	5	5	7	9	8
Rent equivalent per acre	44	47	49	50	49
Profit after rent and finance	44	137	150	94	72
Unrealised profit adjustment	1	(2)	1	4	(4)
Deferred income	(6)	7	(4)	1	(10)
Net farm income per acre	40	142	147	99	58

[Page 18]

Alpha Beta Estates

Livestock enterprise statistics: for the year ended 31 March 1998

Year end	*1998*	*1997*	*1996*
(Harvest year)	*(1997)*	*(1996)*	*(1995)*
Dairy			
Average herd size	**95**	95	90
Yield per cow (litres)	**6,400**	6,454	6,512
	£/head	£/head	£/head
Milk sales	**1,518**	1,598	1,494
Gross output	**1,403**	1,667	1,555
Variable costs	**547**	584	595
Gross margin per cow	**£ 856**	£1,083	£ 960

[Page 19]

306

Alpha Beta Estates
Arable enterprise statistics: year ended 31 March 1998

Year end (Harvest year)	**Current cropping**	*1998 (1997)*	*1997 (1996)*	*1996 (1995)*	*1995 (1994)*	*1994 (1993)*
Productive area in acres						
Barley	**190**	**212**	229	201	180	230
Wheat	**563**	**534**	479	485	461	447
Oats	–	–	71	57	51	45
Beans	**51**	**53**	64	65	68	74
Oilseed rape	**190**	**195**	157	119	136	100
Industrial oilseed rape	**61**	**61**	35	48	59	49
Set-aside	–	–	20	80	100	110
	1,055	**1,055**	1,055	1,055	1,055	1,055
Yields in tonnes per acre						
Barley		**2.88**	2.65	2.58	2.31	2.02
Wheat		**3.23**	3.14	3.06	3.23	3.27
Oats		**0.00**	1.78	1.96	2.05	2.01
Beans		**1.37**	1.03	1.18	1.30	1.12
Oilseed rape		**1.42**	1.54	1.42	1.25	1.36
Industrial oilseed rape		**1.05**	1.08	1.01	0.84	0.75
Average price in £ per tonne (exc. area payments)						
Barley		**78**	100	106	95	98
Wheat		**82**	100	116	102	105
Oats		–	100	114	92	98
Beans		**101**	120	113	100	115
Oilseed rape		**170**	180	172	152	161
Industrial oilseed rape		**115**	121	100	100	90
Area payments in £ per acre						
Barley		**104**	109	109	78	57
Wheat		**104**	109	109	78	57
Oats		–	109	109	78	157
Beans		**150**	157	157	145	148
Oilseed rape		**184**	185	193	177	180
Industrial oilseed rape		**132**	138	138	128	102
Set-aside		–	138	138	128	102
Output in £ per acre (inc. area payments)						
Barley		**329**	374	382	298	255
Wheat		**369**	424	464	408	400

[Page 20]

Oats	–	286	332	267	254
Beans	**289**	281	290	275	277
Oilseed rape	**425**	462	437	367	399
Industrial oilseed rape	**253**	268	239	212	170
Set-aside	–	138	138	128	102

Average outout in £ per acre (inc. area payments)

	363	390	392	331	312

Variable costs in £ per acre (inc. area payments)

Seeds	**19**	18	17	17	17
Fertilisers	**33**	29	26	25	25
Sprays	**48**	40	36	33	34
Contract work	**6**	4	4	3	4
Other	**3**	3	4	3	3
	109	94	87	81	83

Average gross margin in £ per acre (inc area payments)

	253	296	305	250	229

[Page 21]

Alpha Beta Estates
Funds flow statement: year ended 31 March 1998

	1998 £	1998 £	1997 £	1997 £
Financial profit		**74,716**		171,966
Adjustments:				
Depreciation	**70,741**		60,578	
Profit on sale of assets	**(2,129)**		(2,508)	
		68,612		58,070
		143,328		230,036
Change in valuation	**147**		16,750	
Change in debtors	**(4,589)**		1,888	
Change in creditors	**3,539**		(7,531)	
		(903)		11,107
Cash generated from trading		**1432,425**		241,143
Add:				
Machinery, tractor and vehicle sales	**3,300**		12,000	
Additional hire purchase and leasing	**30,634**		16,666	
		33,934		28,866
Cash available to meet commitments		**176,359**		269,809
Commitments:				
Private drawings	**59,581**		56,061	
Income tax	**39,810**		34,088	
Hire purchase and leases repaid	**20,459**		8,564	
		119,850		98,713
Cash available for reinvestment		**56,509**		171,096
Capital expenditure:				
Property	**7,336**		21,588	
Machinery, tractors and vehicles	**97,860**		83,559	
		105,196		105,147
Cash surplus		**(48,687)**		65,949

[Page 22]

Movement in liquid funds

	1998		1997	
	£	£	£	£
Opening balances				
Current account	**80,000**		38,387	
Deposit account	**76,860**		52,560	
Cash in hand	**72**		36	
		156,932		90,983
Closing balances				
Current account	**49,521**		80,000	
Deposit account	**58,652**		76,860	
Cash in hand	**72**		72	
		108,245		156,932
Cash (deficit)/surplus		**(48,687)**		65,949

Appendix 2 – Conversion factors

Useful conversion factors: simply multiply by the factor. For example:
15 feet x 0.305 = 4.575 metres.

Metric to imperial		*Imperial to metric*	
AREA			
Hectares (Ha) to acres (ac)	× 2.471	Acres to hectares	× 0.405
LENGTH			
Kilometres (km) to miles	× 0.621	Miles to kilometres	× 1.609
Metres (m) to yards	× 1.094	Yards to metres	× 0.914
Metres to feet	× 3.279	Feet to metres	× 0.305
Centimetres (cm) to inches	× 0.394	Inches to centimetres	× 2.540
Millimetres (mm) to inches	× 0.039	Inches to millimetres	× 25.40
MASS			
Tonnes to tons	× 0.984	Tons to tonnes	× 1.016
Kilograms (kg) to lbs	× 2.205	Lbs to kilograms	× 0.454
Grams (g) to ounces	× 0.035	Ounces to grams	× 28.35
VOLUME			
Litres (l) to gallons	× 0.220	Gallons to litres	× 4.546
Litres to pints	× 1.760	Pints to litres	× 0.568
POWER			
Kilowatt (kW) to horsepower (hp)	× 1.341	Horsepower to kilowatt	0.746
USEFUL FACTORS			
kg/Ha to units/ac	× 0.80	units/ac to kg/Ha	× 1.255
t/Ha to cwt/ac	× 7.95	cwt/ac to t/Ha	× 0.125
l/Ha to gallons/acre	× 0.089	gallons/ac to l/Ha	× 11.24

Appendix 3 – Statistical sources for analytical review

Farm Management Pocketbook by John Nix.
Published in September every year and contains gross margin data projected forward for the following year. Other data includes labour, machinery and other fixed costs, grants and general farm business data.
Current price £8.75
Wye College Press, Wye College, Ashford, Kent, TN25 5AH.

The Agricultural Budgeting and Costing Book by Agro Business Consultants Ltd.
Published every 6 months in May and November. Contains gross margin data with sensitivity tables, fixed costs and general farm business data.
Current price: single copies £31.00, both editions £53.00.
Agro Business Consultants Ltd, FREEPOST LE5272, Twyford, Melton Mowbray, Leicestershire, LE14 2BR.

Farm Business Survey
A survey is carried out regionally on an annual basis detailing the financial performance of farming businesses in the regions. A report is published annually of the findings. As these are regional reports they are particularly useful for analytical review.

Southern
Department of Agricultural Economic and Management, University of Reading, 4 Earley Gate, Whiteknights Road, PO Box 237, Reading RG6 6AR Tel: 01118 9318960.

South Western
Agricultural Economics Unit, University of Exeter, Lafrowda House, St German's Road, Exeter EX4 6TL. Tel: 01392 263839.

South Eastern
Farm Business Unit, Department of Agricultural Economics, Wye College, (University of London), Ashford, Kent TN25 5AH. Tel: 01233 812401.

Eastern
Agricultural Economics Unit, Department of Land Economy, University

of Cambridge, 19 Silver Street, Cambridge CB3 9EP. Tel: 01233 337147.

East Midlands
Rural Business Research Unit, University of Nottingham, Sutton Bonnington Campus, Loughborough LE12 5RD. Tel: 0115 951 6070.

North Western
Farm Business Unit, School of Economic Studies, The University of Manchester, Dover Street Building, Manchester M13 9PL. Tel: 0161 275 4799.

North Eastern
Rural Business Research Survey Unit, Askham Bryan College, Askham Bryan, York YO23 3FR. Tel: 01904 772233.

Northern
Department of Agricultural Economics and Food Marketing, University of Newcastle-upon-Tyne NE1 7RU. Tel: 0191 222 6900.

Wales
Welsh Institute of Rural Studies, Llanbadarn Campus, Aberystwyth, Ceredigion SY23 3AL Tel: 01970 622253.

Appendix 4 – Sources of advice

ADAS (Agricultural Development and Advisory Service)
Oxford Spires Business Park, The Boulevard, Langford Lane, Kidlington, Oxford OX5 1NZ Tel: 01865 842742.
Enquiries will give details of several regional offices in England and Wales.

Agricultural Mortgage Corporation PLC
AMC House, Chantry Street, Andover, Hants SP10 1DD Tel: 01264 334344.

Agricultural Wages Board
Nobel House, Room 716D, 17 Smith Square, London SW1P 3JR. Tel: 0171 238 6540.
A copy of the Agricultural Wages Order is available from the above address.

British Institute of Agricultural Consultants (BIAC)
The Estate Office, Torry Hill, Milstead, Sittingbourne, Kent ME9 0SP. Tel: 01795 830100.
A directory of members is published annually containing names and addresses and detailing areas of expertise.

Country Landowners' Association
16 Belgrave Square, London SW1X 8PQ. Tel: 0171 235 0511.
Has 19 regional offices in England and Wales. Publishes a number of booklets on taxation and estate management topics.

Countryside Commission
John Dower House, Crescent Place, Cheltenham, Gloucestershire GL50 3RA.
Tel: 01242 521381.

English Tourist Board
Thames Tower, Blacks Road, Hammersmith, London W6 9EL. Tel: 0181 846 9000.

Forestry Commission
231 Corstophine Road, Edinburgh EH12 7AT. Tel: 0131 334 0303.

Ministry of Agriculture, Fisheries and Food
3 Whitehall Place, London, SW1A 2HH. Tel: 0171 270 3000.
There are nine regional offices in England and a Welsh Office Agriculture
Department in Wales.

National Farmers' Union
Agriculture House, 164 Shaftesbury Avenue, London WC2H 8HL. Tel:
0171 331 7200.
Has a number of 'Group Secretaries' in all regions of the country.

Royal Agricultural Society of England
National Agricultural Centre, Stoneleigh Park, Warwickshire CV8 2LZ.
Tel: 01203 696969.

Royal Institution of Chartered Surveyors.
12 Great George Street, Parliament Square, London SW1P 3AD.
Tel: 0171 222 7000.

Appendix 5 – Glossary and commonly used terms

Acclimatise accustom flock of sheep, etc., to the geographic area and climate where they live.

Acid soil soil with a pH of less than 7.

Acre 4,840 square yards. In field terms, approximately 70 paces × 70 paces. 0.4 of a hectare.

ACT Agricultural Central Trading Ltd

ADAS: Agricultural Development and Advisory Service

Agist to take another's livestock to feed on your land.

Agistment agisted stock feeding away from the farm.

Agricultural charge substantial assets attributed by court order to creditors as security.

AICC Association of Independent Crop Consultants.

Alkaline soil soil with a pH of more than 7.

ALT agricultural land tribunal.

AMC Agricultural Mortgage Corporation.

Aphid greenfly which draws sap from leaves and shoots of crops reducing vigour and growth.

Arable land under cultivation, including grass leys.

Artificial insemination (AI) the collection of sperm and its use for impregnating females.

ATB Agricultural Training Board.

At foot suckling. A ewe with suckling lambs is said to have lambs at foot.

Auger driven screw in a cylinder for conveying grain or slurry (liquid manure).

AWB Agricultural Wages Board.

Bareland sites with Forestry Commission approval for the planting of commercial forestry.

Barley, malting barley used to provide malt for brewing and feed.

Barley, spring barley drilled in the early spring.

Barley, winter barley drilled in the autumn.

Barrener female animal unable to produce young.

Battery cages metal or wooden cages for housing poultry, egg layers.

Beating up the replacement of trees lost within the first few years after planting.

BIAC British Institute of Agricultural Consultants.

Boar male pig used for breeding.

Break crop crop grown between main crops.

Brewer's grains barley residue after malting. Used wet or dry as animal feed.

Broadcasting machine sowing of seed by scattering.

Broadleaves distinct group of forest trees whose main characteristic is their broad leaves which are usually shed each autumn.

Broiler young chicken less than three months old, reared quickly for poultry meat.

Broken mouthed sheep which has lost some of its teeth.

BSC British Sugar Corporation.

BSE Bovine Spongiform Encephalopathy, commonly known as mad cow disease.

Buffer feeding the conservation of grass into silage during rapid growth for feeding mid summer when grass growth decreases.

Bulling heifer or young cow of right inclination and body condition to be served, the equivalent of being on heat.

Bullock a castrated bull.

Butterfat fat content of milk.

BWMB British Wool Marketing Board.

CAAV Central Association of Agricultural Valuers.

Cad lamb lamb reared on bottle because of death of mother.

Canker various fungal diseases in trees and horses' hooves.

CAP Common Agricultural Policy.

Capping a ceiling on subsidy payments. Current proposals are a taper rather than a ceiling.

Catch crop crop grown on ground for a short time between two main crops.

Calving interval period of time between one calving and the next.

CEE Central and Eastern European countries.

Cereal members of the grass family. Seeds provide animal feed, flour for breadmaking and malt for brewing.

Chain harrow harrow with loosely jointed links with spikes.

Chisel plough heavy cultivator, with tines (spikes) on a frame.

Chitting the process of allowing seed potatoes to sprout before planting, thus improving early growth rate.

CLA Country Landowners Association.

CMA Centre of Management in Agriculture.

Combine drill conventional wheeled drill used for the accurate placement of seed and fertiliser.

Combination drill drill attached to a power harrow to perform two operations; cultivating the soil and drilling seed.

Combine harvester wheeled machine for cutting and threshing crops. Machine for harvesting cereals, herbage seed, peas, beans and oilseed rape.

Concentrate food concentrate food of high nutritive value compared with its volume; a non-bulky food.

Conifer distinct group of forest trees whose main characteristics are narrow, needle-like or scale-like leaves, regular, almost geometrical branching and, except for larch, evergreen foliage.

Coppice broadleaved woodland derived from the cut stumps of previous crops. Usually cut on short rotations.

Co-responsibility levy levy collected from sale of products to finance intervention boards.

Couch a persistent grass weed. Also called 'twitch'.

Couples a ewe and her progeny (singles or twins) for sale.

Cows adult female cattle which have had at least one calf.

Creep barrier system allowing young animals access to feed whilst restricting larger and older animals; usually the parents of the young animals.

Crop rotation system of growing crops in a fixed sequence, year by year.

Cross compliance conditions that have to be complied with before subsidy payments are made, usually environmental conditions.

Crown the branching area of a tree.

Culling removal of animals from breeding herd.

Cultivation the various operations of tilling or tillage in preparation of soil for plant growth.

Daily live-weight gain (DLWG) the increase in liveweight achieved, averaged day to day.

Deep litter poultry system for keeping pullets or hens on litter.

Dip total immersion of sheep in diluted chemical to control sheep scab and parasites.

Direct drill drill capable of sowing seeds directly into uncultivated ground.

Draft ewe ewe, usually from upland, tupped and sold out of flock.

Drill implement which sows seeds in rows. A direct drill sows seed directly into uncultivated ground. A precision drill provides very accurate seed placement for crops, such as sugar beet.

Dry not producing milk.

Dry off to reduce gradually the amount of milk taken from a cow until it ceases to yield any at the end of its lactation.

Early potatoes potatoes planted to be harvested by the end of July.

Easement right of access or use over land.

Effluent waste material from crops or animals in sold or liquid form.

Establishment a term to describe all the operations up to the stage where a crop is growing.

EU European Union.

Euro European currency.

Ewe female sheep.

Fallow ploughed and harrowed but left uncropped for a year.

Farrow give birth to litter of pigs.

Fat hen arable weed.

FEOGA a French acronym for European Agricultural Guarantee and Guidance Fund.

Fertiliser inorganic, non-bulky organic chemicals applied to the soil to increase the amount of plant nutrients available for crop growth.

Fixed equipment buildings and equipment which cannot readily be moved. Normally included in landlord's capital.

Followers heifers destined for the dairy herd at the time of calving.

Food conversion ratio weight units of food consumed by animal in producing a liveweight gain of one weight unit. A measure of the efficiency of the animal in converting food to meat.

Forage crop crop consumed green by livestock either directly or in silage. Also known as fodder crop.

Freehold absolute ownership under English law.

Full-mouthed full-grown sheep with full set of teeth.

FWAG Farming and Wildlife Advisory Group.

Garnishee order a court order requiring a third party who owes money to a farmer to pay direct to the creditor instead.

GATT General Agreement on Tariffs and Trade.

Gestation period time between conception and birth:
　Cows, 283 days
　Sheep, 144–155 days
　Pigs, 116–120 days.

Gilt young female pig which has not produced any young pigs.

Gimmer shearling ewe from 12 to 18 months old, kept for breeding. See *Theave*.

Grain, rolled cereal rolled or crushed between two rotating cylinders for feeding to livestock.

Grazing livestock unit a system of calculating the grazing requirements of animals in relationship to a standard unit 1 GLU equivalent to the standard dairy cow. Also called Livestock Units (LU).

Green Pound the exchange rate for agricultural commodities from euros to sterling.

Greyface cross of Border Leicester ram and Blackface ewes. Also called Mule.

Gross margins value of outputs of enterprise, less the direct or variable costs.

Hardwood commonly the timber of broadleaved trees.

Harrow implement with tines (spikes) or discs, used for cultivation of the soil. The harrow may be powered by tractor power take off (pto) termed power harrow.

Haulm stems and leaves of cereals, potatoes, beans and peas.

Haulm silage silage made from the stems and leaves remaining after harvest of peas and beans.

Hay cut and dried grass. Normally baled.

Heat time period during which female is susceptible to mating.

Heavy land soil with a high proportion of clay and difficult to manage in extreme wet or dry conditions.

Hectare 100 metres square, or approximately 2.471 acres.

Heifer a young cow which has had less than two calves.

Heft a group of sheep grazing a particular range of mountain pasture. A *hirsel* may contain one or more hefts.

Hefted flock of sheep attached to the land and therefore taken over by the incomer when a farm changes hands.

HGCA Home Grown Cereals Authority.

Hirsel area of land over which shepherd has charge.

Hogg young ewe whether from the time of the summer lamb sales until first shorn in the following spring. Also called hogget or teg.

Holding the farm as registered with the Ministry of Agriculture, Fisheries and Food and issued with a holding number.

Homogenised milk milk made homogenous by breaking up the cream fraction.

IACS Integrated Administration and Control System.

IAgS Institute of Agricultural Secretaries.

In-ground valuation value of tillages or cultivations including direct costs of seed, fertiliser and spray.

In-lamb pregnant ewe.

Intervention price price at which the Intervention Board will support the price of an agricultural commodity by intervening in the market and buying up surplus produce, at a certain specification, for storage and eventual sale.

June return MAFF census of farm holdings on area of crops, livestock numbers, yields, labour force, etc.

Kale plant of brassica or cabbage family grown as a fodder crop.

Killing out percentage weight of carcass expressed as a percentage of animal liveweight.

Lactation period during which female animal is producing milk.

Lamb ram lamb or tup lamb is an uncastrated male from birth until first shearing; wether lamb is a castrated male from birth until the summer sale; ewe lamb or chilver lamb is a female from birth until summer sales.

Lambing percentage number of lambs born per hundred ewes in sheep flock.

Landlord's capital value of farm land, buildings and fixed equipment.

Leaching the washing-out of nutrients from the soil by rainfall.

Leasehold an interest in land for a defined length of time.

Legumes plants obtaining nitrogen for plant growth from the atmosphere, e.g., peas and beans.

Less favoured area designated geographical areas eligible to receive additional subsidies.

Ley temporary grassland. Grass down for five years or less.

Light land soil with a high proportion of sand. Prone to drying out but capable of working in a range of moisture conditions.

Litters straw, sawdust or other material used as bedding for animals. Collective name for the progeny from a sow.

Loam soil with balanced ratio of sand, silt and clay with organic matter. Normally easy working but neither light nor heavy. A heavy loam has a higher proportion of clay. A light loam has a higher proportion of sand.

MAFF Ministry of Agriculture, Fisheries and Food.

Maincrop potatoes grown for harvesting in October with higher yields than early potatoes.

Manure farmyard manure, compost or other bulky organic nutrients applied to the soil.

Masham cross of Wensleydale ram and Swaledale ewe.

Mildew various fungi, parasitic on plants. The fungi penetrate plant tissue or grow on the surface.

Milking parlour building containing equipment for milking and feeding cows.

MLC Meat and Livestock Commission.

MMB Milk Marketing Board, no longer exists.

Modulation redistribution of subsidy payments between producers or policies.

Mole drain drain formed by drawing a cylinder through the soil to form a drainage channel.

Monoculture growing the same crop on a field each year.

Movement record record of animal movements on and off the premises under the Movement of Animals Order.

NAC National Agricultural Centre, Stoneleigh.

Nematode parasitic worm, found in plants (eelworm) and animals.

NFU National Farmers' Union.

NFYFC National Federation of Young Farmers Clubs.

Notice to Quit notice from landlord to tenant of the termination of a tenancy agreement.

NPBA National Pig Breeders Association.

NRA National Rivers Authority.

Nurse crop crop providing protection to another crop sown beneath. Also called cover crop.

Oilseed rape plant belonging to brassica family, grown for small black seeds which are oil-rich.

Paddock grazing a system of grazing management where grazing areas are divided into paddocks by fencing.

Pasteurised milk milk heated to kill bacteria.

Peat soil of high organic matter. Well decomposed black soils are characteristic of the East Anglian fens which, when drained, are often very fertile.

Permanent pasture permanently cropped to grass and not ploughed.

pH measure of acidity and alkalinity determined by hydrogen ion concentration.

Phosphate fertiliser used to supply phosphorus (P) to crops.

Photosynthesis process in plants for making carbohydrates from carbon dioxide and water using the energy of sunlight.

Plantation a site with established trees.

Planting mainly a manual operation of tree planting where the plant roots are inserted in a notch cut with a spade. Some machine planting is done.

Ploughing cultivating and draining soil to improve timber yield capacity and to suppress initial weed growth.

PMB Potato Marketing Board.

Potash fertiliser supplying potassium (K) to the soil.

Potato plant grown for the carbohydrate in its swollen underground stem or tuber.

Potato blight fungal potato disease which causes death of the haulm and yield loss.

Poaching damage to soil by cattle moving around during wet weather.

Pre-emergence herbicide herbicide applied after drilling seed but before emergence of plant from the soil.

Protection the need to protect young trees in the early stages of their development from damage by disease, weak growth, deer and rabbits.

Pullet young hen.

Pulse seed or plant of legumes.

Ram uncastrated male sheep. Also called *tup*.

RASE Royal Agricultural Society of England.

Rotation period of years from planting to harvesting.

RICS Royal Institution of Chartered Surveyors.

Sawlog log of a quality and size suitable for conversion into a timber product, such as furniture or construction timber, rather than pulp of chipboard.

Set stocking system of grazing where livestock remain in one area for a long period.

Shearling a young sheep from its first shearing until its second.

Silage forage crop harvested green for preservation in a succulent condition.

Silo tower, pit surface clamp or polythene bag in which silage is made and stored.

Singling reducing multi-stemmed growth to one usually refers to cutting back a coppice stool.

Softwood; commonly the timber of conifers.

Soil profile vertical soil section which reveals the distinctive layers or horizons. Usually as a result of digging a hole in a field.

Soya bean bean rich in oil and protein, imported to balance the cereal content of livestock feed.

Spray liquid application of herbicide, insecticide or fertiliser.

Sporting rights usually included with the freehold of a woodland property, they allow the owner to exercise the sporting (hunting).

Steers male castrated cattle.

Sterilised milk milk treated in sealed air-tight containers to kill all bacteria and extend its storage life.

Stocking rate head of grazing animals allocated to a given land area.

Stool the stump of a broadleaved tree which has been cut with the intention of producing coppice shoots.

Store an animal kept for later finishing or fattening.

Strip grazing system of grazing management which allows cattle access to a limited area of fresh pasture by using an electric fence.

Subsidiarity EU allowing discretion to individual countries in setting detailed rules regarding support systems.

Suckler cow beef cow allowed to suckle its own young.

Sugar beet rootcrop grown for its high sucrose content.

Sugar beet pulp dried residual root material after the extraction of sugar from beet. Used as animal feed.

Super levy levy charged to milk producer who exceeds quota.

Swede rootcrop normally grown for animal feed. Similar to turnip.

Teg see *hogg.*

Tenant's capital total farm capital other than land and fixed equipment.

Tenant right the right to compensation at the end of the tenancy for the value of cultivations and sowings during the tenancy.

TFA Tenant Farmers' Association.

Theave see *gimmer.*

Thinning removing, at about five-year intervals, a number of stems once the trees have reached saleable size. The pattern of thinning benefits the remaining trees.

Tillage activity of working land with implements in preparation for planting or sowing a crop.

Tilth condition of soil after tillage.

Tramlines wheelmarks in a crop, used for all subsequent operations.

Tup entire male sheep, or ram.

UKASTA United Kingdom Agricultural Supply Trade Association.

Vining peas peas grown for harvesting green, before they are ripe.

Virus yellows virus disease in sugar beet spread by aphids and causing loss of sugar and yield.

Weaning removal of young from mother or milk source.

Weed any plant growing in cultivated ground and competing with the crop for water, light and nutrients. Weeds also contaminate crops and harbour pests and diseases.

Weeding removing competing vegetation from around young trees. Chemical treatment is common, although some hand clearing is done.

Wether castrated male sheep.

Wheat, spring cereal grown for its grain. Normally drilled in the early spring, March/April months.

Wheat, winter cereal grown for its grain. Normally drilled in the autumn.

Whey milk residue after removal of the cheese part of milk, curd, has been removed.

Wild oat annual weed which reduces cereal yields.

Windrow crop cut in rows for picking up and harvesting.

WOAD Welsh Office Agriculture Department.

WTO World Trade Organisation.

Yield class forecast of timber growth. Used to classify forest land and plantations according to potential timber yield, e.g., yield class 14 indicates that there is a potential yield of 14 cubic metres of timber per hectare per annum on average throughout the crop rotation.

Index

The index has been referenced to paragraph number. Appendices have been referenced to Appendix number.

M